ENCHANTED GROUND

THE STUDY OF MEDIEVAL ROMANCE
IN THE EIGHTEENTH CENTURY

Enchanted Ground

The Study of Medieval Romance in the Eighteenth Century

by
ARTHUR JOHNSTON

UNIVERSITY OF LONDON
THE ATHLONE PRESS
1964

Published by
THE ATHLONE PRESS
UNIVERSITY OF LONDON
at 2 Gower Street, London W C I
Distributed by Constable & Co., Ltd.
I2 *Orange Street, London* W C 2

Canada
Oxford University Press
Toronto

U.S.A
Oxford University Press Inc.
New York

© *Arthur Johnston*, 1964

First edition, 1964
Reprinted, 1965

First printed in Great Britain by
WILLIAM CLOWES AND SONS LTD., BECCLES
Reprinted by offset-litho by
THE ALDEN PRESS, OXFORD

PREFACE

IT is difficult for any reader of eighteenth-century literature to remain for long unaware of various anecdotes concerning medieval romances. Mr Bickerstaffe's godson and Uncle Toby enjoyed them. But so also did Edmund Burke as a boy, and Dr Johnson, whose fondness for them lasted throughout his life. One of Coleridge's early recollections was of his father burning his copy of *The Seven Champions of Christendom* in an attempt to prevent the boy's becoming an unpractical dreamer. Other items of information add to one's general impression of the importance of the romances in the period. Malory's *Morte Darthur*, for example, enters literary criticism in Thomas Warton's *Observations on the Faerie Queene* (1754). Richard Hurd reassessed 'Gothic superstitions' in his *Letters on Chivalry and Romance* (1762). In 1802 Joseph Ritson printed a collection of texts of romances, and in 1805 George Ellis published a series of prose abstracts. Scott edited the Auchinleck *Sir Tristrem* in 1804, and so provided Swinburne with some of the material for his *Queen Yseult* in 1857.

The attention paid to the romances by the general reader and by the scholar and antiquary is a subject which has interested me for some years. It is an important by-way in eighteenth century studies, and it has a good deal to tell us about the early development of English literary scholarship. I have concentrated in the chapters which follow on what was known of the romances in the period between Dryden and Scott. This, of course, is arbitrary. I have simply taken what could be adequately discussed in one book, and have necessarily had to isolate the interest in romances from the other medieval, or more generally antiquarian, studies of the period. This seemed to me legitimate, since the scholars from Percy to Scott attached greater importance to the romances than they did to any other medieval texts, or indeed to any other texts at all except the works of Chaucer, Spenser, Shakespeare and Milton. The middle ages were for them the ages of romance. Medieval drama, *Piers Plowman*, Gower, Lydgate, the lyrics—none attracted such intense interest as the romances. While, therefore, I should have liked to include discussions of the interest in the ballads, of Chatterton's Rowley poems and Macpherson's Ossian, of Tyrwhitt's work on Chaucer, of Gray's interest in Old Norse and Welsh, of Horace Walpole and other related topics, I have been content to provide some of the background against which these better known topics may be seen. Similarly, I have not attempted to study the revival of interest in medieval architecture, art, sculpture, tapestries, wall-paintings, political institutions and social organization. Before any adequate study of the Medieval Revival as a whole can be written, these separate topics need to be studied thoroughly.

When I look at what I have done I am tempted to voice my response in the words of Locke, 'he that hawks at larks and sparrows has no less sport, though a much less considerable quarry, than he that flies at nobler game'. Many of my readers will doubtless be able, from their own special knowledge, to suggest areas into which I might well have entered. I hope that I have covered some ground which is sufficiently new to excuse my reluctance to take in a wider territory. 'It is ambition enough to be employed as an underlabourer in clearing the ground a little' in preparation for some future study of the Medieval Revival.

But for the friendly interest of people whose names I have no right to parade here, I would perhaps have been content to read and collect until the larger study was within my grasp. Instead, I have paused to extract what seems to me a fairly self-contained unit. Some of the material in the book was originally incorporated in a doctoral thesis, and here I should like to record my debt to the late Professor David Nichol Smith, Dr J. A. W. Bennett and Miss Ethel Seaton. I have spent many hours in the Bodleian Library and the Reading Room of the British Museum, and so discovered for myself the unfailing helpfulness of those who make the life of the scholar possible. I am grateful to them for making the most enjoyable part of research so pleasant and easy. I am grateful also to the advisers of the Athlone Press, and to its Assistant Secretary, Mr A. G. Dewey, who saved me from many an incoherence and many an error. My greatest debt is to my wife without whose encouragement, vigilance, tactful criticism and uncomplaining labour, I doubt whether the book would have been written at all.

Birkbeck College, London   A. J.

CONTENTS

CHAPTER I

INTRODUCTION

WHEN Thomas Percy published the *Reliques of Ancient English Poetry* in 1765 he did more than introduce a collection of ballads and poems of 'pleasing simplicity' and 'artless grace'. In these volumes he demonstrated the ability of the literary scholar to produce an anthology of poems which would appeal not only to his fellow antiquaries, but also to the general cultured reader. In achieving such a wide audience he made the work of the literary antiquary acceptable to the man of culture, while at the same time making respectable to the scholar a range of literature that had hitherto been neglected. It was not the texts alone, in the collecting of which Percy displayed great energy and care, that made the *Reliques* a new departure. Collections of texts had been made earlier. The originality of Percy's venture lay even more in the scholarship presented in the introductory notes to each poem, in the four essays (on minstrels, the origin of the stage, the metre of *Piers Plowman*, and the metrical romances), and in the sense of the development of English poetry which lay behind the arrangement of the texts. The order in which they were printed would, he hoped, 'shew the gradation of our language, exhibit the progress of popular opinions, display the peculiar manners and customs of former ages, or throw light on our earlier classical poets'. There is evidence enough for the influence on later English poetry of the texts of the *Reliques*, which Wordsworth described as 'collected, new-modelled, and in many instances (if such a contradiction in terms may be used) composed by the Editor'. English poetry, to quote Wordsworth again, was 'absolutely redeemed' by these volumes. 'I do not think that there is an able writer in verse of the present day who would not be proud to acknowledge his obligations to the Reliques.' From them, poets learned to abandon the 'vague, the glossy, and unfeeling language' of the day, for 'true

I

simplicity and genuine pathos'. But poets, like other men, learn only what they have a propensity to learn. Where Wordsworth learnt from the *Reliques* to seek simplicity and pathos in 'incidents and situations from common life', in 'low and rustic life' such as he had experience of, expressed in a 'selection of the language really spoken by men', both Scott and Southey were more impressed by the scholarship in the *Reliques*. This encouraged their own eagerness to seek out subjects for poetry in the past, and to annotate their poems with a wealth of learning and of antiquarian detail, which would support the authenticity of the 'customs and manners of former ages' that their poems displayed. Coleridge found in the ballads a narrative form in which to express his own imaginative myth of the Ancient Mariner.

The immediately-preceding generations of poets, from Dryden to Pope, had been interested in the type of poem collected by Percy. But their main preoccupation had been to create a literature in English that could stand beside that of Augustan Rome, and to disentangle themselves from what they felt to be the barbarisms and provincialisms that characterized the literature of their own immediate past. This they did mainly by subjecting themselves consciously to classical models. Their aim had been so perfectly realized in the poetry of Pope, that it was only to be expected that new interests and ambitions would be sought. 'For the genius of every age is different.' As Dryden looked back to the Elizabethans and realized that he must either not write at all, or attempt some other way, so any poet in the second half of the eighteenth century, looking back on Dryden and Pope, must have felt 'there is no bays to be expected in their walks'.[1] What had been a liberating influence on Dryden and his successors came to be regarded as a restraining force. The revolution they ushered in had brought, in Hurd's words, 'a great deal of good sense', but we had lost 'a world of fine fabling'. There was no going back, but there was something to be learned from literatures other than those of Greece and Rome. Thus, aspects of earlier English literature which had been the object of conscious rebellion in the previous century, or which had interested only a few pedants, or which

[1] W. P. Ker, *Essays of John Dryden* (Oxford, 1926), i. 99.

had been read and enjoyed and occasionally imitated, began to attract attention after 1760.

As the century advanced, the range of literary studies expanded steadily, taking in wider and wider areas. 'Primitive' poetry—Old Norse and Old Welsh—Chaucer, the Scottish Chaucerians, Elizabethan and Jacobean drama and lyric, ballads, all were printed or reprinted. Earlier literature was read in order to provide notes to the growing editions of Spenser, Shakespeare and Milton. Macpherson and Chatterton produced serious imitations of 'medieval' poetry, and expressed their genius most forcefully in the contexts of the past. One body of early texts attracted particular attention—the metrical romances of the middle ages, the stories of King Arthur and his knights, of Bevis and Guy, Valentine and Orson and Libeaus Desconus. Some of these stories were well known in the prose chapbooks read by children. The original texts still hidden in collections of manuscripts became a centre of interest for a series of scholars whose work in discovering and editing them forms the subject of this study.

There can be no simple explanation why the rediscovery of earlier English literature should have gathered momentum about 1760. Pepys had collected ballads, Dryden had loved them, Addison had praised their simplicity and nobility, their 'beauties of nature' and 'true poetical spirit' in his *Spectator* papers on *Chevy Chase* and *The Two Children in the Wood*. Texts had been reprinted in Dryden's *Miscellany Poems* (1684–1708), in the *Collection of Old Ballads* (1723), in Allan Ramsay's *Evergreen* (1724) and in *The Muses Library* (1737). But no ballad revival had ensued.[1] Yet the highly apologetic collection of Percy in 1765 worked a revolution. Not only do the poets acknowledge their debt to it, but from it there developed a flood of publications devoted to earlier literature, until we find that modern literary scholarship has been born.

Study of the medieval romances has its origin in Percy's essay in the third volume of the *Reliques*. This is a characteristic piece of work, combining enthusiasm, in its arguments for a serious

[1] See J. W. Hales, 'The Revival of Ballad Poetry in the Eighteenth Century', reprinted in *Folia Litteraria* (1893), H. B. Wheatley (ed.), *Reliques* (1887), Introduction, and A. B. Friedman, *The Ballad Revival* (Chicago, 1961).

interest in these texts, with careful scholarship in the appended list of romances, their manuscript and printed sources. If we read it now, it is not so much to learn about the romances, as about Percy and the early stages of literary scholarship. To the modern professional scholar, working in the context of the accumulated information of the last two hundred years, there is a pleasure in looking back on the origins of the activities to which he devotes his life. That pleasure is the greater because literary scholarship in its origin was in the hands of amateurs, who often combined literary research with creative writing. They were actively interested in contemporary literary developments, and consciously put their discoveries to the service of modern poetry, or at least urged that they should be so used. When Percy, Thomas Warton, George Ellis and Scott turned over the leaves of manuscripts of romances for the first time after a lapse of four hundred years, they were animated not simply by a love of what was old, but by a delight in what for them was new. Of the five scholars who discovered the romances, only Joseph Ritson was a 'mere scholar', a man who was cut off from all but antiquarian investigations, and who delighted more in authenticity of detail than in the value of his discoveries as a source of inspiration for the modern poet. He, perhaps, is the true ancestor of the modern literary scholar and, exercising as he did a profound influence on the development of English scholarship, has his own interest. But the 'scholars of taste and genius' had a greater influence on the general culture and literature of their day. The work they did on the romances and the hopes they entertained of the influence their discoveries would have will be described in the following chapters.

2. ENCHANTED GROUND

The scholars with whom I am concerned were intent on opening windows on to the literature of the 'dark ages'. For them the middle ages were predominantly the ages of romance. 'Romance and minstrelsy', wrote Richard Price in 1824, were 'the prominent characteristics' of the middle ages.[1] But this

[1] In his Preface to Warton, *History of English Poetry* (1824), i. (14).

was not a view that would have been endorsed by a study of the works of Chaucer, and many a reader in the eighteenth century must have found a window into the remote past through the *Canterbury Tales*. At the end of the seventeenth century, Dryden showed by his poetic paraphrases in the *Fables* and by his critical arguments in the Preface, that the poetry of Chaucer, stripped of its 'antique' language, spoke interestingly to his own age. Chaucer, however, even without the benefit of translation, had never ceased to find readers.[1] It was not merely 'some old Saxon friends' who venerated his 'old language'; Dryden mentions that the Earl of Leicester was of the same opinion. But Dryden's own concern was to pay homage to Chaucer by making some of his work available to readers who, like the young Addison, found him too antiquated in his language and too obscure in his wit to be easily intelligible,[2] and to those who, like Dryden himself, could not accept Speght's opinion that Chaucer's verse could be scanned. Modernizing Chaucer went on throughout the eighteenth century, and of course still continues. The process of making at least one medieval poet available to the modern reader was begun long before the scholars with whom I am concerned began their work.[3]

The literature of the middle ages, outside Chaucer, with which a reader in 1700 was most intimately acquainted, was the romances. In part his knowledge was gained from the late prose redactions of *Guy of Warwick*, *Bevis of Hamptoun* and *Valentine and Orson*. But these were not distinguished in his mind from the modernized and abbreviated versions of sixteenth-century Peninsular romances such as *Amadis* and *Don Bellianis*, and the middle ages would be further extended for him by the addition of the romantic epics of Ariosto, Tasso and Spenser. From a knowledge of these three a reader judged the middle ages to have been a time of chivalry and knight-errantry. As such, they attracted by their strangeness while they repelled by their

---

[1] The evidence is assembled in C. F. E. Spurgeon, *Five Hundred Years of Chaucer Criticism and Allusion* (Cambridge, 1925).

[2] Addison, 'An Account of the Greatest English Poets' (1694), ll. 13–14.

[3] In addition to Spurgeon, see G. Tillotson (ed.) Pope, *The Rape of the Lock and Other Poems* (1962), pp. 3–12.

unnaturalness. In a survey of English poetry before Waller and Dryden, the young Addison saw only Chaucer and Spenser, and of Spenser he wrote

> Old Spenser next, warmed with poetic rage,
> In ancient tales amused a barbarous age;
> An age that yet uncultivate and rude,
> Where'er the poet's fancy led, pursued
> Through pathless fields, and unfrequented floods,
> To dens of dragons and enchanted woods.
> But now the mystic tale, that pleased of yore,
> Can charm an understanding age no more;
> The long-spun allegories fulsome grow,
> While the dull moral lies too plain below.
> We view well-pleased at distance all the sights
> Of arms and palfreys, battles, fields, and fights,
> And damsels in distress, and courteous knights;
> But when we look too near, the shades decay,
> And all the pleasing landscape fades away.[1]

When he wrote these lines, Addison later confessed to Spence, he had not read Spenser. He was merely repeating what he believed to be a common attitude. But in 1712, in *Spectator* 419, he gave the traditional characterization of the middle ages. They were, he said, a period of darkness and superstition, when men looked on nature with 'more reverence and horror' and 'loved to astonish themselves with the apprehensions of witchcraft, prodigies, charms, and enchantments'. This was the inference commonly made from the legacy of superstitions and of 'legends and fables, antiquated romances, and the traditions of nurses and old women'. The Englishman naturally felt at home with such tales, not merely because he imbibed them in infancy, but also because he belonged to the Northern race that had originally elaborated them. Given to 'gloominess and melancholy of temper', he was by nature fanciful, with a fancy that was disposed 'to many wild notions and visions' such as his ancestors had delighted in. One could see this manifested, Addison thought, in the Englishman's

[1] Addison, loc. cit. ll. 17–31. For an account of Spenser's reputation, see H. A. Beers, *A History of Romanticism in the Eighteenth Century* (1926), ch. 3, and H. Cory, *The Critics of Edmund Spenser* (Berkeley, California, 1911).

6

superiority to other modern nations, and to the writers of Greece
and Rome, in creating worlds outside nature, peopled by fairies,
witches, magicians, demons, spirits and giants, conversing 'with
different objects' and thinking 'in a different manner from
that of mankind'. One could see it at work in the power of
Shakespeare to 'touch this weak superstitious part of his
readers' imagination' and to give to the 'speeches of his ghosts,
fairies, witches and the like imaginary persons' so much of
wildness and solemnity 'that we cannot forbear to think them
natural, though we have no rule by which to judge them'. The
only classical writers with whom Addison could draw any
comparison were Ovid in the *Metamorphoses* and Homer in the
Odyssey. He wrote of the *Metamorphoses* in terms drawn from
medieval romance: 'we are walking on enchanted ground, and
see nothing but scenes of magic lying round us'.[1] Milton he
regarded as Ovidian in his accounts of the creation, the
metamorphoses of the fallen angels, and the adventures of
Satan in search of Paradise.

The *Odyssey* had long been considered a work of Homer's
old age, from the predominance in it of marvellous tales.
Longinus had characterized the Homer who wrote it as a
garrulous old man, with an old man's fancy 'roving in the
fabulous and incredible'.[2] Thus Steele could compare the
imaginativeness of Sir John Mandeville in the *Travels* with that
of Homer and Spenser; 'all is enchanted ground and fairy
land'.[3] The phrase 'enchanted ground' occurred most com-

---

[1] *Spectator* 417. 'Enchanted Ground' was the term used to describe any territory
in a romance that was subject to a magician, e.g. the 'Inchanted Wood' in
Tasso's *Jerusalem Delivered*, Books 13 and 18. Bunyan's Enchanted Ground in
Pilgrim's Progress is a dark forest in which the pilgrims become drowsy. Dryden
uses the phrase twice,

> Passion's too fierce to be in Fetter's bound,
> And Nature flies him like Enchanted Ground.
> (Prologue to *Aurungzebe* (1675) ll. 9–10)

> For *Happiness* was never to be found;
> But vanished from 'em like Enchanted ground.
> (*Religio Laici* (1682) ll. 28–9)

[2] Longinus, *On the Sublime*, ed. W. R. Roberts (Cambridge, 1907), ch. 9, p. 67.
[3] *Tatler*, 254.

monly in descriptions of the *Faerie Queene*. James Thomson, for example, wrote of

> Fancy's pleasing son;
> Who, like a copious river, pour'd his song
> O'er all the mazes of enchanted ground.
> *(Summer* (1744), ll. 1573–5)

Spenser had created a world where walled castles are besieged by dragons, where knights in armour quest in search of adventure, where magicians have power to change their shapes and create illusory beings, where the magic girdle, the blatant beast, Prince Arthur and the Faerie Queen exist in a timeless forest. Such a world was regarded as the essence of romance, and, said Addison, it never lost its power to absorb the imagination of the 'gloomy and melancholy' Englishman, even of those who bent their thoughts most strenuously to dwell only on 'classic ground'. Many a scholar pointed out that even Milton had felt the fascination of the world of romance,

> Of Turneys and of Trophies hung;
> Of Forests and inchantments drear.

'Men of cold fancies, and philosophical dispositions', wrote Addison, might object to the lack of probability, but most readers were prepared to give themselves up to 'so agreeable an imposture'. The 'cold' critic was more likely to burst out, as did Sir Richard Blackmore, that the writers of romance

were seized with an irregular Poetick phrenzy, and having Decency and Probability in Contempt, fill'd the World with endless Absurdities . . . While this sort of Writing was in fashion, the Imaginations of the modern Poets . . . imbib'd a strong tincture of the Romantick Contagion, which corrupted their Taste, and occasion'd their neglect of Probability.[1]

Both Addison and Blackmore are agreed that 'modern' poetry had derived its excessive imaginative characteristics from the vogue of chivalrous romances in the middle ages, a vogue that reached its culmination in England in Spenser's *Faerie Queene*. As long as critics and poets were trying to escape from

---

[1] Blackmore, 'Essay on Epic Poetry', *Essays upon Various Subjects* (1716–17), i. 31–2.

the 'Romantick Contagion', and to dwell only on 'classic ground', it was not to be expected that the romances themselves would attract serious attention. By the middle of the eighteenth century, however, various forces were at work to modify the long-standing attitude towards the middle ages and their literature. Since the romances had long been regarded as the characteristic literary product of the middle ages, it is not surprising that when interest turned to the origins and development of English literature, the romances should become the centre of attention.

'Enchanted ground', the phrase made famous by Hurd but really quite common in the century before he wrote, signified the world of magic and faerie found in the romances. The aim of the scholars and critics discussed in the later chapters of this book was to capture some of the imaginative spirit displayed in that world. They were not attempting to put back the literary clock, but to rejuvenate contemporary poetry by encouraging 'fine fabling' and a more daring imaginativeness than most modern poets displayed. They felt that the poet could best learn how to be more imaginative by the study of poets who had been bold to an excess.

3. MEDIEVAL ROMANCES

Throughout the seventeenth and eighteenth centuries the medieval romances were characterized as narratives, in verse or prose, in which the author had given free rein to his imagination in the invention of marvellous beings and wonderful happenings. The writer's judgement was held to have been in abeyance, otherwise he would have seen that his stories were full of impossibilities, that 'blows which cleave a man in two' were not made more credible by the invention of a magic sword with which the feat was performed. Romance was synonymous with magic, with the incredible and the impossible, with the abandoning of accounts of plain matter of fact, in actions and characters. From the point of view of the modern critic of romance,[1] who can draw on a much greater body of

[1] In the following pages I am indebted to various modern discussions of the romances. The literature is voluminous and no single work adequately surveys the field. Many of the editions of single romances have valuable introductions. Useful

detailed study of medieval life and literature, this sweeping characterization is inadequate. It attempts to define a wide range of texts without the benefits of close study of a large number, and without any realization of the variety of audiences for whom they were written. It fails to take into account the varying literary skills of the original authors. As we find it expressed at any time before Hurd, it implies a condemnation of the use of magic and the supernatural. Even at the end of the eighteenth century, we do not find critics asking of the romances how the author has treated the marvellous elements in his story, or whether the reader is willing to suspend his disbelief because the marvellous is integral to the motivation of the characters and the structure of the plot. Opinion swings from general distaste to vague approval.

Most critics of the period were prepared to accept Homer's and Virgil's gods and goddesses, and the epic equivalents of giants and enchanters, but were not willing to extend the same charity to the romances. This was largely because the artistic skill of the authors of the romances known to them would not bear comparison with that of Homer or Virgil. But there were subsidiary reasons. Latin and Greek were more highly regarded than English, especially English in its earlier 'unpolished' forms. The marvellous of romance seemed more childish than that of the classics, mainly because it survived in folk-tale and children's stories. It was rarely combined with any deep understanding of human nature in the probable parts of the stories. Moreover, the marvellous of romance was thought of as a product of the superstitious attitude engendered by Roman Catholicism. Minerva and Zeus were remote figures who might well have been worshipped in the distant past, but medieval 'superstitions' were still a subject of controversy. Enlightened readers had extricated themselves from such beliefs too recently to be able to admire a literature where they were, apparently, presented in all seriousness. It was not until 1762 that Hurd was

general surveys include A. C. Baugh (ed.) *A Literary History of England* (1950), pp. 165–99; R. S. Loomis (ed.) *Arthurian Literature in the Middle Ages* (Oxford, 1959); L. A. Hibbard, *Medieval Romance in England* (New York, 1924); R. M. Wilson, *Early Middle English Literature* (1939), ch. 9 and *The Lost Literature of Medieval England* (1952), ch. 6; D. Everett, *Essays on Middle English Literature* (Oxford, 1955), pp. 1–22; G. Kane, *Middle English Literature* (1951), pp. 1–103.

able to look at 'Gothic' machinery and regard it as more suited to the poetic temperament than classical mythology.

Thus even the scholars who began the study of medieval romance, and who were dimly aware of the ancient origin and cumulative growth of romance themes and motives, wrote at times of romances as though they all conformed to one pattern and had been invented by over-imaginative minds. In fact the romances of the middle ages display a wide range of skills. Equally, the surviving texts—and there are over eighty romances, some in more than one version[1]—were written for widely varying audiences, from the courtly to the popular. They are written in a variety of metrical forms—couplets, stanzas, alliterative verse—and in prose. They vary considerably in length. Though the majority have a happy ending, the *Morte Arthur* and the *Knight of Courtesy* do not. The stories are drawn from many sources, from the Matters of Britain, France and Rome, from legends of heroes like Bevis, Guy and Havelock, from accounts of historical figures like Richard I. They are embellished by material from oriental and Celtic sources. The heroes may be motivated by mere love of adventure, or by love of a lady, by religion (e.g., Guy's desire to expiate his selfishness by adventures in the Holy Land, or the quest of the Holy Grail undertaken by the knights of the Round Table), by friendship, or by the desire to recover a kingdom. They were written at different times over a period of three hundred years. Even where we can date a particular text with accuracy, we often do not know whether it is the earliest or the latest version of that story in English, or whether other forms of the same story once existed but have not survived.[2]

The description of such a body of fiction is by no means simple. It is some help to group together all the stories told of a particular hero—Charlemagne—or group of knights—the Arthurian romances. But such a category is useful only for tracing the development of particular themes. In any such

[1] For descriptions of the romances see J. E. Wells, *A Manual of the Writings in Middle English, 1050–1400* and supplements (New Haven, 1916ff.). The MSS of romances are listed in C. Brown and R. H. Robbins, *The Index of Middle English Verse* (New York, 1943).

[2] H. S. Bennett shows that of 84 romances written between 1100 and 1500, 65 exist only in fifteenth century MSS, *Library*, 5th series, i. (1946–7), 167–78.

group we shall find good, bad and indifferent romances, the poems will be written for different audiences, in different metrical forms, in different centuries. We shall, of course, find that almost all the romances are written for entertainment, that didacticism, even where it exists, does not take first place in the author's mind. Most obviously, in all the romances the story is treated in terms of medieval chivalry. Whatever the source of the story—and there are romances recounting the stories of Troy, of Alexander, of Orpheus—there is no attempt on the part of the author to lend interest to it by exploiting the sense of remoteness in time or strangeness in modes of behaviour of a past civilization. A modern reader finds the romances 'romantic' as did his eighteenth-century counterpart, precisely because they evoke the sense of the remote and strange. To the original audience, however, they must have seemed remarkably up to date and contemporary.

The eighteenth-century scholar enjoyed the romances because they were portraits of a vanished age, much as we enjoy *Tom Jones*. An age becomes romantic as it recedes, and even its careful records of its way of life acquire a romantic aura. But it was not until the end of the eighteenth century that men began to manufacture the 'romantic', by turning in their fictions from the contemporary scene to the evocation of a past age.[1] The medieval author of a romance held the interest of his audience by recounting exciting adventures of noble knights, by introducing giants, dragons, enchanters, magic castles, fairyland, enchanted ladies, and by describing contemporary aristocratic activities in a heightened manner. Feasts, costumes, architecture, jewellery, armour, the knightly skills in hunting, often receive detailed treatment, realistic in the sense that they are accurately portrayed, but idealized in the sense that the account goes beyond what would normally be found. The heroes and heroines themselves do not behave like

[1] For the development of the historical novel, see J. M. S. Tompkins, *The Popular Novel in England*, 1770–1800 (1962), pp. 223–42. The antiquary Francis Douce assisted John Kemble in the costuming of Shakespeare's Roman plays and later, in 1823, provided details from his collection of illuminated mss for the historical costumes used in *King John* at Covent Garden. Here the designer was J. R. Planché (see Planché, *Recollections and Reflections* (1872), i. 54, and *Costume of Shakespeare's Historical Tragedy of King John* (1823).)

men and women in real life. They live in a world in which men
fight on the merest pretext and the ladies fall in love with as
little justification. The presence in the romances of so much
description, however, led eighteenth-century scholars to look to
the romances for facts about medieval life. The picture of
aristocratic life and manners that emerged was naturally more
in accord with the romancer's idealization than with reality.
But even if, in the middle ages, one would rarely have found
assembled such a feast of delights as the king in *The Sqyr of
Lowe Degre* offers to his daughter, from such a list we can
discover what delights *could* be offered.

In turning to the romances the scholars from Percy to Scott
were attracted partly by the accidental quality which the
lapse of time had created—the pleasure that springs from a
sense of the 'otherness' of the past, conveyed in entertaining
fiction. Partly they were interested in the 'realistic' details
which made them romantic antiquarian documents for the
eighteenth century; and partly they were eager to revive early
examples of fictions in which, it seemed, the authors had been
free to indulge in the marvellous.

4. THEORIES OF THE ORIGIN OF ROMANCE:
HUET TO CAYLUS

Most contemporaries of Addison felt, with him, that 'romantic'
literature possessed a quality, or perhaps simply a type of
subject matter, that was easily identifiable. It seemed to them
that one sort of 'modern' literature was full of the fancifulness
that delighted in dragons and enchanters. Classical literature
on the other hand appeared to be comparatively free from such
things. Whence, then, had this material come? Attempts to
explain the origin of romantic fabling, and to trace its progress
began in the late seventeenth century. The attraction which all
such investigations held for the eighteenth century may be
seen in the number of philosophers, scholars, critics, historians
and antiquaries who wrote on the origin and progress of some
established institution or genre. Gothic architecture in particular, which like romantic fabling had made its appearance in
Europe after the collapse of the Roman Empire, was the object

of many different theories of origin; so many that by the end of the century John Britton was able to list sixty-six different theories.[1] Its origin was held to be Saracenic by Wren, Arabian by Stukeley, Norman by Godwin. Warburton distinguished between 'Saxon' and 'Norman' styles, the former he thought being an imitation of the debased Grecian architecture found in Palestine, the latter originating with the 'Gothic' invaders of Spain, who created the pointed arch in imitation of their sacred groves, with the help of 'Saracen architects'.[2]

The same races—the Goths or Northern nations of Europe, the Moors or Saracens, and the Normans—occur in various combinations in the attempts to describe also the origins of rhyme and of romance. 'The Moors', wrote Stephen Riou in 1768, 'or what is the same thing . . . The Arabians or Saracens, . . . have expressed in their architecture the same taste as in their poetry, both the one and the other falsely delicate, crowded with superfluous ornaments, and often very unnatural. The imagination is highly worked up in both, but it is an extravagant imagination.'[3] The Arabic poetry to which Riou vaguely refers was generally regarded as the germ of medieval romance, and, since it was in rhyme, of European rhymed verse as well. The architecture, the fables and romances, and the addiction to rhyme, of the middle ages, were commonly seen as of Eastern origin, treading the path to Europe by way of the Moorish invasion of Spain, and through the contact of Crusader and Saracen in the Holy Land. When Thomas Warton began to study the literature of the middle ages it was 'an established maxim of modern criticism, that the fictions of Arabian imagination were communicated to the western world by means of the crusades'.[4] Many believed that the Crusaders brought with them also a style of architecture

[1] John Britton, *The Architectural Antiquities of Great Britain* (1807–26), v. 33 f. See also Charles L. Eastlake, *History of the Gothic Revival* (1872), pp. 132–3.

[2] In a note to Pope's *Moral Essay*, iv. l. 29, in *Works of Pope* (1760), iii. 372. The theory was also held by Wren (*Parentalia* (1750), pp. 354–5, 361). For a survey of ideas about Gothic architecture in the period see A. O. Lovejoy, *Essays in the History of Ideas* (Baltimore, 1948), pp. 136 ff.

[3] S. Riou, *The Grecian Order of Architecture* (1768), p. 9.

[4] T. Warton, *History of English Poetry* (1774), i. sig. al. See also T. Warton, J. Bentham and others, *Essays on Gothic Architecture* (1800), pp. 1–14.

The King's Library

based on the pointed arch, 'ramified windows' and spires. But 'among the Germans it was strenuously maintained that [rhyme] derived its origin and use from the Northern Scalds'.[1] The origin of rhyme was one of the few topics on which Gray had compiled a dissertation for his intended history of English poetry.[2] Avoiding conjecture, he cautiously traced the origin of rhyme in Europe not to the Arabs but to late Latin examples, and he dated the introduction of rhyme into England in the twelfth century. He also showed that some of the Germanic tribes (the 'Goths') used rhyme before the Norman Conquest. Of particular interest to him were the sixth-century examples of rhyme in Welsh poetry; in so far as Gray held to a theory of the origin of rhyme, it was to a Celtic theory.

The commonly received opinion in the seventeeth century was that rhyme and romance had been learned by the Spaniards from the Moors. This, the view of Salmasius,[3] was not accepted by Pierre Daniel Huet, whose *Traité de l'Origine des Romans* was prefixed to Madame de la Fayette's romance *Zayde*, in 1670.[4] The *Traité* is important as the first attempt to write a history of fiction, setting the pattern for later surveys by Clara Reeve (1785), John Moore (1797) and John Dunlop (1814). In part, Huet's plan is to give instruction for writing fiction by judicious appraisal of particular works, and to warn his readers of the precautions necessary when reading romances. His main interest is in tracing the development of the seventeenth-century French romances and in providing the

[1] Isaac D'Israeli, *Amenities of Literature* (1841), 'Origin of Rhyme'. This gives a survey of the various theories. Jean-George Wachter in his *Glossarium Germanicum* (Leipsig, 1736–7), p. 1304 suggested that *Roman* (i.e. historia fabulosa) was developed from the 'Gothic' 'RIMAN, RIEMEN (Gallicé *rimer*), *metricé scribere*'.

[2] Gray, *Poems, Letters, and Essays* (Everyman Library, 1946), pp. 349–65.

[3] Salmasius, Preface to *Achilles Tatius* (Leyden, 1640); Francis Vavasseur, *De Ludicra Dictione Liber* (Paris, 1658), p. 137; P. D. Huet, *Huetiana* (Paris, 1722), p. 191; G. Massieu, *Histoire de la Poésie Françoise* (Paris, 1739), p. 89; Quadrio, *Storia d'Ogni Poesia* (Milan, 1739–52), iv. 299.

[4] The *Traité* was frequently reprinted with editions of *Zayde*, and appeared separately in French, in Latin (1682), Dutch (1679, 1715) and English (1672, 1715, 1720). Huet made additions and alterations in the second (1678) and seventh (1693) editions. It has been edited by A. Kok (Amsterdam, 1942). For Huet's account of writing the *Traité*, see his autobiography, translated by John Aikin (1810).

genre with a pedigree. He limits his definition to works in prose, 'Romances, properly so called, are Fictions of Love Adventures artfully formed and delivered in prose, for the delight and instruction of the Readers', the chief design of such works being the instruction of the reader by representing the reward of virtue and the chastisement of vice. He excludes such 'fabulous' histories as that of Herodotus, and all entirely false histories of the 'imaginary Originals of nations'. 'For a Romance is the Fiction of things that might have happened, but never did happen, whereas Fables are of Things that never were, and never can be.'[1] Huet's predecessors in the discussion were Giraldi and Pigna,[2] but they had treated only of romances in verse, recommending Boiardo and Ariosto as models. Huet, who has in mind the contemporary romances in France, those in which love is the principal subject, with war and politics as incidentals, dismisses the old French romances of the middle ages as not 'regular', since they are predominantly concerned with fighting.

The origin of fiction, 'this agreeable Amusement of a harmless Idleness', he traces not to Provence or Spain, but to the East—to the Egyptians, Arabs, Persians and Syrians, with their fondness for allegory, fable and metaphor. From this area he follows its path to the rich and voluptuous Ionians of Asia Minor, and so to the Greeks; by another route, from the luxurious and pleasure-loving Milesians to the Sybarites and to Italy. With the decline of these rich civilizations, the art of romantic fabling for pleasure declined also. The romances of the middle ages were born of ignorance. Lack of proper materials for histories led to the production of fabulous histories. The works of Taliessin, Melkin [i.e. Merlin], Hunibaldus Francus, the Pseudo-Turpin, and Geoffrey of Monmouth, show how history 'began to degenerate into Romance'.[3] Seizing upon the easy credulity of their audience, 'Your Poetasters, Ballad-mongers, story-Tellers, and Jugglers of Provence; in short all Those of that Country, who practised what they called "The Gay

[1] *Upon the Original of Romances,* in Samuel Croxall, *Select Collection of Novels* (1720), i. pp. ii, v.

[2] *Discorsi di M. Giovambattista Giraldi Cintio* (Venice, 1554); *I Romanzi di M. Giovan Battista Pigna* (Venice, 1554).

[3] Croxall, p. xxxvii.

16

Science", began in the Days of Hugh Capet to Romance in good Earnest.'[1]

Provence, according to Huet, gave birth to the romances of the middle ages, and from France, both Spain and Italy borrowed the stories and the art. A further infusion of romantic fabling came from the Normans, whose singing of the exploits of Roland at the battle of Hastings was evidence of their propensity to romance. The 'cloud of ignorance' which then covered Europe is for Huet sufficient explanation for the spontaneous outburst of romancing. All barbarous peoples like fabulous stories, whether the Goths with their Runic memorials or the savages of North America. 'This inclination to Fables . . . is common to all Men, [and] is not the effect of Reasoning, nor does it arise from Imitation or Custom; it is natural to them, and is rivetted in the very Frame and Disposition of the Soul.'[2]

Huet thus reverses his position, and from tracing the path of romance from Provence to Spain and Italy, turns to a theory that all romances 'are of the Country's Growth, born upon the place, and not transplanted thither'.[3] It was therefore possible for later scholars to claim Huet's support for the theories that fiction originated in the East, and that medieval romance had its origin either in Provence or in the spontaneous productions of the barbarians of Northern Europe. Evan Evans later interpreted the references to Taliessin and Merlin as giving 'the honour to the Britons'.[4] Thomas Warton was not the only person to claim Huet as a supporter of the Arab–Spanish theory; an anonymous writer of 1695 had already done so.[5]

The reputation of Huet, 'than whom *France* never produced a more learned man',[6] made it difficult for later scholars to neglect his theories. The interest of the topic made it inevitable that the origin of romance should become a subject for lengthy

---

[1] Most of Huet's information about the middle ages is drawn from C. Fauchet's *Recueil* (Paris, 1581).

[2] Croxall, p. xliii.

[3] ibid., p. xlvi.

[4] *Percy–Evans Correspondence*, p. 76.

[5] 'The Rise, Progress and Destruction of Fables and Romances' in *Two Essays sent in a Letter from Oxford. by L. P.* (1695), p. 31. cf. Warton, *History of English Poetry*, i. 112 n.

[6] Gregorio Mayáns y Siscár (1699–1782), *Life of Cervantes*, trans. John Ozell, in *Don Quixote*, trans. Charles Jervas (1742), i. 68.

and sometimes acrimonious discussion. Thomas Warton, for example, rejoiced that the 'sophistry and ignorance' of Huet—who had confounded 'romances of chivalry, romances of gallantry, and all the fables of the Provencial poets'[1]—had been 'detected and exposed' by Warburton. Warburton indeed returned so often to the subject, with his customary dogmatism and tenacity, that few readers could be unaware either of his views or of the importance of the subject to him. His first treatment of it, in a supplement to Jervas's translation of *Don Quixote* (1742), so delighted Pope that, in all probability, both subject and opinion were thereafter endeared to him. 'I never read a thing with more pleasure', Pope wrote, 'Before I got over 2 paragraphs I cryed out, Aut Erasmus, aut Diabolus! I knew you as certainly as the Ancients did the Gods, by the first Pace & the very Gait'.[2] 'Neither the translating painter, nor the simple poet', observed Isaac D'Israeli, 'could imagine the heap of absurdities they were admiring. Whatever Warburton here asserted was false, and whatever he conjectured was erroneous'.[3] Reprinted as a note on Armado in *Love's Labour's Lost* (I.i.) in 1747,[4] Warburton's views were repeated in commentaries on Shakespeare for the rest of the century. In abbreviated form the article reappeared as part of his preface to volumes three and four of *Clarissa* (1748), and as a note in the edition of Pope in 1751.[5]

Warburton's theory elaborates one put forward by Sir William Temple in 1695. Temple found the origin of romances in the 'adventures and successes of the first Christian, pretended heroes and their combats with Pagans and Saxons', instancing the wars of Arthur against the Saxons. The later elaboration of Geoffrey of Monmouth's account of Arthur he attributed to the influence of Spanish romances 'which many years after filled the world with so much of that idle trash'.[6] Warburton, equally

---

[1] Warton, *History*, i. 112 n.

[2] Pope, *Correspondence*, ed. George Sherburn (1956), iv. 455.

[3] *Quarrels of Authors* (ed. 1840), p. 168 n.

[4] Warburton's edition of *The Plays of Shakespeare* (1747), ii, a gathering of four leaves between pp. 288 and 289.

[5] *Works of Pope*, ed. W. Warburton (1751), iv. 166–9; reprinted in J. Warton's edition of Pope (1822), iv. 166–7.

[6] Temple, *Works* (1720), ii. 532.

unaware of the late date of the Peninsular romances, and, like Hurd after him, unacquainted with their contents, boldly asserted that the 'elder romances', headed by *Amadis of Gaul*, treated of the driving of the Saracens from France and Spain, that the later romances, headed by *Amadis of Greece*, dealt with the crusades into Greece and Asia to support the Byzantine Empire and recover the Holy Sepulchre, that the elements of magic in romance derived from Crusaders and Eastern travellers, and that Arthurian material passed from Geoffrey of Monmouth to Spanish romancers, who changed Geoffrey's Saxons into Saracens. Warburton's views are of no value in themselves, but serve to show the depth of ignorance on romance subjects that existed before Percy. Thomas Warton's unwarranted deference to Warburton in the *History of English Poetry*, a constant source of irritation to Ritson, probably led Tyrwhitt[1] to undertake a detailed refutation of the 'hasty and imperfect view' that Warburton had adopted.

Other views were also put forward before Percy and Warton began to study the subject. Humphrey Wanley, commenting on *Le mort Arthure* in Harley MS 2252, writes, 'This I take to be translated from the French Romance of K. Arthur, which seemeth to have been invented by the Armorican Britons'.[2] The same theory was held by Mattain Veysière La Croze[3] and later by Richard Hole[4] and John Leyden. But such a limited undertaking as to attempt to trace the beginnings of Arthurian romance in Brittany was rare. Theorizers preferred to trace the origin of romantic fiction in general, rather than the sources of particular stories.

While English writers still theorized from grossly inadequate knowledge, French scholars were pouring the results of their researches into the volumes published by the Académie des Inscriptions et Belles Lettres. One of the most brilliant of their number, the Comte de Caylus, studied medieval French romances closely and attempted to show the links that bound

[1] Supplement to the *Edition of Shakespeare's Plays Published in 1778* (1780), i. 373–80.

[2] *Catalogue of the Harley MSS* (1759), MS 2252, art. 49.

[3] M. Jordan, *Histoire de la Vie et des Ouvrages de Mr. de la Croze* (Amsterdam, 1741), pp. 220–1. Warton refers to the theory in *History*, iii. 477.

[4] R. Hole, *Arthur, or the Northern Enchantment* (1789), pp. vii, 160.

modern France to the middle ages.[1] He was, in all probability, the first scholar to show that stories had been transmitted from age to age and from peoples to peoples, at each stage being remoulded by their new narrators, who adapted them to the customs and manners of their own time and nation. In examining the romances,[2] he agrees with Huet that they originated in France. He compares the Pseudo-Turpin Chronicle with the authentic records of the reign of Charlemagne and shows that it must have been fabricated two hundred years after Charlemagne's death, that is, about 1095.[3] It was, he thought, written in order to encourage the princes to take part in the Holy War against the Infidel, on the model of Charlemagne's wars. But he was also able to show that the Chronicle was not in itself a romance; chivalry and knighthood are not fully elaborated in it. What he found supported his theory of the slow elaboration of fables; the Chronicle, especially in its later manuscripts, contained elements that were normally thought of as characteristic of romance—giants, individual combats, exaggerated accounts of valour, and a wonderful sword called Durandel. The presence of these indicated to Caylus that by the eleventh century romantic accretions were transforming the historical Charlemagne into a hero of romance.

Caylus found the source of some of the stories incorporated into historical narratives in the Old Testament. In particular he pointed to Goliath and the fall of the walls of Jericho. Other modifications he traced to social changes in the attitude towards women, in the institution of the orders of chivalry and in the establishment of tournaments. He fills out his account with much scholarly detail. When he turns to Arthurian story, however, his explanation of the growth of this body of legends is based on his theory of jealousy or noble emulation. Just as

[1] See Samuel Rocheblave, *Essai sur le Comte de Caylus* (Paris, 1889), p. 79.

[2] Caylus became a member of the Académie des Inscriptions in 1742. His articles include 'Les féeries des anciens comparées à celles des modernes', 'Origine de l'ancienne chevalerie et des anciens romans' (*Histoire de l'Académie des Inscriptions*, xxiii. 144 f., 236 f.) 'Les Fabliaux', 'Guillaume de Machaut' (*Mémoires de l'académie*, xx. 352 f., 399 f.).

[3] This was the view of Bartholin, *De Holgero Dano* (Copenhagen, 1677), p. 145.

the French and English imitated the Romans in tracing their ancestry back to the Trojans, so the English, jealous of the French Charlemagne, invented an English hero, Arthur. He sees the proof of this in the parallels between the two. The way in which both legends grew slowly from historical accounts suggested to him that the same principle was at work in both. In both, romantic material accumulated slowly, in the case of Arthur the initial impetus being given by Geoffrey of Monmouth's *Historia*. Because the legends of the Grail are told in romances of Arthur's knights, Caylus believed that they were of English origin. Whatever the ultimate sources of these stories may be, we know now that they were first attached to Arthurian heroes by French authors. But Caylus believed that the story of Joseph of Arimathea's coming to England with a 'graal' containing the blood of Christ, was an English invention in imitation of the French tradition that Lazarus came to France and was the first Bishop of Marseilles. The invention of the graal story he attributed to the translation of the body of Lazarus at Marseilles in 1172 and to the religious excitement produced by the opening of the tomb of St Maximin in 1279. Supported by his hitherto unparalleled reading in medieval literature, Caylus's account was persuasive.[1] His method too was scholarly, based on close knowledge of the texts in manuscripts. Greater things might have been expected of him had his attention not turned from medieval literature to classical art. Interesting as the details of his researches are, however, it is his general attitude towards medieval studies that is most revealing. 'Rien n'est indigne de recherches, principalement sur des choses qui regardent notre langue et le progrès que l'esprit a fait dans notre nation.'[2] Interest centred on the origin of romantic fiction because it was generally accepted that the French and English nations had been nurtured on romance.

[1] I have used the full text of Caylus's *De l'ancienne Chevalerie et des Anciens Romans* printed at Paris (1813). An abridged form of the article as printed in the *Histoire*, xxiii, appears in the *Encyclopédie, ou Dictionnaire des Sciences, des Arts et des Metiers* (Neufchastel, 1765), xiv. 342 f. Caylus prints (loc. cit., pp. 41–2) the opinion of the historian Millot, that the Fisher King represents Pope Gregory VII, the successor of St Peter, the fisherman. The Fisher King's wound is Gregory's gout! This is surely the earliest attempt to explain this mystery.
[2] Quoted by Rocheblave, p. 81.

5. ROMANCE SCHOLARSHIP IN FRANCE

The antiquarian spirit, which was once confined to inquiries concerning the manners, the buildings, the records, and the coins of the ages that preceded us, has now extended itself to those poetical compositions which were popular among our forefathers, but which have gradually sunk into oblivion through the decay of language, and the prevalence of a correct and polished taste. Books printed in the black letter are sought for with the same avidity with which the English antiquary peruses a monumental inscription, or treasures up a Saxon piece of money. The popular ballad, composed by some illiterate minstrel, and which has been handed down by tradition for several centuries, is rescued from the hands of the vulgar, to obtain a place in the collection of the man of taste. Verses, which a few years past, were thought worthy the attention of children only, or of the lowest and rudest orders, are now admired for that artless simplicity which once obtained the name of coarseness and vulgarity.

Vicesimus Knox *Essays, Moral and Literary* (ed. 1823), i. 257

It was not only in England that 'a certain antiquarian tendency in literature, a fonder, more earnest looking back into the Past'[1] began to manifest itself in the middle of the eighteenth century. Carlyle dated the beginning of the similar movement in Germany at the publication in 1757 of Bodmer's *Chriemhildens Rache und die Klage,* a part of what was later called the *Nibelungen Lied.* In Germany, as in England, 'Manuscripts, that for ages had lain dormant, . . . issued from their archives into public view; books that had circulated only in mean guise for the amusement of the people, [became] important, not to one or two virtuosos, but to the general body of the learned.'[2]

It is more difficult to decide when such a movement began in France, since there is an almost unbroken tradition of the study of early French literature, from Jean de Nostredame's largely fictitious *Les Vies des plus Célèbres et Anciens Poètes Provençaux* in 1575, and Claude Fauchet's *Recueil de l'origine de la langue et poésie françoise, ryme et romans,* in 1581, to the study of medieval history and literature undertaken by the Benedictines of St Maur in the seventeenth century. These great historical surveys of French literature were supplemented by

[1] Thomas Carlyle reviewing *Das Nibelungen Lied* in *Westminster Review*, No. 29, repr. in *Miscellaneous Essays* (1872), iii. 111.
[2] Carlyle, p. 112.

shorter accounts, like that of Massieu in 1739, by studies of smaller topics in the transactions of the Académie des Inscriptions, and by monographs on chivalry by Sainte-Palaye, on the uses of romances, with a bibliography, by du Fresnoy, and on the Norse Edda by Mallet.[1]

When English scholars such as Gray, Thomas Warton, Percy, Hurd and Gibbon began to be interested in medieval English literature, they turned naturally for information to the earlier French work; to Fauchet, for example, who had traced the development of the French language and of romances, described the origin of poetry and rhyme—topics of great interest in England in the eighteenth century—and discussed Trouvères, Chanteurs and Jongleurs. From the *Recueil* they derived the view that romances were first written in the time of Hugh Capet, when Jongleurs and Trouvères wandered from court to court singing their songs and stories in the common language, 'Romain rustique'.[2] From Fauchet again, via Massieu, came Warton's statement, so scornfully attacked by Ritson, that before the Crusades romances were about Arthur and Charlemagne, afterwards, about Godfrey of Bulloigne, Solyman, Nouraddin, Caliphs and Sultans.[3] Similarly, information about the *Roman de Brut* by 'Eustache' was taken from Fauchet by Massieu and copied by Joseph Warton, Percy and Thomas Warton.[4] Percy's *Essay on the Ancient English Minstrels* is much indebted to Fauchet. Without the work of Sainte-Palaye and Chapelain in the transactions of the Académie des Inscriptions, Hurd's *Letters on Chivalry* would never have been written. Sainte-Palaye is the constant source of information about chivalry, not only for Hurd, Percy and

---

[1] The Benedictine *Histoire Littéraire* was published in 12 vols. (Paris, 1732–63). G. Massieu, *Histoire de la Poésie Françoise* (Paris, 1739); J. B. de la Curne de Sainte-Palaye, *Mémoires sur l'ancienne chevalerie*, 2 vols. (Paris, 1759), with addit. vol., 1781; Paul-Henri Mallet, *Introduction à l'Histoire de Dannemarc* (Copenhagen, 1755), *Monumens de la Poésie des Celtes et . . . des Scandinaves* (Copenhagen, 1756), trans. Percy, *Northern Antiquities* (1770). For Du Fresnoy, see below, p. 24.

[2] Fauchet, *Recueil* (Paris, 1581), p. 32. This is repeated by Massieu, Huet, and Akenside (*Pleasures of Imagination* (1744), note to ii. 19).

[3] Fauchet, pp. 75–6; Massieu, pp. 105–6; Warton, *History*, i. 110; Ritson, *Observations* (1782), p. 8.

[4] Fauchet, p. 82; Massieu, p. 109; J. Warton, *Essay on Genius of Pope* (ed. 1806), i. 227–8; Percy, *Reliques*, (1767), iii. p. ix; Warton, *History*, i. 64.

Thomas Warton, but for Gibbon, Joseph Sterling and later even Byron.[1] The sciences of palaeography and diplomatics were also born of earlier French scholarship. Charles Dufresne, Seigneur Du Cange (1610–88), was the founder of Medieval Latin philology. Warton was very much indebted to his Latin glossary in the edition of Carpentier (Paris, 1733–6). One of the bibliographical guides much used by the English scholars was the Abbé Lenglet du Fresnoy's *De l'Usage des Romans* (Paris, 1734)[2] which Francis Douce[3] regarded as 'extremely useful and the only one of its kind', in spite of its errors and omissions. Du Fresnoy listed editions of romances, arranging them in fourteen sections, which included Greek and Latin Romances, Political, Satirical, and Heroic. The section on Romances of Chivalry is subdivided into Romances of Arthur, Charlemagne, Amadis and others. There is also a list of French metrical romances still in manuscript. The whole work was to prove invaluable to English scholars and collectors. We cannot say that the impetus to study the romances came from France; but without the vast body of French scholarship, Percy and Warton would have found their task even more difficult than it was. Earlier medieval scholarship in England had been directed at subjects far removed from the romances, and though there was help to be gained from Hearne's edition of medieval chronicles, it was largely with a sense of rebellion against Hearne's antiquarianism that the new generation of English scholars worked.[4]

6. ROMANCES AS HISTORICAL DOCUMENTS

The explanation offered most frequently by the eighteenth-century English scholars for their interest in the medieval

[1] See Gibbon, *Decline and Fall*, Ch. 58 (ed. J. B. Bury (1896–1900), vi. 284 n.), 'Hints relating to Chivalry', *The Bee* (April, 1793); J. Sterling, 'Dissertation on Chivalry', prefixed to *Chevalier Bayard* (Dublin, 1781); Byron, Additions to Preface to *Childe Harold*. Warton sent his copy of Sainte-Palaye to Percy in January, 1763 (*Percy-Warton Correspondence*, pp. 77, 82).

[2] Fresnoy published his *De l'Usage des Romans* under the pseudonym M. le C. Gordon de Percel. He also edited *Le Roman de la Rose*, 3 vols. (Amsterdam, 1734 and Paris, 1735).

[3] See Douce's MS note in his copy in the Bodleian Library (Douce, L. 619). Ritson's Catalogue of Romances was compiled to fill the need that Du Fresnoy's work satisfied imperfectly. See p. 132 below.

[4] For an account of earlier medieval scholarship in England, and the response of Percy and Warton to it, see Appendix I.

romances was that in such texts were to be found details of the manners and customs of our ancestors which were otherwise unobtainable. The accumulated work of previous generations of English scholars, had, it seemed to Percy and Warton, been directed to political and theological ends no longer interesting. The new race of scholars had different aims. 'N'y aura-t-il que l'antiquité Grecque et Romaine qui mérite notre attention et nos recherches?' asked Nicholas Freret in 1737.[1] The plea was for an interest in medieval literature, and in particular in the romances, and was heard in England as well as France. The quest was for light on the manners of life and modes of thought of the past, 'les moeurs du siècle de l'Auteur, . . . ses opinions et sa manière de penser',[2] where the richest sources were the romances. Tapestries, paintings and sculptures showed that the authors of romances were faithful to the dress of their day. Though 'fabuleux pour les événements', romances were 'historique pour le reste'[3] and thus were valuable supplements to the bare recitals of the chronicles. Chapelain was the first writer, it would seem, to have propounded this opinion, and did so as early as 1647. But after him there is a host of French scholars who drew on romances for such detail. They are listed by Sainte-Palaye,

Du Cange, dans son Glossaire latin et dans ses savantes Dissertations, du Chesne dans ses Généalogies, le P. Ménestrier, dans ses divers Traités sur la Chevalerie, le Blason, la Noblesse, les Tournois, &c. Pasquier et Fauchet dans leurs immenses recherches sur tous les pointes de nos Antiquités, Favin et la Colombière dans leurs *Théatres d'Honneur et de Chevalerie*, la plupart de ceux qui ont écrit l'histoire, particulière des Provinces et des Villes, M. le Président de Valbonnais, D. Vaissette et D. Calmet, tous généralement sont souvent usage de nos anciens Romans. Auguste Galland, Catel, Caseneuve, Salvaing, et ceux qui ont écrit avec le plus de profondeur sur les matières féodales, n'ont point dédaigné de s'appuyer de l'autorité des Romanciers, dans les plus grandes questions de notre jurisprudence; et plusieurs nous ont laissé des témoinages formels

[1] In his preface to the Comte de Caylus's translation of *Tiran le Blanc* ('London', i.e. Paris, n.d. [c. 1737]), i. p. xxv.
[2] ibid., p. xxviii.
[3] Jean Chapelain, *De la lecture des Vieux Romans* (c. 1647) ed. A. Feillet (Paris, 1870), p. 15.

du profit qu'on peut tirer de la lecture des Romans. Tels sont entre les autres, Etienne Pasquier, le Président Fauchet, André Favin, Chantereau le Fèvre, et sur-tout Jean le Labourer.[1]

One could not provide a comparable list of English scholars before Percy who had used the romances in their researches. But, influenced by the French tradition, Percy chose the ballads in the *Reliques* to 'shew the gradation of our language, exhibit the progress of popular opinions, display the peculiar manners and customs of former ages, or throw light on our earlier classical poets'.[2] For the antiquary, the romances were becoming 'the veritable registers of their ages', valuable to illustrate 'many obscure points in geography and history'.[3] Lord Lyttelton was commended by Thomas Warton for using the *Brut* of Wace in his *History of Henry II* and thereby showing that 'important facts and curious illustrations of history may be drawn from such obsolete but authentic resources'.[4] Joseph Strutt, in his *Sports and Pastimes of the People of England* (1801), draws on such romances as *Bevis*, *Launfal*, *Eglamore*, *Richard*, *Ipomydon* and *Morte d'Arthur* to illustrate medieval games, minstrelsy and jousting.[5] For all who found the 'history of manners' the 'most interesting part of *all* history'[6]—and in 1774 Thomas Warton was able to congratulate his age as one of 'curiosity, distinguished for its love of historical anecdotes and the investigation of antient manners',[7]—the romance was a source of delight. 'Works of fancy, written in remote ages, are the most authentic historical documents with respect to the manners and customs of the time in which they are composed.'[8]

This view of the romances exercised a fascination over those

[1] *Mémoires sur l'Ancienne Chevalerie* (Paris, 1759), ii. 111–12.
[2] Percy, *Reliques* (1765), i. p. ix.
[3] Isaac D'Israeli, *Amenities of Literature* (1841), i. ch. ix 'Gothic Romances'.
[4] Warton, *History of English Poetry* (1774), i. 64; Lyttelton, *History of Henry II* (1767–71), iii. 180.
[5] *Sports and Pastimes* (ed. W. Hone, 1830), pp. xli, xlvii, 12, 41, 44, 65, 129, 184, 185, 193, 375.
[6] J. Warton, *Works of Pope* (ed. 1797), iii. 305.
[7] Warton, *History*, iii. p. lxxvii.
[8] G. Ellis, Preface to G. L. Way, *Fabliaux or Tales* (1796–1800), i. p. ii. Even Warburton came to approve of the study of romances and persuaded himself that he was the 'first who gave the hint, that these extravagant compositions were a rude picture of life and manners' (*Percy–Warton Correspondence*, Appendix II).

who wrote on them. It had the appeal of a paradox—here in the wildest imaginative stories were embedded facts of social history. It found easy acceptance also, because the authors of romances were universally regarded as men lacking sufficient judgement to realize how improbable their tales were, but equally incapable of inventing new costumes or manners. The great danger in this approach was the difficulty of drawing a distinguishing line between what was purely fictional in any romance, and what was based on direct observation of everyday aristocratic life. Much of the later idealization of the middle ages stems from this propensity to take as fact the codes of behaviour extracted from the purely fictitious behaviour of many knights-errant in romances. Thus Warton and Hurd often write as if convinced that medieval aristocrats were constantly on the alert to protect damsels in distress, or to set out in pursuit of adventures at the whim of a superior baron. And, trying to fit the giants of romance into his sociological picture, Hurd explained that this is what oppressive feudal lords became in the hands of the romance-writer.

Study of the romances as 'authentic historical documents' was believed to bring about the humanizing of medieval history, which the later scholars regarded as necessary after the arid work of the previous two hundred years. This was one of the justifications for the attention bestowed on them by the scholars. The study of a literature which had descended to the nursery, and been the subject of so many moral and aesthetic objections, called indeed for many justifications.

7. THE PRINTING OF THE ROMANCES

It is impossible that anything should be universally tasted and approved by a multitude, though they are only the rabble of a nation, which hath not in it some peculiar aptness to please and gratify the mind of man.

Addison, *Spectator*, 70

In their search for manuscripts of the metrical romances of the middle ages, the scholars were discovering the original forms of some stories with which they were already quite familiar. Few nurseries in the eighteenth century can have been without the chapbook versions of the romances, little twenty-four page booklets, badly printed on poor paper with crude illustrations, of *Guy of Warwick, Bevis of Southampton, Valentine and Orson, Don Bellianis* and *The Seven Champions of Christendom*. Caxton had recommended the *Morte Darthur* 'unto all noble Princes, Lords and Ladies and Gentlewomen', and three hundred years later the 'Romances in sheets', their 'coats in tatters and the cuts in wood'

> are the Peasant's joys, when, placed at ease,
> Half his delighted offspring mount his knees.[1]

The romances were often part of a nostalgic memory of childhood. Crabbe, for example, regretted the passing of those days 'to care unknown' when he 'Winged round the globe with Rowland or Sir Guy', when the child

> in magic themes
> O'er worlds bewitched, in early rapture dreams.

With the coming of mature judgement, however, 'Enchantment bowed to Wisdom's serious plan', and the 'ancient worthies of Romance' pleased no more.

> My doughty giants all are slain or fled,
> And all my knights—blue, green and yellow—dead!
> Magicians cease to charm me with their art,
> And not a griffin flies to glad my heart.[2]

Addison had plenty of evidence, besides Spenser, Shakespeare and Milton, for his assertion that the 'naturally fanciful' Englishman loved the romances. The period from 1660 to 1720 was the most prolific in the printing of editions of them. Johnson recorded of Edmund (Neale) Smith (1669?–1710) whose life coincided with this period of printing, that he 'had diligently perused, and accurately remembered, the old romances of Knight-errantry'.[3] According to William Nicolson, in 1714, 'King *Arthur*'s Story in *English*' was 'often sold by the Ballad-singers, with the like Authentic Records of *Guy of Warwick* and *Bevis of Southampton*'.[4] George Ellis, writing in

---

[1] *Life and Poetical Works of George Crabbe* (1847), p. 134.

[2] Crabbe, *The Library* (1781), in *Works* (1847), p. 110 n. (The original version.)

[3] Johnson, *Lives of the Poets*, ed. G. Birkbeck Hill (1905), ii. 20. The information he had from Gilbert Walmsley.

[4] W. Nicolson, *The English Historical Library* (1714), p. 38. The ballad of Arthur was probably Thomas Deloney's, reprinted in 1680, 1690 and 1700.

1805, remarked of *The Seven Wise Masters* that it was 'so truly delectable, till lately, to every schoolboy',[1] while Scott recorded that *Roswal and Lillian* was 'the last metrical Romance of Chivalry which retained its popularity in Scotland, & indeed was sung in Edinbr. within these 20 years by a sort of reciter in the streets'.[2] *Eger and Grime* now exists only in three copies, all deriving from the seventeenth and early eighteenth centuries, one in the Percy Folio Manuscript, one in an edition dated 1687, and one in an Aberdeen edition of 1711.[3]

The printing of Malory's *Morte Darthur*, however, is not typical of the romances. It was printed six times between 1485 and 1585, only once in the seventeenth century (1634), and not again until 1816, when two reprints of the 1634 edition appeared, closely followed in 1817 by Southey's reprint of Caxton's text. But Raoul Lefevre's *Recuyell of the historyes of Troye* reached its eighteenth edition in 1738 and seems to have been remarkably popular in abridged form throughout the late seventeenth and early eighteenth centuries, editions being dated 1617, 1636, 1663, 1670, 1676, 1680, 1684, 1702, 1708, 1728 and 1735. Similar lists could be given for the medieval collection of exempla, the *Gesta Romanorum* and *The Seven Wise Masters*, generally known as *The Seven Sages of Rome*. Towards the end of the seventeenth century short prose versions of the romances were written, and these were the bases of the texts read in the eighteenth and nineteenth centuries. John Shurley abridged and rewrote *Guy* in 1681, *Don Bellianis* in 1683, *Bevis* in 1689 and *Amadis of Gaul* in 1702. Lawrence Price published his version of *Valentine and Orson* in 1673. The reductions in length are considerable. William Watson's voluminous *Valentine* of the mid-sixteenth century[4] was reduced to fifty-two chapters in 1637, and by the time of the sixteenth edition in 1736, to forty-two. But the eighteenth century chapbook versions contained only eight short chapters.

[1] Ellis, *Specimens of Early English Metrical Romances* (1805), iii. 16.
[2] Scott, *Letters*, ed. Grierson, xii. 194; repeated in note to *Sir Tristrem* (1804), Fytte II, Stanza 13.
[3] See David Laing, *Early Metrical Tales* (Edinburgh, 1826) and J. R. Caldwell, *Eger and Grime* (Cambridge, Mass., 1933).
[4] See Arthur Dickson's edition in E.E.T.S. (1937) and his *Valentine and Orson. A Study in Late Medieval Romance* (1929) for list of references to *Valentine*.

Guy of Warwick underwent the same series of abridgements. Samuel Rowlands's version in twelve cantos of six-line stanzas, which was steadily reprinted from 1609 to 1700, was rewritten in couplets and in prose about 1700, the couplet version being an eighty page octavo, with woodcuts, at one shilling. In 1706 it was again altered by G.L., who produced a very florid version by simply writing out Rowlands's highly poetic account as though it were prose. This version reached a fifth edition in 1711, a tenth in 1759, a twelfth about 1780, and was still being printed in the provinces in 1840. This is in addition to the versions by Shurley (1681) and Samuel Smithson (1680) which also continued in print.[1] The editions of the lasty forty years of the seventeenth century were usually black letter quartos, adorned with worn woodcuts which served for many different texts.

In addition to such 'authentic' medieval romances, which circulated in various forms and formats, there were imitations, such as Richard Johnson's *Tom a Lincolne, the Red-Rose Knight* (1599) which reached a thirteenth edition in 1704 and was later reduced to a chapbook, and his *Seven Champions of Christendom* (1596, 1597), steadily printed for over a hundred years, then abridged in 1679 and in this form reaching a seventeenth edition about 1815. The story of St George and the fair Sabra, which is a version of the romance of *Bevis*,[2] was extracted from Johnson's romance more than once before 1700, and printed in chapbook form later. Translations (and, later on, abridgements) of some of the sixteenth-century Peninsular romances appeared also in the seventeenth century—*Amadis of Gaul, Palmerin d'Olivia, Palladine of England, Palmerin of England, The Mirror of Knighthood,* and *Don Bellianis*.[3] Of these, only *Don Bellianis* seems to have survived throughout the eighteenth century in chapbook form. But it was one of the most popular of children's books. Mr Bickerstaffe's godson, at the age of seven, had turned from Aesop to *Don Bellianis, Guy,* and the *Seven Champions,* and

[1] For *Guy* see R. S. Crane 'The Vogue of "Guy of Warwick" from the close of the Middle Ages to the Romantic Revival', *PMLA*, xxx (1915), 125–94.

[2] Percy realized Johnson's debt to *Bevis* here, see *Percy–Warton Correspondence*, p. 39.

[3] For a survey of these romances and their popularity throughout Europe, see H. Thomas, *Spanish and Portuguese Romances of Chivalry* (1920).

could 'find fault with the passionate temper in Bevis of Southampton, and loved St George for being the Champion of England; and by this means had his thoughts insensibly moulded into the notions of discretion, virtue and honour'.[1]

In the prefaces to the romances in the seventeenth century we find many encomiums on the heroes and incitements to imitate them. Shurley, for example, holds up the 'Elder times' to admiration, at the expense of modern days 'which are too much divolved into effeminacy', and offers Bevis as a pattern of heroic virtue 'that by imitating him, [we] may raise the very name of the British Empire, as formerly it was, to be the Terror of the World'.[2] Valentine and Orson are represented as 'Art' and 'Nature' and the romance recommended as giving 'a Working to the Minds of the dull Country-Swains, and, (as it were) lead[ing] them to search out for Martial Atchievements'. Here 'may the Princely Mind see his own Model; the Knightly Tilter his Martial Atchievement, and the Amorous Lady her *dulcet Passages of Love* . . . it is a Garden of Courtly Delights'.[3] *The Seven Champions* is offered as 'suited to the meanest Capacity, to enrich the Fancy, as well as to divert the Learned' and valuable as encouraging the virtues of '*Honour, Justice, Love,* and *Compassion* to the *Distressed*'. 'It is a Garden of Delight, out of which may be gathered a POSIE to delight and improve the Understanding and refresh the Memory, in the Knowledge of Things past'.[4] Though presenting the romances to a lower class of readers, the writers of the prefaces still clung to the courtly quality of the works and feel that the 'newest and quaintest Dialect'[5] in which they write them will be a recommendation.

Francis Kirkman[6] seems to have stocked all the available romances and in his preface to *Don Bellianis* (1672) outlines the 'Order and Method' whereby the reader may run through the

---

[1] Steele, in *The Tatler*, 95 (17 November 1709).
[2] *Bevis of Southampton* (1689), sig. A2.
[3] *Valentine and Orson*, sixteenth edition (1736), sig. A3ᵛ.
[4] *Seven Champions of Christendom* (1719), sig. A3.
[5] John Shurley's *Don Bellianis* (1683), Parts II and III, sig. A2.
[6] See Strickland Gibson, *A Bibliography of Francis Kirkman*, Oxford Bibliographical Society Publications (1949), and R. C. Bald, 'Francis Kirkman, bookseller and author', *Modern Philology*, xli (1943), 17–32.

whole list with 'Profit and Delight'. He recommends beginning with *The Seven Wise Masters*, because it is fitted with pictures, as a first reader after the Horn Book; then *Don Bellianis*, made more attractive by having the second and third parts specially written by Kirkman with 'Stories acted and done in *England and Ireland*'. Then to follow are *The Destruction of Troy*, a useful primer of classical mythology, and others, leading up to the *Arcadia* and the French romances of the seventeenth century. But Kirkman, in offering his three parts of *Bellianis* in 1763 at three shillings and sixpence (the price of *Paradise Lost*), was aware that the market at this level was declining. 'They are not worth the Printing agen', he complains; they have been 'thrust out of use, by the present slighting and neglect of all Books in general, & by the particular esteem of our late *English Stage Plays*'. The drastic abridgements that followed were dictated by the necessity to find a lower market, which would buy the inferior and shorter black-letter quartos in 1700 at threepence, and which later still would purchase a chapbook printed 'for the Company of Walking-Stationers'.

8. READERS OF ROMANCES

Give me the works which delighted my youth! Give me the *History of St George*, and the *Seven Champions of Christendom*, which at every leisure moment I used to hide myself in a corner to read.
Coleridge, *Letters*, ed. E. M. Coleridge (1895), i. 11 n.

The gradual descent of the romances to the literature of the nursery, though in one sense an embarrassment to the scholars who tried to revive interest in them in their original forms, was also an encouragement to the historically minded antiquary, who could thereby trace an unbroken link with the literature of the middle ages. Thomas Warton, for example, collected references to the reading of romances in the sixteenth and seventeenth centuries to show that 'however monstrous and unnatural these compositions may appear to this age of reason and refinement',[1] they were not only popular reading in previous ages, but the reading of poets and men of letters whom it was impossible not to admire. They were the source 'from

[1] T. Warton, *Observations on the Faerie Queene* (1762), ii. 267.

which young readers especially, in the age of fiction and fancy, nourished the SUBLIME'.[1] Since the romances were in his own day the literature of children, it was natural for Johnson to argue that the ages in which they were the predominant imaginative literature were ages when learning was in its infancy.[2] The nation, like the individual, grew out of such a taste for 'very wild improbable tales' that 'exhibited only the superficial appearances of action, related the events but omitted the causes, and were formed for such as delighted in wonders rather than in truth'.[3] The revival of interest in them was an attempt to return to sources of inspiration which had been invaluable for Spenser, Shakespeare and Milton, but not an encouragement to 'common Readers', amongst whom, thought Percy, 'it would do hurt'.[4]

For Johnson an understanding of the literary expectations of Shakespeare's audience was to be derived from a study of the romances on which Elizabethan popular taste was built. But he justified such reading by the modern scholar by pointing also to the

fertility of invention, the beauty of style and expression, the curiosity of seeing with what kind of performance the age and country in which they were written was delighted: for it is to be apprehended, that at the time when very wild and improbable tales were well received, the people were in a barbarous state, and so on the footing of children.[5]

There had always been uneasiness about the reading of romances, whether on literary or moral grounds. The decline of the medieval stories to the lowest level of literacy in the community did not result in the disappearance of the age-old arguments against them. These flourished in application to their descendants, the modern romances and novels.[6] The

[1] ibid., i. 188.
[2] Johnson, Preface to *The Plays of Shakespeare* (1765), i. xl.
[3] ibid.   [4] *Percy–Farmer Correspondence*, p. 7.
[5] Boswell, *Life of Johnson*, ed. G. Birkbeck Hill and L. F. Powell (Oxford, 1934–50), iv. 17.
[6] For examples of attacks on the novel see such periodical essays as *The World*, Nos. 19, 25, 79; *The Lounger*, Nos. 20, 74, 92; *The Observer*, No. 27; *The Miniature*, No. 2; Vicesimus Knox, *Essays* (ed. 1823), No. 14; and George Colman's *Polly Honeycombe* (1760).

apologetic and sometimes defiant tone of the scholars from Percy to Ellis is to be attributed to the centuries of abuse which had been heaped on works of romantic fiction in every country of Europe, by Erasmus, Vives, Anton Possevin, Thomas Lansius, François de la Noue, Montaigne, Cornelius Agrippa, Tyndale, Ascham, Henry Crosse, Nashe, Cervantes, Ben Jonson, Robert Burton, Arthur Dent, Drayton, George Wither, John Davies of Hereford, and Richard Baxter, to mention only the more familiar names.[1] Ascham's attack on Malory's 'open mans slaughter and bold bawdrye', and E.K.'s reference to the romance writers as 'fine fablers and loud lyers' are only later examples of the objections that Caxton faced in his preface to the *Morte Darthur*. Both Catholic and Protestant moralists in the sixteenth century condemned romances as undermining virtue in young people by filling the mind with stories and images of unlawful love and of cruel and irresponsible behaviour. The views of the canon in *Don Quixote* summarized the opinions of all serious thinkers: 'their style is hard, their adventures are incredible, their love affairs lewd, their compliments absurd, their battles long-winded, their speeches stupid, their travels preposterous, and, lastly, they are devoid of all art and sense, and therefore deserve to be banished from a Christian commonwealth, as a useless tribe.'[2]

'O seculi insaniam! O morum infamiam! O bibliothecarum ulcera!' cried Thomas Lansius,[3] when he thought of the popularity of the romances at the court of the Valois in the sixteenth century. 'The reading of the bookes of Amadis de Gaule, & such like is no less hurtful to youth than the works of Machiavel to age', was the Protestant's lament.[4] Where a Catholic like Possevin believed that Satan inspired the trans-

[1] H. Thomas, *Spanish and Portuguese Romances of Chivalry* (1920), surveys most of the attacks. See also M. Bataillon, *Erasme et l'Espagne* (Paris, 1937), pp. 663–4; V. Hall, *Renaissance Literary Criticism* (Columbia, 1945); R. P. Adams, 'The English New Humanist Attack on Medieval Romance', *Huntington Library Quarterly*, xxiii (1959–60), 33–48.

[2] *Don Quixote*, Part I, ch. 47, transl. J. M. Cohen (1950), p. 425.

[3] Thomas Lansius, *De Principatu inter Provincias Europae* (Tubingen, 1620), p. 312. See also J. Schwering, 'Amadis und Faustbuch in den Hexenprozessen', *Zeitschrift für Deutsche Philologie*, li (1926), 106–16.

[4] François de la Noue, *Discours politiques et militaires* (Lausanne, 1587), transl. into English by Edward Aggar in the same year; *The Sixt Discourse*.

lation of *Amadis* into French, to divert readers from the *Lives of the Saints*, and so make their conversion to Protestantism easy, Protestants like Tyndale, Edward Dering and Lawrence Ramsey accused the Catholics of denying the Scriptures to the layman while encouraging romance reading.[1] 'Fantasticall dreames of those exiled Abbie-lubbers' sneered Nashe; 'Abortives of the fabulous dark cloister, Sent out to poison courts and infest manners', was Jonson's contemptuous dismissal.[2] But the editions increased in number; the playwrights—Dekker, Chapman, Thomas Tomkis, Thomas Nabbes, Richard Brome, Henry Glapthorne, Beaumont and Fletcher, Marston, Shirley, Rowley, Massinger, Thomas Killigrew, Lord Barry, Shadwell and George Granville—expected their audience to be familiar with the stories: character writers like Overbury and Saltenstall, poets like Carew, Corbett and Milton, prose writers like Burton, Browne, Bunyan, Glanvill, Locke, Addison and Steele, witness to the widespread reading of the romances.

Richard Baxter classed the romances with card-playing, dicing, hunting, hawking, bowling, cock-fighting, horse-racing and dancing as 'powerful baits of the devil'. 'Are you travailling towards another world', he wrote, 'with a Playebook in your hand?'[3] 'What is knight-errantry?' asked a correspondent in the *Athenian Mercury* for 1691, and was told

Loving, Sighing, Whining, Rambling, Starving, Tilting, Fighting, Dying, Reviving, Waking, Staring, Singing, Crying, Praying, Wishing, Composing, Writing, Serenading, Rhyming, Hoping, Fearing, Despairing, Raving.[4]

At a lower level, another anonymous writer attempted to laugh away the romances by composing an English *Don Quixote*

[1] See Anton Possevin, *Bibliotheca Selecta Qua agitur De Ratione Studiorum* (Rome, 1593), p. 113; Tyndale, *The Obedience of a Christen Man* (1528) repr. in W. W. Skeat, *Specimens of English Literature, 1394–1579* (1890), p. 179; E. Dering, *A Sparing Restraint, of many lavishe Untruthes* (1586), p. 6; L. Ramsey, *Practise of the Divell* (c. 1571), sigg. B2, C2.
[2] Nashe, *Anatomie of Absurditie* (1589) in G. Gregory Smith, *Elizabethan Critical Essays*, i. 323; Ben Jonson, *The New Inn*, I, vi.
[3] R. Baxter, *A Treatise of Self-Denyall* (1660), pp. 126–7; see also his *Christian Directory* (1673), p. 61.
[4] *The Athenian Mercury*, iii, No. 1, Question 3, 28 July 1691.

entitled *The Essex Champion: or, The Famous History of Sir Billy of Billericay* (c. 1690). In format and presentation it is indistinguishable from the late seventeenth-century quarto versions of the romances themselves, and tells the story of the education of a farmer's son by a course of romance-reading, and of his adventures as a knight errant, equipped with squire and lady. Sir Billy does not emerge from his Quixotic adventures as a sympathetic figure. He ends his life a lunatic, who beats out his brains against the bars of his cage. Only one character, a Justice, believes that the romances are harmless,

for the subjects of them being known to be fabulous and figments, no man's faith is beguiled, nor any persuaded to believe them as a truth; rather on the contrary, where the minds of the vulgar are not busied in some such pleasant arguments, they fall upon matters which less concerns them, and become troublesome Judges of the State and Church wherein they live, and therefore it hath been accounted great Policy to divert Men's Fancies by reading such Romances.

But the Coroner expresses the common view, that they are

very prejudicial to a well-governed Common-Wealth, wherein Men might bestow their time better than in reading Figments, impossibilities, and in many of them incitements rather to looseness and Vanity, than any instructions to vertuous Living.[1]

The moralists provided a ready-made excuse for any one whose life was ill-spent. Stephen Burroughs, for example, attributed his life-time of crime to the chance reading of *Guy of Warwick*. 'Reading and dwelling too much', he wrote, 'on those romantic scenes at that early period of my life, when judgment was weak, was attended with very pernicious consequences in the operations of my after conduct.' The romance had led his mind, he believed,

from the plain simple path of nature into the airy regions of fancy; and when the mind is once habituated to calculate on the Romantic System, error and irregularity are the common consequences.[2]

So widespread was the reading of the romances, in the

[1] *The Essex Champion* (c. 1690), p. 66.
[2] *Memoirs of the Notorious Stephen Burroughs* (Hanover, New Hampshire, 1798), pp. 10–11.

eighteenth century especially, that few could have escaped these consequences had they been as inevitable as the moralists believed. It is true that Johnson, whose passion for them was life-long, attributed to them 'that unsettled turn of mind which prevented his ever fixing in any profession'.[1] Johnson, like many others, had learned to read from *The Seven Champions*.[2] But both Coleridge and Wordsworth recognized that their childhood reading in the romances had been an essential influence on their imaginative development. Coleridge asserted that through the romances his mind 'had been habituated *to the Vast*', so that he never regarded his senses as in any way the criteria of his belief. 'I know no other way of giving the mind a love of the Great and the Whole', he wrote, when recommending the romances for children.[3] Wordsworth regarded them as the 'food' for the child's 'dumb yearnings, hidden appetites', encouraging imaginative identification with others,

> The child whose love is here, at least doth reap
> One precious gain, that he forgets himself.[4]

Reading the romances, the child will meet in a context of 'the shining streams of faery land' scenes that, if later faced in reality, will no longer have the power to evoke terror.

Neither Wordsworth nor Coleridge, however, felt that the stories of the romances were materials for his own poetry. Wordsworth, searching for a subject for the great poem he felt he had the power to write, turned only briefly to

> Some old
> Romantic tale by Milton left unsung,

or to 'dire enchantments' and chivalry, or to the theme of the

---

[1] Boswell, *Life*, i. 49.

[2] Mrs Piozzi, *Anecdotes*, ed. S. C. Roberts (1932), p. 13. See also Burke on his childhood reading in Cobbett, *Parliamentary Register*, 5 Dec. 1787, xxvi. 1276, and A. P. Samuels, *Early Life of Burke* (1923), pp. 48–9; *Tristram Shandy*, Book vi, ch. 32; Robert Nares in his copy of *The Seven Champions* (1696) in the British Museum (12450 d. l); Samuel Bamford, *Passages in the life of a Radical* (1893), i. 87; C. Kegan Paul, *William Godwin* (1876), ii. 119–20; Robert Southey, *Life and Correspondence*, ed. C. C. Southey (1850), ii. 110; Carlyle, *Life of John Sterling* (1851), ch. 3.

[3] *Collected Letters of Samuel Taylor Coleridge*, ed. E. L. Griggs (Oxford, 1956), i. 354.

[4] See *The Prelude* (1850), v. 341 f., 453–5, 496 f.; vii. 79, 455, 506, 713; ix. 300, 451.

migration of Odin.[1] The 'moving accident', the 'dragon's wing, the magic ring', were not for the adult poet. Coleridge's attitude is summed up in his pronouncement, 'as to Arthur, you could not by any means make a poem on him national to Englishmen. What have *we* to do with him?'[2] In common with many writers of the previous two hundred years, Coleridge thought of the romances as works in which free rein was given to the imagination. This imaginative play fostered in its turn 'a considerable vigour of imagination' in the child, necessary 'to cause a generous expansion of the passions by giving the most lively aspect to the objects by which they ought to be interested'.[3] According to the orthodox account, the imaginative person saw the things of everyday life as though they existed in a supernatural world, and this imaginative view of 'reality' Wordsworth and Coleridge hoped to perpetuate into adult life. They explained their aims in *Lyrical Ballads* in such terms,

to choose incidents and situations from common life, and . . . to throw over them a certain colouring of imagination, whereby ordinary things should be presented to the mind in an unusual way.[4] to excite a feeling analogous to the supernatural by awakening the mind's attention to the lethargy of custom, and directing it to the loveliness and the wonder of the world before us.[5]

For the traditionalist, however, the perpetuation into adult life of a vision admittedly valuable in childhood rendered the adult incapable of attending coolly to reality. As Foster explained, in the adult

the influence of this habit of dwelling on the beautiful fallacious forms of imagination, will accompany the mind into the most serious speculations, or rather musings, on the real world, and what is to be done in it and expected; . . . The vulgar materials, that constitute the actual economy of the world, will rise up to its sight in

---

[1] *The Prelude* (1850), i. 169 f. The migration of Odin is discussed by Mallet, *Northern Antiquities* (1770), i. 58 f., and Warton, *History of English Poetry* (1774), Dissertation I. Wordsworth did use Geoffrey of Monmouth for *Artegal and Elidure* (1815) and Malory for *The Egyptian Maid* (1830).

[2] Coleridge, *Table Talk*, 4 September 1833.

[3] John Foster, 'On the Application of the Epithet "Romantic",' in *Essays in a Series of Letters to a Friend* (1806), i. 251.

[4] Wordsworth, Preface to *Lyrical Ballads* (1802).

[5] Coleridge, *Biographia Literaria* (1817), ch. xiv.

fictitious forms, which it cannot disenchant into plain reality, nor will even suspect to be deceptive.[1]

This view was a legacy from the late seventeenth century, when the 'world in imagination' was distrusted. To John Smith, the 'Imaginative Powers . . . will be breathing a gross dew upon the pure Glass of our Understandings'.[2] The romances, whether medieval, Peninsular or modern, were condemned as filling the mind with false notions, hindering 'the *true understanding* and *real notions* of things as they are in the World, which *true histories* set forth'.[3] Even serious thinkers were troubled by false notions of *things*, thought Obadiah Walker, 'wandering and insignificant fancies *in the brain* (Romances in thought)'. How much more troubled were weak-minded people by the romances themselves. As with the novel later, the enemies of romance were almost as numerous as the readers of it. Those who supplied the stories argued that 'Romantick Poetry' had as its end

1. Either to attract the Curious and Careless Eyes of such, who can be no otherwayes induc'd to cultivate their wits and inform their Minds; or 2. To Recreate (not without some profit) the over-intense Spirits after more serious Reading; or 3. To Reprove Powerful Vice without danger to the Mythologist; or 4. Lastly, to Affect those with Vertue thus set off by Fable, whose Luxuriant Fancies cannot descend to the looking on more plain Morality.[4]

Those who opposed them complained that

they commonly do more Mischief than Good. For besides misspending of time, giving an ill-Tincture to the Imagination, and stuffing the Head with Rubbish, they paint good Qualities out of Character, give false Images of Life, teach young people to be indiscreet in Friendship and Passions, put them in a Way how to cheat their Parents with more Dexterity, and steal a Misfortune for their Life-Time.[5]

Dr Johnson, however, was in agreement with Coleridge, Wordsworth, Lamb and Godwin when he pointed out that

---

[1] Foster, i. 249. [2] John Smith, *Discourses* (1673), p. 21.
[3] Obadiah Walker, *Of Education, Especially of Young Gentlemen*, (Oxford, 1673), ch. v, §6.
[4] *Arnaldo, or The Injur'd Lover*, Made English by T. S. (1660), Preface, sig. A7.
[5] Jeremy Collier, *Appendix to Morey's Great Historical, Geographical, and Poetical Dictionary* (1721), sig. 602.

'Babies do not want to hear about babies; they like to be told of giants and castles, and of somewhat which can stretch and stimulate their little minds.'[1]

In 1851 Henry Mayhew's penny bookseller was still selling *The Seven Champions*. 'There's plenty of "Henry and Emmas", and . . . "Good Books for Good Boys and Girls"; but when people buys really for their children, they buys the old stories—at least they does of me.'[2]

9. DISCOVERING THE TEXTS

> Manuscripts, that for ages had lain dormant, . . . issued from their archives to public view; books that had circulated only in mean guise for the amusement of the people, [became] important . . . to the general body of the learned.
>
> Carlyle, *Misc. Essays* (1872) iii. 112

In the households of Percy and Scott, to move from the nursery to the study, from the chapbook to the manuscript, must have been no unusual experience. Once in the study, the scholar's attitude towards the romances was coloured by the recollection that these stories had fired the imaginations of Spenser, Shakespeare and Milton. As they worked, Percy, Warton, Ritson, Scott and Ellis began to give recognizable shape to various branches of literary study that we now take for granted. Percy, for example, collected the Peninsular romances in order to illustrate the satirical basis of *Don Quixote*, wrote essays on minstrels, alliterative poetry and the development of the drama, and printed the first bibliography of metrical romances. Ritson and Ellis wrote on the development of the English language in the middle ages, and both followed Warton in mastering some of the medieval French romances in order to assess the dependence of English romances upon them. Warton traced the development of romance and allegory in the middle ages in order to illustrate Spenser's heritage. Scott, in his edition of *Sir Tristrem*, set a pattern for the thorough presentation of medieval texts, providing full notes, glossary, and a discussion of authorship, dating, analogues, and a description of his manuscript source. All their work was discovery—of texts that had probably not been read for centuries. On their

[1] Mrs Piozzi, *Anecdotes*, p. 13.
[2] Henry Mayhew, *London Labour and the London Poor* (1864), i. 324.

discoveries they imposed patterns, elucidating the chronology of the romances by internal and external evidence, or arranging them according to subject matter. They engaged in only rudimentary analysis of the language of their texts and were all capable of making mistakes in their glossing. But in Scott's discussion of the language of *Tristrem*, in which he concluded that his manuscript preserved a Southern minstrel's version of a Northern poem, and in Ritson's irritated corrections of errors made by Warton and Percy, one can see the uncertain beginnings of the study of Middle English. Standing as they did so close to the initial discovery of the texts, their excitement was confined to the larger issues of seeing specific debts by Shakespeare, Spenser and Milton to the romances, or of tracing the origin of romantic fiction as a part of the study of the development of fiction in general.

The work of discovering the texts was aided by the publication of catalogues of manuscripts, and by the opening of the British Museum in January 1759. A key to the manuscript treasures of the more important libraries, including those at Oxford and Cambridge, was provided by Edward Bernard's *Catalogi librorum manuscriptorum Angliae et Hibernae*, published at Oxford in 1697. This work, compiled by a team of scholars including Humphrey Wanley, guided Percy and Warton to many of the romances, in particular to those that had been in the collection of John Moore. The opening of the British Museum made generally available the collections of Sir Robert Bruce Cotton (1571–1631), and of Robert (1661–1721) and Edward Harley (1689–1741). But collections without catalogues are not of immediate use. The scholars were helped by Thomas Smith's catalogue of the Cottonian manuscripts (1696) and David Casley's catalogue of the manuscripts in the King's Library (1734). Later came Samuel Aynscough's catalogue of the Sloane manuscripts (1782). The most important of the catalogues was that of the Harley manuscripts, which was finally published in 1762.[1] With its dating of each manuscript, quotation of opening and closing lines of each work contained

---

[1] *A Catalogue of the Harleian Collection of Manuscripts*, 2 vols., 1759 (actually published in 1762). MSS 1 to 2407. 13 are described by Wanley, MSS 2407. 14 to 5797 by Casley. The catalogue was revised by Douce and Nares (4 vols., 1808–12).

in every manuscript, and Wanley's comments on the texts, this provided a most valuable tool to medievalists, and led Percy, Warton, and Ritson to many of the romances for the first time. But even a catalogue is imperfect without an index. Percy thought the Harleian catalogue 'almost useless'[1] until in 1763 Thomas Astle published an index to it. One can almost date the beginning of later medieval literary studies at the publication of this index.

Without such catalogues as have been mentioned, Warton's task of writing the history of English poetry would have been impossible, at least for the period before the beginning of printing. We can see the difficulties faced by these scholars in attempting to discover the literature of the past in a letter of Warton to Malone on 22 June 1781. He describes his attempts to use the collection of books left to the Bodleian by Tanner. They were crammed in a confused order, without any classification and without a catalogue. 'I have often been unable to find a book a second time which I have seen not half a year before.'[2] Since, for all but Warton and Ellis, literary researches were occupations for hours left after the business of the day, any shortcomings in their works should be judged in the light of the difficulties they faced in discovering their subject. 'Much is due to those who first broke the way to knowledge, and left only to their successors the task of smoothing it.'[3]

10. ROMANCES AND 'OUR EARLIER CLASSICAL POETS'

In studying the romances the scholars were convinced that they were examining the springs from which English literature at its best had drawn its inspiration. They hoped to 'throw new light on the rise and progress of English poetry' and to illustrate innumerable passages in 'our ancient classic poets'.[4] They saw the romances as preserving 'many curious historical facts', and throwing light on the 'nature of the feudal system'.

They are [wrote Thomas Warton] the pictures of ancient usages and customs; and represent the manners, genius, and character of

[1] Percy–Farmer Correspondence, p. 30.
[2] Quoted by C. Rinaker, Thomas Warton (Illinois, 1916), p. 81. Warton's printed sources for his History are listed in Rinaker, pp. 177–232.
[3] Johnson, Journey to the Western Isles of Scotland (1775), sub Aberdeen.
[4] Percy, Reliques (1765), iii. p. ix.

our ancestors. Above all, such are their Terrible Graces of magic and enchantment, so magnificently marvellous are their fictions and fablings, that they contribute, in a wonderful degree, to rouse and invigorate all the powers of imagination: to store the fancy with those sublime and alarming images, which true poetry best delights to display.[1]

The scholars were conscious that the romances were not only central to a study of the development of English literature, but could be of value in revivifying contemporary poetry. Their scholarly interests were directed to a true understanding of the past, but, by presenting their findings in a form that would appeal to the cultured reader, they sought also to encourage antiquarian studies as a valuable stimulus for the modern poet. Thomas Warton combined the rôles of scholar and Poet Laureate, and advocated new forms of poetry, 'Poetry endued with new Manners and Images'.[2] He agreed with Percy that 'the appetite of the public is so palled with all the common forms of poetry', and looked to 'some new Spenser' to revive it.[3] Both shared Hurd's belief that 'the manners of romance are better calculated to answer the purposes of pure poetry, to captivate the imagination, and to produce surprise, than the fictions of classical antiquity'.[4] Since they could point to Spenser and Milton for their examples, they were confident in their assumptions. The Elizabethan age appeared to them to have possessed the qualities most 'favourable to the purposes of poetry', since it lay in time 'between the rude essays of uncorrected fancy', as exemplified in the romances themselves, and 'the refinements of reason and science'[5] which were the virtues of the literature of their own age. In turning to the romances, they were exploring the immediate background of the Elizabethans, whom Hurd, for example, praises for virtues that derive from the practice of chivalry, 'in their festivities, their exercises, and their poetical fictions'.[6]

Interest in chivalry, romance and feudalism was a byproduct of interest in Shakespeare, Spenser and Milton and to explain

---

[1] Thomas Warton, *Observations on the Faerie Queene* (1762), ii. 268.
[2] Warton to Percy, 4 September, 1762, in *Percy–Warton Correspondence*, p. 47.
[3] ibid., pp. 44–5.   [4] Warton, *History* (1774), i. 434.
[5] Hurd, *Dialogues* (1798), i. 198.   [6] ibid., pp. 201–2.

these authors, scholarship was brought to the aid of criticism. The scholar-critic began to read the books, especially the imaginative works, which had helped to mould the literary masterpieces of the past. Until Warton's *Observations on the Faerie Queene* in 1754, Johnson could justly complain that no help was borrowed 'from those who lived with them, or before them'.[1] Johnson himself adds little of this type of annotation in his edition of Shakespeare, but what he does witnesses to the prevailing interest in romances. He instances *Guy of Warwick, Morte Darthur*[2] and Caxton's *Recuyel of the Histories of Troy*, and pauses to refute at length Warburton's view that belief in witchcraft was brought to Europe by the Crusaders.[3] Johnson's main interest in this type of scholarship is the light it throws on the critical suppositions of the audience for whom the plays were originally written. Thus he explains the crowding of incidents, the show and bustle, by Shakespeare's need to satisfy an audience whose taste was formed by the romances, which 'invigorated the reader by a giant and a dwarf'. For Thomas Percy, however, minutiae of annotation provided sufficient excitement. He discovered that the words of the Fool in *King Lear* (III, iv, 138–9)

> But rats and mice and such small deer
> Have been Tom's food for seven long year

were adapted from *Bevis*, and that the reference in *King John* to Richard's encounter with a lion was to an episode in the romance of *Richard Coeur de Lion*.[4] These were two strong points in his argument that the romances deserved study.

With the same sense of triumph Thomas Warton and Hurd pointed to Milton's 'predilection for the legends of chivalry',

---

[1] Boswell, *Life of Johnson*, i. 270.

[2] See Mary Lascelles, 'Sir Dagonet in Arthur's Show', *Shakespeare–Jahrbuch*, 96 (1960), 145–54.

[3] In a note on the witches in *Macbeth*, which, like the note on Prospero, draws on Hooker and on King James' *Daemonologie*. Both Johnson and Swift assert that Milton's 'and on their Hinges grate Harsh thunder' (*Paradise Lost*, ii. 881–2) was borrowed from *Don Bellianis*, Part 2, ch. 19 (Johnson's *Shakespeare* (1765), vi. 424–5; H. J. Todd ed., *Poetical Works of Milton* (1852), i. 511 n.). I have not found the phrase in any edition of the romance.

[4] *Percy–Farmer Correspondence*, pp. 49–50; *Reliques* (1765), iii. pp. ix–xii; Johnson, *Shakespeare* (1765), viii. Appendix, Notes to vi. 92.

his references to them in *Il Penseroso*, *Paradise Lost* and *Paradise Regained*, his projected *Arthuriad*, his use of material from Geoffrey of Monmouth in *Comus*, his intended ·treatise on Geoffrey, and his telling over the materials of the *Historia* in the *History of Britain* 'be it for nothing else but in favour of our English Poets, and Rhetoricians, who by their Art will know, how to use them judiciously'.[1] Chaucer provided an example of an English poet who had actually composed romances, one of which, the *Squier's Tale*, had attracted both Milton and Spenser. The value of romance studies was further vindicated, however, by the realization that Chaucer had also seen the foolishness of romances and in *Sir Thopas* had anticipated Cervantes, exposing 'with infinite humour' 'the leading impertinencies of books of chivalry'.[2] In 1762 Hurd, acting on a suggestion made to him by Warburton,[3] put forward this view as part of his explanation of the lack of any great romance which could rival classical epic; Chaucer had laughed the romances out of court before they were used by any great medieval poet. Hurd does not name any great poet between Chaucer and Spenser who might have been tempted to use the stories had Chaucer not mocked them. Nor, of course, did he realize that Chaucer's satire was directed more at those authors whose method of telling the stories and whose attitude towards their material betrayed incompetence. Percy, however, did come close to recognizing this. His main evidence for saying that Chaucer's poem was an 'express imitation of the manner, style and Meter of these Old Ballads' was *The Sqyr of Lowe Degre*, which he read in the only two complete texts that have survived—in his Folio MS and in Garrick's copy of Copland's edition (c. 1555–60). Unfortunately this poem is a late romance, written about 1475; it cannot have been known to Chaucer. Percy had no means of dating the text accurately. His opinion was formed at the very beginning of his studies and his account was printed by Thomas Warton from the letter in which

[1] Milton, *History of Britain* (ed. 1695), p. 7. See Warton, *Observations on the Faerie Queene* (1762), ii. sect. vii; Hurd, *Letters on Chivalry* (1762), Letter vii.

[2] Hurd, *Letters on Chivalry* (1762), Letter xi; the account was expanded in the 1765 edition.

[3] See *Percy–Warton Correspondence*, pp. 168–9.

Percy had put forward his conjecture.[1] Discoveries of this type were, for Percy, indications of the riches waiting to be unearthed.

II. ROMANCES AND THE MODERN POET

Of old the world on dreaming fed,
Grey Truth is now her painted toy.
Yeats, 'The Song of the Happy Shepherd'

By the 1760s there was a sufficiently large audience for the literature of the Elizabethan and medieval periods. Goldsmith noted in *The Vicar of Wakefield* (1766), 'Dryden and Rowe's manner . . . are quite out of fashion! Our taste has gone back a whole century' (ch. 18). The narrower antiquarianism of the previous century, the scholarship that had concerned itself with non-literary texts, had gradually filtered through to a wider public. Interest was aroused by the publication of evidence that our ancestors had been not merely politically and religiously conscious, but also creators of works of literature. Of course many a scholar and collector of the seventeenth century had been interested in earlier literature. Pepys and Anthony Wood had collected ballads, including many of the Elizabethan age. The collectors of manuscripts had rescued many medieval texts. Nameless men, like the person who compiled Percy's Folio MS, had transcribed texts. Ballads ancient or modern had found ready readers in Dryden and Addison, they had been imitated, and one at least, *Hardyknute*, had been forged. Scott, in his autobiographical fragment, commented that Percy's collection in the *Reliques* was a new departure not so much in the assembling of texts, as in the 'sober research, grave commentary, and apt illustration' with which they were presented. And this task had been performed, said Scott, not by a dull antiquary but by an editor of 'poetical genius' who was 'capable of emulating the best qualities of what his pious labour preserved'. In collecting texts, and in 'improving' the versions he printed, Percy had been preceded by Allan Ramsay, who had drawn on the Bannatyne MS to print pieces of Dunbar and Henryson in his *Evergreen* (1724–7). The Scottish Chaucerians were frequently printed in the century, from Edmund Gibson's

[1] Warton, *Observations* (1762), i. 139; *Percy–Warton Correspondence*, pp. 20 f.; *Percy–Farmer Correspondence*, Letter iii.

edition of *Christ's Kirk on the Green* (1691) and Francis Fawkes's edition of the Prologues to Gavin Douglas's translation of the *Aeneid* (1761), to the work of Lord Hailes, Pinkerton and Sibbald at the end of the century.[1]

The great labours on the plays of Shakespeare in the period represent only part of the interest in earlier drama. Ben Jonson, Beaumont and Fletcher and Massinger were edited; Dodsley's (1744) and Chetwood's (1750) collections of plays contained many Elizabethan and Jacobean texts. In the field of poetry, we find reprints of Davies's *Nosce Teipsum* and of the works of Drummond, Daniel and Drayton, parts of Hall, Marston, Phineas Fletcher, Fairfax, Tottel's *Miscellany*, Skelton and Sackville. The study and reprinting of sixteenth-century prose works, as of Ascham, Sidney, More, Raleigh, Lyly, Elyot, also went on apace.[2]

The rich scholarly activity throughout the period provided poets with numerous literary models and encouraged a prosodic inventiveness, and a concern with new subject matter for poetry. The texts reprinted made writers vividly aware that there were more methods of composition than the classical. The older antiquarianism, centred on detailed historical study had occasionally brought to light something of literary interest, like the fragment of Old Norse, the *Incantation of Hervor*, which found its way from Hickes's *Thesaurus* into the *Miscellany of Poems* published by Tonson in 1716. A great deal of the pleasure derived from such pieces came from the sense of being authentically in touch with the primitive outpourings of one's own ancestors. There was a powerful local patriotism in the support of Scotsmen for the authenticity of Ossian, in the printing of the Edda by Mallet as part of the history of Denmark, and in the invention of Chatterton's Rowley. The romances might be despised, but Frenchmen were anxious to claim their origin for Provence, Welshmen for Wales, and Scotsmen for the Celtic kingdom of Strathclwyd.

Patriotic tendencies also underlay the division of poetry

[1] For a fuller account of the interest in earlier English and Scottish literature, see R. Wellek, *The Rise of English Literary History* (Chapel Hill, 1941), esp. ch. 4.

[2] See Wellek, op. cit. and E. R. Wasserman, *Elizabethan Poetry in the Eighteenth Century* (Urbana, 1947), W. B. C. Watkins, *Johnson and English Poetry before 1660* (Princeton, 1936).

lovers into two camps, the admirers respectively of the 'French' school, which comprised Dryden and Pope—thought of as deriving from Boileau—and of the 'English', which included Spenser, Milton and their imitators. The cosmopolitanism of Pope's admirers contrasts with the attitude of the upholders of the 'English' tradition, in which the Augustan age was seen as a mere interpolation. Yet those who looked furthest back had also the clearest view forward. Johnson and Goldsmith were able to show that the school of Pope still had life, but they were less able to point out a path for the new poet. Percy, Gray and the Wartons, looking back, like many others, to Spenser and Milton and beyond to the romances, Welsh and Old Norse, saw a possibility of rejuvenating poetry by returning to models and sources of fiction which had not been used for centuries. The hold that an idealized Roman civilization had exercised over the imagination, and which, in conjunction with the improvements in society and manners, had produced 'much good sense', was waning, its function being achieved. To continue to go forward demanded a new model. What is interesting is that in literature the suggested model was not something higher, but something lower; no longer the *Aeneid* and Horace, but the *Death Song of Ragnar Lodbrok*, Gwalchmai's 'Ode to Owen Gwynned', and the romances; not a new Virgil but a new Spenser was looked for.

'Shall we feel the fire of heroic poetry in translations from Greece and Rome, and never search for it in the native products of our own country?' asked John Aikin.[1] The world of fine fabling had been raided by Dryden, and made acceptable to the modern reader in the volume of *Fables* from Ovid, Boccaccio and Chaucer. The popularity of these throughout the century witnesses to the delight in narrative poetry,[2] which the scholars studied here encouraged. Gray, for example, thought *Theodore and Honoria* 'stood in the first rank of poems';[3] George Ellis

---

[1] J. and A. L. Aikin, *Miscellaneous Pieces in Prose* (1773), p. 140.

[2] H. G. Wright, 'Some sidelights on the reputation and influence of Dryden's *Fables*.' *RES*, xxi (1945), 23–37.

[3] *Correspondence of Thomas Gray*, ed. P. Toynbee and C. Whibley, (Oxford, 1935), iii. 1291.

placed it 'on the very top shelf of English poetry'.[1] Wordsworth remarked on the same taste for narrative when he noted that any well-used copy of Thomson's *Seasons* 'generally opens of itself . . . with one of the stories'.[2] Joseph Warton, whose critical opinions reinforced those of the scholars, considered that Pope was at his best in the poems with a narrative basis— *The Rape of the Lock* and *Eloisa to Abelard*—since 'a tale or a story more strongly engages and interests the reader than a series of precepts or reproofs, or even of characters themselves, however lively and natural'.[3] Macpherson's Ossian, Chatterton's Rowley poems and the ballads owed not a little of their appeal to their narrative content, their supposed origin in a world of fine fabling. To restore this world was the aim of the scholars. They saw the poet as 'more a poet by the fictions he invents than by the verses he composes',[4] and advocated new narratives. 'Some old Romantic tale by Milton left unsung' attracted Wordsworth and Southey,[5] and William Taylor was urged by Southey to seek subjects for poems in Ritson's *Metrical Romanceës* and Scott's edition of *Sir Tristrem*. Thomas Warton tried to use the new material in *The Grave of King Arthur* (1777), Richard Hole in *Arthur: or the Northern Enchantment* (1789), Reginald Heber in *Morte Arthur* (pr. 1830), and *The Masque of Gwendolen* (1816), Scott in *The Bridal of Triermain* (1813) and John Hookham Frere in *Arthur and his Round Table* (1817).

Scott's love of all that belonged to chivalry and to legendary story inspired his voluminously annotated series of narrative poems. He aimed to give an imaginative presentation of the past, mingling authentic customs and manners, as the romance-writers of the middle ages did, with a fictitious story. But since

[1] Lockhart, *Life of Scott*, ch. xvi (ed. 1896, p. 153).
[2] Wordsworth, *Essay, Supplementary to the Preface* in *Poetical Works* ed. E. de Selincourt (Oxford, 1944), ii. 421.
[3] *Essay on Genius and Writings of Pope* (1782), i. 211.
[4] Ritson, *Metrical Romanceës* (1802), i. p. xii. This is Aristotle's view, 'the poet must be more the poet of his stories or Plots than of his verses, inasmuch as he is a poet by virtue of the imitative element in his work, and it is actions that he imitates.' *On the Art of Poetry*, trans. Ingram Bywater (Oxford, 1947), pp. 44–5.
[5] *The Prelude* (1850), i. 169; J. W. Robberds, *Memoirs of William Taylor of Norwich* (1843), i. 515, 517.

49

the customs and manners which he represented were those of a past age, his annotations proved the authenticity of his picture and gave added entertainment.[1] Scott had, however, been preceded as a commentator by Southey. His *Joan of Arc* and *Thalaba* and later *Madoc*, *The Curse of Kehama* and *Roderick*, are as learnedly annotated as any of Scott's poems. The fashion for poems set either in the past or in an alien civilization produced many imitations—such as *Lalla Rookh* (Thomas Moore), *Theodric, Gertrude of Wyoming, The Pilgrim of Glencoe* (Campbell), and Byron's *The Bride of Abydos, The Corsair* and *Mazeppa*. In these, the notes grow thinner until they disappear altogether. But the narrative poem was firmly re-established, as Keats, Shelley and the succeeding poets prove. By 1809 Malone might well write 'the whole world is to be "bespread with the dust of antiquity" and what was formerly thought a good subject of ridicule, is now quite the fashion'.[2]

Scott's poems 'brought chivalry again into temporary favour'. Jeffrey wrote 'again' because its original favour, in the middle ages, had also been only 'temporary'. To Jeffrey the new passion was 'as much a phantasy as to build a modern abbey or an English pagoda'.[3] One might see the narrative poem with notes as the outcome of the labours of Percy, Warton, Ellis and Scott; their enthusiasm for annotating earlier poetry resulted in a literature of new works in the guise of learned editions. The poet was now his own scholar, the scholar his own poet.

'The poem is narrative, not didactic. It is a series of pictures', Shelley wrote in the Preface to the *Revolt of Islam*. To turn the poet from didacticism to fabling, to narrative, to fiction, was the aim of Percy and the Wartons. Their influence is seen partly in the wealth of narrative verse produced in the following generation.

[1] Later he added notes to the Waverley novels, as well as autobiographical and informative prefaces to novels and poems.

[2] *Percy–Malone Correspondence*, p. 260. It will be remembered that Erasmus Darwin's *Botanic Garden* (1792) was heavily annotated. Selden's notes to Drayton's *Poly-Olbion* (1612–13) were probably not without influence on Southey and Scott.

[3] Jeffrey, reviewing *Marmion* in *Edinburgh Review*, 1808, quoted in Lockhart, *Life of Scott*, ch. 16.

12. THEORIES OF THE ORIGIN OF ROMANCE:
WARTON TO SCOTT

> The generality are so much in the dark about these matters,
> they neither know whence they spring, nor how they got the
> name of Romances.
>
> *A Treatise of Romances and Their Original* (1672), sig. A3ᵛ

The attraction of the romances themselves naturally led to a
more fervid discussion of the one topic connected with them
which had engaged the attention of earlier writers—the origin
of romance. Under this heading was conceived the history of
fictitious writing, of allegorical compositions, of figurative
language, and of imaginative excesses in creating giants, dragons
and enchanters. It was a great rag-bag into which was poured
what was known of Norse literature, of Greek and late Latin
romances, of the Old Testament and the Koran seen as
literature, of Arabic and Persian literature, of Provençal
poetry, of medieval and Peninsular romances and early Welsh
poetry. Homer, Ovid and Virgil were by no means excluded.
Any literature that went beyond the clear description of the
everyday affairs of men and women—and this meant almost
all that was known of early narrative literature—was fitted into
the mould of 'romantic fabling'. Most of those who discussed
the subject accepted that the propensity to fabling was natural
in all men, and likely to find expression in all primitive states of
society. Yet most were also prepared to believe that fabling
had originated in some particular region—in the Middle East,
among the Arabs and Persians, or in Scandinavia—and from
its source spread to the rest of Europe. Those who favoured an
Arabian origin did so on account of a belief that excessive
imaginative qualities could only be developed in warm climates.
For some reason they believed that a cold Northern climate
could only produce a 'cold' imagination. If a romance was the
product of a 'heated' imagination, it was not likely to be the
original work of a Scandinavian shivering in the Nordic snows.
The 'giants, enchanters, dragons, and the like monstrous and
arbitrary fictions', were the product of an alien mode of

thinking, and must have been introduced into Europe by communication with the East.[1] 'Dragons are a sure mark of orientalism',[2] Warton assured his readers.

Other abstractions which found easy acceptance determined alternative theories of the origin of romance. Hurd, for example, accepted that literature was the product of a particular type of society, and took its form from the predominant interests of that society. This long established view enabled critics to explain literature in terms of society, and to deduce a society from its surviving literature—whether the epics of Homer, the poems of Ossian, or the plays of Shakespeare. Holding to this doctrine, Hurd argued that the spirit of romance was born of the ages of chivalry, which were in turn the product of the feudal organization of society. Feudalism and chivalry had a particular attraction for many eighteenth-century writers. Johnson, in the *Journey to the Western Islands of Scotland* (1775), is in quest of a feudal society and expounds its organization while regretting that he had come too late to see it in full operation. Historians, like William Robertson, Gilbert Stuart, and John Dalrymple, sympathetically survey the main aspects of feudalism and the civilizing quality of chivalry,[3] much in the manner of Thomas Warton. The very scenery of the Highlands Johnson saw as that portrayed in the medieval romances: 'the adventurer might suddenly pass from the gloom of woods, or the ruggedness of moors, to seats of plenty, gaiety, and magnificence'.[4] Those who sought for the origin of romance were really looking for the source of 'giants, dragons, and enchantment', which they held to partake more of the essence of romance than the customs and manners fortuitously added during a single period of its development. Hurd thought that at least he could explain the giants in medieval romance, when he declared that 'giants

[1] Thomas Warton, *History of English Poetry*, i. sig. c3. A warm climate was regarded as conducive to imaginative writing, a cold climate to rational thought, see V. Knox, *Essays* (1823), iii. 224–7.

[2] ibid., i. sig. c1. The absence of giants and dragons from the poems of Ossian was to Warton 'a striking proof of their antiquity', ibid., sig. h3.

[3] For a survey of the eighteenth-century attitude to feudalism, see H. Weisinger 'The Middle Ages and the late Eighteenth-Century Historians', *P.Q.*, 27 (1948), 63–79.

[4] *Journey to the Western Islands* (1924), p. 113.

were oppressive feudal lords'.[1] But no theorizer chose to follow him.

Thomas Percy could not accept the view that the romances developed only after the establishment of chivalry as a distinct military order, for he had found giants and dwarfs, fairies, spells and enchantments, dragons and monsters, at an earlier period, in Northern literature. When his reading of Mallet's *Introduction à l'Histoire de Dannemarc* and *Monumens de la Poésie des Celtes et . . . des Scandinaves . . .* also assured him that the Northern nations were fond of going in quest of adventure, and of single combat, and were respectfully complaisant to the fair sex, then all the elements of romance seemed to stem from the North. What more obvious, at least to Percy, than that they were brought to England by the Saxon invaders, and carried by the Danes to France, whence, with the Norman conquest, they returned once more to England. All theorizers believed that primitive societies gradually romanticized their historical narratives. Percy merely showed that this activity had been common in Northern Europe, and he naturally concluded that romance-writing must have originated there. He was sure that stories of Arthur were Celtic in origin, that *Bevis* and *Guy* were by English minstrels, and that romances of chivalry were first composed in France, whence they had their name.[2]

The Eastern and the Northern theories were not so irreconcilable as may at first sight appear. They were, as Thomas Warton showed, really only partial views of the truth. Warton himself began by holding the simple Eastern theory of Warburton, which attributed the development of romance in Europe to the returning Crusaders.[3] But under the influence of Sainte-Palaye, Mallet, and Percy, he modified his view. Percy's letter to him, outlining the Northern theory, was taken over into the second edition of the *Observations* (1762).[4] To it Warton

[1] *Letters on Chivalry and Romance* (1762), Letter iv. Hurd found this idea in Boullainvillier's *Essai sur la Noblesse de France* (Amsterdam, 1732), p. 141.

[2] Percy, *Essay on the Ancient Metrical Romances* in *Reliques* (1765), iii, expanded in 2nd, 3rd, and 4th editions. On Arthurian romances, see *Percy–Evans Correspondence*, pp. 59–60, 68–70, 74–6.

[3] *Observations on the Faerie Queene* (1754), pp. 42–3.

[4] *Observations* (1762), i. 64; Percy's letter is in *Percy–Warton Correspondence*, pp. 12–13.

added the suggestion that was later to be the basis of his 'dazzling theory'—that the Northern nations are descended from an Eastern people who migrated, 'under the command of their general, or god, ODIN', from Georgia to Scandinavia in the time of Mithridates. Thus Warton could continue to talk of 'the romances of the dark ages, founded on Saracen supersitions, and filled with giants, dwarfs, damsels, and enchanters',[1] since the Eastern theory is his ultimate theory; the Northern theory merely explains one way in which romantic fabling entered Europe. Considered as abstract theory, Warton's view was certainly attractive. Romantic fiction could not have had its origin in 'the cold and barren conceptions of a western climate', therefore it was necessary 'to trace the manner and the period of its introduction into the popular belief, the oral poetry, and the literature, of the Europeans'.[2] In order to do this, Warton had to show that the links between Arabs, Moors, Saracens, and Europeans, were many and of early date. Here the value of the story of the migration of Odin from Georgia, after the defeat of Mithridates by Pompey, was obvious. Warton was familiar with it from Mallet, and earlier accounts in Bartholin and Olaus Wormius.[3] Seemingly well-authenticated, it showed how the Northern nations had obtained their oriental cast of imagination, and explained the similarities which Warton saw between the religion and customs of the Scandinavians and the Arabs and Persians. Odin's Goths had taken with them their skill in poetry, which was exercised in praise of their heroes, and included the supposedly 'oriental' extravagances, 'a sublime and figurative cast of diction', and the use of circumlocutions and comparisons. In time 'the piny precipices, the frozen mountains, and the gloomy forests, acted on their imaginations, and gave a tincture of horror to their imagery'.[4]

Thus, Warton argued, the seeds of romance were carried from the East to Northern Europe, and spread by the invasions of the descendants of Odin's Goths. He saw the Saxon invasion

---

[1] *Observations* (1762), ii. 84.
[2] *History of English Poetry*, i. sig. a1.
[3] Warton gives his sources in the *History*, i. sig. c4^v.
[4] ibid., sig. d4.

of England in the sixth century, and the Danish in the ninth as an explanation for the spreading of romantic fabling to the Celtic peoples in Wales, Scotland and Ireland. To account for its more general distribution throughout Europe, he had recourse to the conjecture that the Nordic Scalds were welcomed at the courts of European monarchs before the Crusades. Wild as the conjecture seems now, Warton had some authority for it. He was relying on a statement by Thormodus Torfaeus to the effect that the Scalds 'were sought for and caressed by the *British* as well as *Saxon* Princes of this Island' and that 'Islandic was a kind of court language, as French is now, and was understood in all the northern courts of Europe and in this Island'.[1] So, he explains, the basic ideas of romance were present throughout Europe from an early date. But a second wave of influence from the East began in the eighth century, when the Moorish conquest of Spain not only brought the science and philosophy of the Greeks to Europe, but also disseminated 'those extravagant inventions which were so peculiar to their romantic and creative genius'. From Spain, the new impetus to romantic fabling spread, via the trade routes, to France and Italy, and in particular to Brittany, whence, as a result of the kinship between the Bretons and the Welsh, it passed to Cornwall and Wales.[2] Warton's theory was created in order to explain the presence in Wales, before the composition of Geoffrey of Monmouth's *Historia* in the eleventh century, of the elements that Warton regarded as basic to romance. It also explained their presence in France before the writing of the Pseudo-Turpin Chronicle of Charlemagne. These two seminal works, regarded by Warton and Caylus[3] as the source of later romances on Arthur and Charlemagne, were therefore infected by oriental fabling at their very inception.

Feudalism, for Hurd the parent of romance, was for Warton

---

[1] The quotation is from Percy's explanation in *Percy–Evans Correspondence*, pp. 61–2. See Thormodus Torfaeus, *Orcades seu Rerum Orcadensium Historiae Libri Tres* (Copenhagen, 1697), Preface. Percy quotes the relevant passage in *Reliques* (1767), i. p. lxii.

[2] *History*, i. sig. a2.

[3] Caylus (see pp. 20–1 above) was anticipated by G. Naudé, *History of Magic*, trans. G. Davies (1657), p. 9, 'It is out of all controversie, that our old Romances took their rise from the *Chronicles* of Bishop *Turpin*'.

no more than a systematization in Northern Europe of political and social ideas having their origin in the East. Medieval feudalism and romance were in his view only accidentally connected. The romances of the feudal middle ages 'complimented the ruling passion of the times, and cherished in a high degree the fashionable sentiments of ideal honour and fantastic fortitude'.[1] Warton saw the Crusades simply as introducing a new and final wave of Eastern influence which provided specific oriental topics and elevated the Saracens to the place of eminence as enemies of the Christian knights.

Warton's lengthy dissertation 'Of the origin of romantic fiction in Europe' prefixed to the first volume of his *History of English Poetry* shows how important the subject was to him. Far from wishing to avoid such a vague and ultimately sterile topic, he was eager to cast all existing theories into his system, and so at last explain a phenomenon that puzzled his contemporaries and predecessors. For the elements of romance had attracted writers and readers for centuries and had only with difficulty been exorcized from polite literature, and from general belief. Many a reader must have shared Warton's satisfaction in looking back from the eminence of an age which had at last restored canons of good taste and reasonable customs and manners, to the dim centuries that had delighted in, and been enchained by, superstition and dread. There was also the serious consideration of what modern civilization owed to that past, so well expressed by Gilbert Stuart:

The spirit of humanity, which distinguishes modern times in the periods of war, as well as of peace; the gallantry which prevails in our conversations and private intercourse; in our theatres and in our public assemblies and amusements; the point of honour which corrects the violence of the passions, by improving our delicacy, and the sense of propriety and decorum; and which, by teaching us to consider the importance of others, makes us value our own; these circumstances arise out of chivalry, and discriminate the modern from the ancient world.[2]

The romances as the literary expression of the ideals of that chivalry were thus of great interest; to trace the origin of the

[1] *History*, i. 117.
[2] Gilbert Stuart, *A View of Society in Europe* (Edinburgh, 1778), p. 66.

romances was to trace to their source the ideals which had slowly transformed civilization. The disposition to believe that this source was the East was deeply ingrained. William Robertson was not alone in believing that it was contact with the East during the Crusades that, by bringing the West in touch with a more refined culture, gradually dispelled barbarism and ignorance.[1]

The myth of the migration of Odin, on which Warton depended, was challenged by John Richardson[2] as being totally improbable. Yet Richardson also accepted that chivalry and knight-errantry, tournaments, armorial bearings, respect for women and belief in fairies and giants were Eastern in origin. He argued that while the feudal system in Europe was an exotic plant, in the East it was indigenous, universal and immemorial.[3] But 'romance, whose characteristic genius rolls entirely on a peculiar and distinct species of machinery, could not have originated in Arabia', since the Arabs had to adopt words to describe the strange creatures of romance, whilst the Persians had indigenous terms. Persia, therefore, may be presumed to be the original home of all the typical elements of romance. To illustrate the Persian love of single combat, he instances the story of Sohrab and Rustam. A century later, the Persian theory received further support, when W. A. Clouston argued that the Persian story of the Bedoin poet-hero Antar contained episodes very similar to incidents in *Guy of Warwick* and *Bevis*.[4]

Theorizing about the origins of romance held an unfailing attraction for the eighteenth century. James Beattie, for instance, elaborated the views of Huet and Hurd, in a 'Dissertation on Fable and Romance'. Though only one of a lengthy series of *Dissertations Moral and Critical*,[5] it was chosen by the reviewer in the *London Magazine* as the main subject for

---

[1] See Herbert Weisinger, op. cit., p. 71.

[2] *Dissertation on the Language, Literature and Manners of the Eastern Nations* (Oxford, 1777), p. 138. This was prefixed to his *Dictionary, Persian, Arabic and English*.

[3] ibid., p. 153.

[4] W. A. Clouston, *Popular Tales and Fictions, their Migrations and Transformations* (1887), i. 39–48.

[5] *Dissertations* (1783), pp. 505 f.

his article.[1] Clara Reeve, in her history of fiction *The Progress of Romance*, summarized existing opinions and concluded sensibly that 'Romances are of universal growth, and not confined to any particular period or countries. They were the delight of barbarous ages, and they have always kept their ground. . . . Epic poetry is the parent of Romance'.[2] Similarly, both John Moore and Mrs Barbauld begin their histories of fiction with summaries of the various theories of the origin of romance.[3]

Into the unwieldy quest for the origin of fiction was swept the more manageable problem of who first wrote a romance of King Arthur or of Charlemagne. John Leyden,[4] 'with all his many-languaged lore', and a thorough knowledge of all the romances in the Auchinleck MS, began promisingly with the *Lais* of Marie de France, and, working back from Brittany to Cornwall and Wales, concluded that though stories of Arthur originated in Celtic Britain, the first literary treatment of them was in Brittany. Arthurian traditions in Scotland also supported his general Celtic theory of the origin of Arthurian romance. Leyden argued further that since the late Pseudo-Turpin chronicle attributed to Charlemagne the exploits of Charles Martel, this other prime source of romance may have been fabricated in Armorica. But, though he realized that this 'most curious subject of investigation' was 'involved in the greatest obscurity', he rashly pushed his theory of Armorican origin to the same exclusive point as Percy and Warton.

Joseph Ritson, however, was careful not to offer an exclusive system. He follows Tyrwhitt's note on Warburton's theory in denying the pre-eminence of Spain in the production of romances, and in suggesting that it is unnecessary to limit the origins of romance to one time and place. In 1782 he was prepared to accept a Celtic origin.[5] But in the 'Dissertation on

[1] *London Magazine*, July, 1783, pp. 49–55.

[2] *Progress of Romance* (Colchester, 1785), i. pp. xv–xvi, 25. Here Landor found the 'Egyptian' romance, on which he based his poem *Gebir*.

[3] John Moore, 'Commencement and Progress of Romance', prefixed to *Works of Smollett* (1797); reprinted 1872. Mrs Barbauld, *The Origin and Progress of Novel-Writing*, prefixed to *The British Novelists* (1810).

[4] John Leyden (ed.), *The Complaint of Scotland* (Edinburgh, 1801), pp. 254 ff. The Armorican theory was also adopted by Sharon Turner, *History of the Anglo-Saxons* (1799).

[5] *Observations on the three first volumes of the History of English Poetry* (1782), p. 3.

Romance' in 1802 he dismisses earlier theories in favour of the more cautious belief that 'the Engleish acquire'd the art of romance-writeing from the French'.[1]

George Ellis was the first scholar to confine his attention to the medieval romances proper, and to realize that stories were taken from various sources, Armorican, Celtic, Scandinavian, French and Eastern, so that any exclusive theory was unlikely to be valid.[2] On the transmission of the Celtic Arthurian stories to the Norman minstrels, he agreed with Scott that the Normans 'borrowed very many (though certainly not all) . . . from the minstrels of the "north country"'.[3] The northern minstrels derived their knowledge from the traditions surviving in what had been the Celtic kingdom of Strathclwyd. This theory was elaborated by Scott in his edition of *Sir Tristrem* (1804). Scott's more general position, expressed in his article on *Romance* in the *Encyclopaedia Britannica* (1824), is akin to Ellis's—that romance sprang from the real or fabulous histories of each nation, which were gradually embellished with materials derived from Celtic, classical, Norse and Arabian stories. Romance, Scott concluded, 'was like a compound metal, derived from various mines, and in the different specimens of which one metal or another was alternately predominant'.[4] The clear thinking of Caylus had taken over half a century to penetrate English views.

---

[1] Ritson, *Metrical Romanceës* (1802), i. p.c.
[2] Ellis, *Metrical Romances* (1805), i. 36. [3] Scott, *Letters*, i. 113 n.
[4] Scott, *Miscellaneous Prose Works* (1847), ii. 559.

CHAPTER II

EPIC AND ROMANCE:
RICHARD HURD

RICHARD HURD (1720–1808) has already been mentioned as one who theorized on the origin of romance. His *Letters on Chivalry and Romance*, which appeared in 1762, the same year as the second edition of Thomas Warton's *Observations on the Faerie Queene*, constitute an attempt to reassess the romantic epics of the Renaissance, in particular the *Faerie Queene*, and to look afresh at chivalry, knight-errantry and medieval superstitions—belief in fairies and witchcraft—as the material of poetry. Like Thomas Percy, of whom he was an almost exact contemporary, Hurd's career was in the Church. In 1775 he became Bishop of Lichfield, and was translated to Worcester in 1781. Two years later, being then sixty-three, he refused the Archbishopric of Canterbury. He is remembered as the friend of Warburton, Gray and Mason, and as the author of a commentary on Horace (1751), a valuable *Letter to Mr Mason on the Marks of Imitation* (1757), and a series of *Moral and Political Dialogues* (1759). Though not a deeply learned man, he had the ability to present his material in a very attractive manner.

The *Letters on Chivalry* are brief and persuasive. They are concerned only incidentally with medieval romances, with which Hurd was barely acquainted. What knowledge he had, he openly declared to be derived from Sainte-Palaye's *Mémoires sur l'ancienne chevalerie*, which he had read in the proceedings of the Academy of Inscriptions. He omitted to mention, though, that he had also read, in an earlier volume of their proceedings, a work by the seventeenth-century poet and critic, Jean Chapelain, called *De la Lecture des Vieux Romans*.[1] Sainte-

---

[1] Sainte-Palaye's *Mémoires* he read in vol. 20 of the *Recueil de l'Academie des Inscriptions*. Chapelain's *De la Lecture*, written c. 1647, was printed in *Continuations des Mémoires de Littérature* (Paris, 1728), vi. Part i, pp. 281–342. See V. M. Hamm, 'A Seventeenth-Century French Source for Hurd', *PMLA*, lii (1937), 820–8.

Palaye's work gave him the knowledge of knight-errantry and of chivalry as an institution, which he used to persuade his reader that the manners portrayed in romances had once been practised by living human beings. Chapelain gave him the form of the dialogue with hostile interlocutors, which Hurd changed to a series of letters to an incredulous but trusting correspondent. More important were the critical points in Chapelain from which Hurd's own argument springs. It is this contact with an early seventeenth-century commentary which probably explains why Hurd's *Letters* read like a reopening of the discussion of epic and romance that had begun in Italy in the sixteenth century.[1]

Serious discussion of the rules for composing epic was still going on, however, when Hurd wrote. John Wilkie, in the Preface to his epic, *The Epigoniad* (1757), was still writing in the tradition of Dryden and Rapin, long after Pope had burlesqued such critical occupations by his sarcastic recommendations in the *Guardian*: 'take out of any old poem, history book, romance, or legend (for instance Geoffrey of Monmouth, or Don Bellianis of Greece) those parts of story which afford most scope for long descriptions.'[2] But for Hurd the discussion was no longer concerned with the present possibilities of epic; he was reviving a long-dead issue, the choice of subject-matter and form by Ariosto and Spenser. The *Letters* are a piece of historical criticism, though the justification of Spenser's choice is not simply in terms of the critical background of the age in which he wrote. Hurd goes further, to argue that a work need not adhere to an abstract ideal form, that the form of a work might be expected to develop out of the nature of the subject of which it treats. He is indulging in special pleading on behalf of the subject-matter and form of the romances, boldly trying to reverse the judgement of the previous two centuries.

Hurd was conscious that the *Faerie Queene*, like the plays of Shakespeare, could not easily be fitted into accepted critical

[1] For this discussion see W. L. Renwick, *Edmund Spenser* (1949); J. B. Pendlebury, *Dryden's Heroic Plays* (1923); C. B. Millican, *Spenser and the Table Round* (Cambridge Mass., 1932); V. Hall, *Renaissance Literary Criticism* (Columbia, 1945).

[2] *Guardian*, 78, 10 June, 1713. Scott thought this 'the first instance in which common sense was applied to this department of poetry'. (Preface to *The Bridal of Triermain* (1813).)

canons. The *Faerie Queene* had always delighted readers. Spenser was the object of numerous imitations, burlesque and serious, by poets who include Prior, Thomson, Akenside, Shenstone, Mason, Smart, Mickle and Beattie.[1] But he also received scholarly attention. John Hughes' edition came out in 1715, John Upton's in 1758. Jortin's *Remarks on Spenser's Poems* (1734) and Upton's *Letter concerning a New Edition of Spenser's Faerie Queene* (1751) prepared the way for Warton's *Observations* (1754). This was the context in which Hurd wrote his *Letters*, a context which already included the germ of his contention that Spenser should not be tried by classical rules. Hughes, in the preface to his edition, had gone back to sixteenth-century Italian apologies for Ariosto, drawn a parallel between Gothic architecture and the structure of the *Faerie Queene*, and stressed the influence of chivalry on Spenser. Hurd simply took these points a step further. His important addition to the discussion was his sketch of the medieval background of chivalry, based on Sainte-Palaye, and his forthright support for the superiority of Gothic superstitions over classical mythology. Without knowing any medieval romances himself, he yet called for a new attitude towards them, basing his appeal largely on the evidence that Spenser, Shakespeare and Milton had been attracted to them.

The *Faerie Queene* was the last great epic to make use of what was regarded as the form of romance. Judged by classical standards it was, of course, formless. But if the form of romance had been abandoned after Spenser, the subject-matter had continued to attract poets. In particular, the story of Arthur had been seriously considered by Milton and Dryden.[2]

Their interest was sufficient excuse for the historically-minded scholars of the later eighteenth century to investigate the romances which had so nearly been the subject of national epics. But Hurd was the first critic to look back on the controversy of romantic subject and epic form and see it as one

---

[1] See the works of Beers and Cory referred to above (p. 6) and W. L. Phelps, *Beginnings of the English Romantic Movement* (Boston, 1893), ch. 4.

[2] See R. F. Brinkley, *The Arthurian Legend in the Seventeenth Century* (Baltimore, 1932); H. W. MacCallum, *Tennyson's Idylls of the King and Arthurian Story from the Sixteenth Century* (Glasgow, 1894).

that merited reopening. It was not unusual to test a romance by the structural rules for epic. Percy, for example, described *Libius Disconius* as 'as regular in its conduct' as any classical epic, and inferior only in diction and sentiments,[1] in much the same way that Addison had approached *Chevy Chase*. Burke declared also that the *Aeneid* and *Don Bellianis* differ only in respect of language. The 'refined language' of the epic is an obstacle to the admirer of the romance. But if the epic were 'degraded into the style of Pilgrim's Progress' then both epic and romance would be seen to have the same basis, 'in both . . . a tale exciting admiration is told; both are full of action, both are passionate; in both are voyages, battles, triumphs, and continual changes of fortune'.[2] The similarity of the fables used in classical epic and romance had led Cowley to reject both, the 'mad stories of the gods and heroes' being 'no better argument for verse than those of their worthy successors the knights-errant'.[3] Dryden had compared Aeneas with Amadis and Lancelot. Jean Chapelain, in 1647, had argued that it was only in point of style that *Lancelot* was inferior to Homer's epics, that since both were extravagant fables, 'je ne voy pas grande différence entre l'errant Hercule & l'errant Lancelot', 'pour les choses elles ne sont guères plus vrayes les uns que les autres'.[4] Chapelain also repeated the argument of Pigna and Cinthio that the romances were not known to Aristotle, and therefore not subject to his rules, but were themselves so good that

Si Aristote revenoit, & qu'il se mit en tête de trouver une matière d'Art poétique en Lancelot, je ne doute point qu'il n'y réussit aussi-bien qu'en l'Iliade & en l'Odyssée.

Hurd probably met this argument in Chapelain's essay. But comparisons between classical and romantic machinery were not uncommon when Hurd was writing. The romances could by

---

[1] *Reliques* (1765), iii. xvi. Percy also praised the selection of circumstances in *Richard* as 'not unworthy the selection of any epic poet' (iii. p. xii), but withdrew this in the fourth edition.

[2] Burke, *Philosophical Enquiry into the Origin of our Ideas of the Sublime and the Beautiful* (1757), eighth edition, 1776, pp. 24–5.

[3] Cowley, Preface to *Poems* (1656).

[4] J. Chapelain, *De la Lecture des Vieux Romans*, ed. A. Feillet (Paris, 1870), pp. 9, 22. Even Fielding came to wish that Homer had treated of true history instead of fable, Preface to *Voyage to Lisbon* (1755).

this means be made to seem not quite so ludicrously extravagant. Thomas Warton, for example, anxious to trace the origin of romantic fiction to the East, asserted that Homer also was indebted to the East for 'his giants, and other incidents of romance, scattered in different parts of the Iliad and Odyssey, particularly the latter'. He gave as a further example the story of Jason, which has 'the cast of one of the old romances', and in which the elements of romance are 'found in the aggregate, and form a series of romantic adventures'.[1] Joseph Warton developed the same ideas, arguing that 'facts and events have been indeed verified and modified, but totally new facts have not been created'. Hence, 'the writers of old romances, from whom Ariosto and Spenser have borrowed so largely' may be indebted

for their invulnerable heroes, their monsters, their enchantments, their gardens of pleasure, their winged steeds, and the like, to Echidna, to the Circe, to the Medea, to the Achilles, to the Syrens, to the Harpies, to the Phryxus, and the Bellerophon, of the Ancients ... Some faint traditions of the ancients may have been kept glimmering and alive during the whole barbarous ages, as they are called. . . . To say that Amadis and Sir Tristan have a classical foundation, may at first sight appear paradoxical; but if the subject were examined to the bottom, I am inclined to think, that the wildest chimeras in those books of chivalry with which Don Quixote's library was furnished, would be found to have a close connexion with ancient mythology.[2]

It is a theory that has attracted the modern scholar, Roger Sherman Loomis,[3] as well as Robert Southey,[4] and was noted by the philosopher of romance, Kenelm Henry Digby. Digby justified his use of classical allusions in a review of chivalry by comparing classical and romantic heroes, and concluding that many instances in classical epic 'present a strong resemblance to the spirit and character of our later chivalry'.[5] That this should become a commonplace of criticism is largely

[1] T. Warton, *Observations* (1762), i. 178; cf. *History*, iii. 497–8.
[2] J. Warton, *An Essay on the Genius and Writings of Pope* (1782), ii. 3.
[3] R. S. Loomis, *Celtic Myth and Arthurian Romance* (New York, 1927).
[4] In his Preface to *Amadis of Gaul* (1803).
[5] Kenelm Henry Digby, *The Broad Stone of Honour. Godefridus* (1829), pp. 77, 78 f., 83.

the result of Hurd's statement of it in the *Letters*, but in fact he is merely echoing Chapelain, Cowley, and indeed Cervantes when he asks 'And what are the Grecian Bacchus, Hercules, and Theseus but Knights-errant, the exact counter-parts of Sir Lancelot and Amadis de Gaul', and when he observes that 'the Grecian romances were just as extravagant and as little credible, as the Gothic'.[1]

To convict the fables of the classical epics of extravagance and incredibility, was not intended to debase the epics, but to show that no critic could justifiably be content to dismiss the romances on these grounds alone. And if not on these grounds of wildness of fable, then on what? For the medieval romances, the grounds of diction and sentiment were adequate, but these features could be shown to be due to the state of the language and society, as well as to the failure of any poet of commanding genius, other than Chaucer, to use the Gothic fables during the height of the chivalrous ages.[2] There was also the ground of structure, for it had long been accepted that the classical structure was superior to the romantic shapelessness of the *Faerie Queene*. For a particular romance, like *Libius*, it was possible to show that it conformed to Aristotle's rules. But to attempt to force such works into Aristotle's mould was to admit that the classical structure was the only possible one. Hurd, seizing on Chapelain's dictum, that a romance had its own structure, good of its kind but different, urged the reader to look on the *Faerie Queene* 'as a Gothic, not a classic poem'. While, therefore, pressing the argument that as fables the classic and Gothic were in-distinguishable, Hurd used the differentiation in structure to plead for a recognition that a work could have 'that sort of unity and simplicity, which results from its nature', in Spenser's case 'a unity of *design*, and not of action'.[3] With Chapelain, Hurd believed that a romance like the *Faerie Queene* was composed according to the rules of its own nature, and therefore a true appreciation of the poem must depend on a knowledge

[1] *Letters* iv and v (in the expanded form of 1765).

[2] *Letter* xi.

[3] *Letter* viii. John Hughes, in the introduction to his edition of Spenser in 1715, realized that Spenser had not designed his poem by the rules of epic, and compared it to Gothic architecture, in the manner of Hurd later. Upton in the preface to his edition (1758) saw the poem as unified in the figure of Arthur.

of such rules and an understanding of the poet's observance of them.

Hurd is Chapelain's returning Aristotle, prepared to find 'Une matière d'Art poetique' in Spenser, which could be applied to test romantic or Gothic structure. Thus, in the eighth Letter, he defines the Method and Unity of the *Faerie Queene*. The Method of the twelve knights undertaking adventures he derives from the 'established modes and ideas of chivalry', instancing the 'feast made at Lisle in 1453, in the court of Philip the Good'. The Unity he describes as 'the relation of it's several adventures to one common *original*, the appointment of the Faery Queen; and to one common *end*, the completion of the Faery Queen's injunctions'. This unity of *design* in the narrative is further elaborated by Spenser—though injudiciously—by the intermingling of the several actions together, and by the creation of Arthur as a superior character with a part to play in each separate action. Hurd considered that the real justification for the creation of Arthur, lay not in the narrative design, but in the Moral Unity of the poem, to which the narrative is subservient. The knights function not simply as part of the narrative, but, as allegorical figures representing virtues, in the Moral Design as well. The double unity thus imposed—resulting, presumably, in the intermittent weakening of the narrative in the interests of the moral, and of the moral in the interests of the narrative—Hurd found to be the source of perplexity and confusion, the 'only considerable defect of this extraordinary poem'.

Hurd, it would seem, was led to this elaboration of a set of rules for a Gothic poem, by the statement of Chapelain. From his application of them in the ninth Letter to the *Gierusalemme Liberata* of Tasso, it is clear that he is prepared to use them as rigidly as other critics had applied the rules of Aristotle. As a preliminary to the justification of Gothic structure, however, he had of necessity to show that Spenser and other writers of romances were, like the authors of classical epic, engaged in imitating nature. Bougainville, in his *Avertissement* to the 1759 edition of Sainte-Palaye's *Mémoires sur l'ancienne chevalerie*, a work to which Hurd acknowledges his debt, had said that the average reader looked on the system of chivalry as 'un système bizarre, imaginé par nos anciens Romanciers'.[1] In England too most readers found it impossible to believe that the romances described a form of society and manners that had ever existed. 'Not one in ten-thousand knows enough of the barbarous ages, in which [Gothic manners] arose, to believe that they ever really existed'.[2] The behaviour of knights-errant was as remote from that of eighteenth-century gentlemen as from the ideal behaviour that the sixteenth- and seventeenth-century moralists had tried to inculcate in their readers, and from the ordinary life of any human being since the Crusaders. The behaviour of Homer's warriors was truer to human experience. 'Homer copied true natural manners', wrote Hume, 'which, however rough and uncultivated, will always form an agreeable and pleasing picture; but the pencil of the English poet [Spenser] was employed in drawing the affectations, and conceits, and fopperies, of chivalry, which appear ridiculous, as soon as they lose the recommendations of the mode.'[3]

There were two means of arguing against this position; first, to show that 'they had not ceased to be the mode in Spenser's time',[4] and secondly, to show that the manners of chivalry 'are to be accounted natural'.[5] The interest in primitive societies which the reading of travel books had for long encouraged stimulated interest also in the barbarians who had succeeded to the Roman Empire. Compared with the social structure and manners of the Romans, those of the barbarians of the Middle Ages were 'unnatural'. But since they had been the practice of human beings for centuries, there must be something in them that is consonant with human nature. For, as John Foster observed, human nature is

a mere passive thing, variable almost to infinity, according to climate, to institutions, and to the different ages of time. Even taking it in a civilized state, what relation is there between such a form of human nature as that displayed at Sparta, and, for instance, the modern Society of Friends, or the Moravian Fraternity?[6]

[1] Sainte-Palaye, *Mémoires* (1759), i. p. viii.   [2] *Letter* xi.
[3] Hume, *History of England*, ii. (1759), 739.
[4] Joseph Warton, *Essay on the Genius and Writings of Pope* (fifth edition, 1806), ii. 32 n.
[5] *Letter* xi.
[6] John Foster, *Essays in a Series of Letters to a Friend* (1806), i. 262–3.

But Hurd was dealing with 'nature' in a barbarous state, and even here, he argues, barbarians have their own 'reason' since 'nothing in human nature . . . is without its reason'. Fresh from a reading of Sainte-Palaye's *Mémoires*, he undertakes in the first four letters to show that neither 'Gothic Chivalry' nor 'the spirit of ROMANCE' can be simply dismissed as 'the usual caprice and absurdity of barbarians'. By considering the institution of Chivalry, 'the time of its birth, the situation of the barbarians amongst whom it arose . . . their wants, designs, and policies', he proves that the manners of the ages of chivalry 'are to be accounted natural'.

Sainte-Palaye had 'opened a new and extensive field of information concerning the manners, institutions and literature of the feudal ages',[1] by his exposition of the education of a knight, his exercises, tournaments, the ideals of chivalry and the civilizing influence of its institutions. From him, Hurd obtained 'an idea of what Chivalry was in itself', his account of tournaments,[2] and his definition of chivalry as 'a distinct military order, conferred in the way of investiture, and accompanied with the solemnity of an oath and other ceremonies'.[3] Sainte-Palaye provided the information 'at a cheaper rate' than the perusal of the romances themselves, and successfully showed that while the authors of romances were inventive, in their accounts of marvels, they were also authentic, in their descriptions of such things as costume, food, sports and pastimes, tournaments, social relations, the attitudes of the sexes towards each other, codes of conduct, heraldry, law and customs.[4] Though this was well in the tradition of French medieval scholarship, it was new and exciting to English scholars. It is to Hurd's credit that he realized how fundamentally it disturbed traditional attitudes towards the romances and to Spenser.

Settling therefore to the task of showing that 'Gothic manners' are not 'visionary and fantastic', he sketches a history of Europe after the collapse of Rome, the division of Europe into 'petty tyrannies' giving rise to societies centred on

---

[1] Thomas Warton, *History* (1774), i. 149.
[2] *Letter* ii, Sainte-Palaye, *Mémoires* (Paris, 1759), i. 153–4.
[3] *Letter* ii, Sainte-Palaye, i. 68.   [4] See Sainte-Palaye, ii. 107–37.

military arts. If to this be added the attitude towards women that, Tacitus informs us, was common in Germanic peoples, and the superstitition of their religion, we can account for the growth of an Order of Chivalry with ideals of Courtesy, Courage, Faith, Justice and Adventurousness. Chivalry is the natural product of Feudalism, so runs Hurd's argument, no 'absurd and freakish institution, but the natural and even sober effect of the feudal policy'.[1] But, though natural, as arising from the organization of Europe, both Feudalism and Chivalry were short-lived, and with the political constitution went the manners that belonged to it.

There was no example of any such manners remaining on the face of the earth: and as they never did subsist but once, and are never likely to subsist again, people would be led of course to think and speak of them, as romantic and unnatural. The consequence of which was a total contempt and rejection of them; while the classic manners, as arising out of the customary and usual situations of humanity, would have many archetypes and appear natural even to those who saw nothing similar to them actually subsisting before their eyes. Thus, though the manners of HOMER are perhaps as different from ours, as those of Chivalry itself, yet as we know that such manners always belong to rude and simple ages, such as HOMER paints; and actually subsist at this day in countries that are under the like circumstances of barbarity; we readily agree to call them *natural*, and even take a fond pleasure in the survey of them.[2]

Thus the naturalness of Gothic manners is not that of a 'true' primitive human condition, but a special, almost an aberrant form of primitive behaviour. Hurd considered it an impossible task to persuade the generality of readers to accept the naturalness of Gothic manners, and therefore abandoned the *Faerie Queene* to the admiration of 'a few lettered and curious men'. Yet, far as he was from encouraging any modern poet to imitate the romances or to revive their fables as the matter for contemporary poetry, he nevertheless believed that there was something in such fables that was particularly suited to poetry.

'Some ages are not so fit to write epic poems in, as others', Hurd wrote, thus voicing the realization not only that literature

[1] *Letter* ii.   [2] *Letter* xi, *ad fin.*

is conditioned by complex social, ethical and political conditions, but also that the Renaissance ideal of producing
national epics which would vie with the *Iliad*, *Odyssey* and
Aeneid, was dead, killed not by lack of poets of genius but by
changes in society. For an epic poem the 'marvellous' was
essential, and the marvellous could only be produced by 'the
agency of superior natures really existing', such as Milton's
angels and devils, or by natures to the existence of which the
imagination of the reader could give willing assent.[1] Gothic
faeries had gone the way of pagan gods; they were no longer
believed in by any poet or reader. Therefore Hurd advises no
modern poet to 'revive these faery tales in an epic poem'. But
for the historical critic, anxious to do justice to the poets of a
past age, and prepared to put himself 'in the circumstances of
the poet, or rather, of those, of whom the poet writes', the
question of the superiority of classical or Gothic machinery was
a question meriting discussion.

Hurd is on the side of the Wartons in preferring poetry of the
imagination to poetry of men and manners or even to poetry
of the passions, and in such 'sublime and creative poetry' those
'cautious rules of credibility' are not necessary.[2] As well
condemn Homer and Virgil for the superstitions in their
poems, as Ariosto and Tasso for the magic and enchantments in
theirs. In fact, the attraction of the romance lay in its magic
and enchantment. 'We are all on fire amidst the magical feats
of Ismen, and the enchantments of Armida'. This view is not
confined to Hurd. Earlier, in 1752, John Hawkesworth had
considered romance as a kind of epic, and declared that 'the
most generally pleasing of all literary performances, are those
in which supernatural events are every moment produced by
Genii and Faeries'.[3] He instances the popularity of the
Arabian Nights and the *Tales* of the Countess d'Anois, read 'by
almost every taste and capacity with equal eagerness and
delight'. These, together with epic and romance, he considered
more entertaining than the novel, which, though it bears a
nearer resemblance to truth, 'is confined within the narrower
bounds of probability, the number of incidents is necessarily

---

[1] *Letter* x, *ad fin.*　　　　　　　　[2] *Letter* x.
[3] John Hawkesworth, *The Adventurer*, No. 4, 18 November 1752.

diminished, and if it deceives us more, it surprises us less'. Hawkesworth, in this fourth *Adventurer* paper, is perhaps consciously replying to Johnson's fourth *Rambler* paper, where Johnson prefers the novel, written from learning, observation and general converse, to the romance with its giants, knights, deserts and imaginary castles, the product of a mind heated with incredibilities. Accordingly Hawkesworth justifies a delight in 'relations which contradict all experience, and exhibit a series of events that are not only impossible but ridiculous'.

Hurd's later contention, that the presence of the marvellous does not extend its baleful influence to the characterization,

> . . . it is not true that all is *unnatural* and monstrous in their poems, because of this mixture of the wonderful. Admit, for example, Armida's marvellous conveyance to the happy Island, and all the rest of the love-story is as natural, that is as suitable to our common notions of that passion, as anything in Virgil or (if you will) Voltaire.[1]

is made at greater length by Hawkesworth. A reader is satisfied if every event appears to have an adequate cause,

> and when the agency of Genii and Fairies is once admitted, no event which is deemed possible to such agents is rejected as incredible or absurd; the action of the story proceeds with regularity, the persons act upon rational principles, and such events take place as may naturally be expected from the interposition of superior intelligence and power: so that though there is not a natural, there is at least a kind of moral probability preserved, and our first concession is abundantly rewarded by the new scenes to which we are admitted, and the unbounded prospect that is thrown open before us.

The relationships between the human characters in such stories must be those of normal human beings, for

> though we attend with delight to the achievements of a hero who is transported in a moment over half the globe upon a griffin, and see with admiration a palace or a city vanish upon his breaking a seal or extinguishing a lamp; yet if at his first interview with a mistress, for whose sake he had fought so many battles and passed so many regions, he should salute her with a box on the ear; or if immediately

[1] *Letter* x.

after he had vanquished a giant or a dragon, he should leap into a well or tie himself up to a tree, we should be disappointed and disgusted, the story would be condemned as improbable, unnatural and absurd, our innate love of truth would be applauded, and we should expatiate on the folly of an attempt to please reasonable beings, by a detail of events which can never be believed, and the intervention of agents which could never have existed.

Hurd has a more authoritative critic than Hawkesworth behind him, however. Addison, describing 'the Faery way of writing', had witnessed to the common reader's delight in giving himself up to agreeable impostures.[1] Hurd is simply restating Addison's point when he argues that, unnatural in one sense though the magical elements may be, there is a naturalness to be found in the consistency of the poet's imagination, in the way in which all that is marvellous and extraordinary in the poet's world is yet agreeable to the 'conceptions that are readily entertained of these magical and wonder-working Natures'.[2]

It is important to remember in all this that Hurd is engaged in laying the foundations for a reassessment of the medieval romances by serious scholars and critics. Hurd may have been, in Gray's term, a 'second-hand savant', culling his information from the volumes of the Académie des Inscriptions et Belles Lettres, but the presentation of his views, in a witty and urbane style, ensured that they made the widest impact. After Hurd's *Letters* it was more difficult to avoid looking at the literature of the middle ages with the eye of the historical critic. To admit that supernatural machinery was essential to epic was not to be original. To see that both classical and romantic machinery were exploded, and to decide, as an academic question, that romantic machinery was superior to classical, was to change the nature of the discussion. While the possibility of writing an epic was still alive, Chapelain had declared both classical and romantic machinery equally extravagant, Cowley had rejected both, Dryden, following Milton, had invented a Christian machinery. Smollett, like Fielding, on the side of Cervantes, had dissociated himself from the 'ludicrous and

---

[1] *Spectator*, 419. [2] *Letter* x. cf. *Spectator*, 419.

unnatural' of the romances, as well as from the 'heathen mythology, which is no other than a collection of extravagant romances'.[1]

For Hurd the discussion exists in a world where justice is to be done in a long-dead dispute, and he does not disguise his pleasure in his own ingenuity in reversing the verdict, by putting a more favourable interpretation on the evidence. In the absence of any great medieval romance—Spenser and Tasso coming too late 'to paint truly and perfectly what was no longer seen or believed'—Hurd is prepared to compare the life and manners of Homer's Greece with those of the middle ages, and to give the preference to the latter on the grounds of 'the improved gallantry of the feudal times; and the superior solemnity of their superstitions'. The usual objection to the romances was the impossibility of believing their stories, in particular their magical elements. Having disposed of this objection, Hurd is free to compare classic and romantic 'incredibilities', as well as Homeric and feudal societies, and with Shakespeare, Spenser and Milton as his exemplars, to award the prize to his own countrymen much as Addison had done. He is comparing the potentialities, never fully realized in literature, of medieval manners and superstitions, with the supreme achievements of Homer. There is no doubt that his historical view has something irresponsible in its constitution. But in revaluing some aspects of the middle ages, not for the antiquary but for the general reader, Hurd is in the forefront of an attempt to revive interest in chivalry and romance.

Thomas Percy, writing to Richard Farmer after reading Hurd's *Letters*, was 'glad to find a taste for the Old Romances' reviving, 'not among the common Readers, where it would do hurt', but 'amongst our Critics and Poets. Mr Hurd's Letters place them in a very respectable light'.[2] Perhaps no literature has needed quite so much to be placed 'in a very respectable light' as did the medieval romances in the middle of the eighteenth century. By arguing the superiority of their magic and manners over the classics, and by showing the interest in

[1] Smollett, Preface to *Roderick Random* (1748).
[2] *Correspondence of Thomas Percy and Richard Farmer*, p. 7.

them of Spenser, Milton and Shakespeare, Hurd encouraged readers 'to think with more respect, than is commonly done of the Gothic manners, I mean as adapted to the uses of the greater poetry'.[1] It was a prologue to the work of Percy and Thomas Warton.

[1] *Letter* vii, *ad fin.*

CHAPTER III

THOMAS PERCY

Percy's attention to poetry has given grace and splendour to
his studies of antiquity. A mere antiquarian is a rugged being.
Johnson to Boswell, 23 April 1778

UNLIKE Hurd, Thomas Percy (1729–1811)[1] equipped
himself to write with authority on the middle ages.
Percy is an example of the truth of Johnson's dictum
that men are directed in their choice of subject 'not by an
ascendant planet or predominating humour, but by the first
book which they read, some early conversation which they heard,
or some accident which excited ardour and emulation'.[2] The
careful side of Percy's character found satisfaction in his career
in the Church. After twenty-five years as rector of Easton
Maudit, he became Dean of Carlyle in 1778, and from 1782
until his death he was Bishop of Dromore. His adventurousness
was reserved for his literary studies, which he pursued in his
early life with a single-minded ardour. Collecting, transcribing,
and collating texts, providing notes to explain their literary
and historical background, extending the range of English
authors to whose works the apparatus of scholarship should be
applied, these were his delight. He planned and worked on
editions of Buckingham and Surrey, *Don Quixote* and the
Spectator, in addition to the works he actually published, each
one of which shows him in the forefront of literary studies. The
accident which determined his lifelong interest in the romances
was the discovery of a manuscript that was 'being used by the
Maids to light the fire' in the house of Humphrey Pitt.[3] Even
in its mutilated form it attracted him. It was a collection of

---

[1] There is no complete modern study of Percy. The more important studies are
listed in the bibliography.

[2] *Lives of the Poets*, ed. G. B. Hill (Oxford, 1905), iii. 174.

[3] Percy's note in the Folio MS, see Hales and Furnivall, *Bishop Percy's Folio MS*
(1867–8), i. lxxiv.

transcripts, made about the middle of the seventeenth century, of poems, ballads, songs and metrical romances. The texts ranged from the fourteenth to the seventeenth centuries, and as Percy read through it, the idea of printing a selection from it took shape.

Percy, at the age of thirty, was married and rector of Easton Maudit in Northamptonshire. To judge from his surviving correspondence of the 1760s, his burning passion was 'Ancient English Poetry'.[1] He was already known to the poet Shenstone and to Johnson, and quickly made himself known to such scholars as Sir David Dalrymple, Thomas Warton, Richard Farmer, and the poet Gray. It was Johnson who suggested printing from the Folio MS, and who even promised to write the notes to the selected poems, 'a work for which he is peculiarly fitted', Percy wrote to Shenstone, 'by his great acquaintance with all our English Romances etc. of which kind of reading he is uncommonly fond'.[2] The manuscript did indeed contain 'many old Romantic and Historical Ballads', such as had interested the original compiler a century earlier. They included *Sir Degare, The Carle of Carlile, The Grene Knight, Sir Triamore, Sir Eglamore, The Emperor and Child* (a version of *Valentine and Orson*), *Libius Disconius, Guy and Colbrand, Sir Lambwell, Eger and Grime* and *Merline*, as well as ballads about Arthur, Lancelot and Gawain. Possession of such a manuscript put Percy in a unique position. He was the only person to own such a varied collection of texts. It is doubtful whether anyone else could even have compiled a comparable list of titles. It is to Percy's credit that he realized the opportunity it gave him.

The romances in their early forms, such as Percy had discovered, were likely to appeal to a talented young versifier who found an absorbing interest in the more out-of-the-run among his predecessors. Percy was attracted to what he called 'Specimens of the ancient Poetry of different nations'. He planned to publish original texts, with literal translations, in

---

[1] The correspondence is being published, under the editorship of D. Nichol Smith and Cleanth Brooks. Some is printed in John Nichols, *Illustrations of the Literary History of the Eighteenth Century* (1817–58).

[2] Percy to Shenstone, 9 January 1758, in Hans Hecht, *Thomas Percy und William Shenstone* (Strassburg, 1909), p. 9.

small pamphlets, and later to collect them in 'two neat pocket volumes'. Describing his plan to the young Welsh scholar, Evan Evans, in 1762, he listed

the *Erse Poetry*: the *Runic Poetry*: and some *Chinese Poetry* that was published last winter at the end of a book called *Hau Kiou Choaan* or *the Pleasing History* 4 vol. Besides these I have procured a MS. translation of the celebrated *Tograi Carmen* from the Arabic: and have set a friend to translate *Solomon's Song* afresh from the Hebrew, chiefly with a view to the poetry; . . . I have myself gleaned up specimens of *East-Indian Poetry: Peruvian Poetry: Lapland Poetry: Greenland Poetry:* and enclosed I send you one specimen of *Saxon Poetry.*[1]

Percy hoped that the Welsh specimens would be provided by Evans, and had sought him out with this in view. An authentic text of an early poem never failed to excite him. He had no small share of 'that temper of mind which makes men set an immense value on an old manuscript'.[2] The welcome that had been given to the supposed Erse fragments of Ossian published by Macpherson in 1759 seemed to Percy to presage a public interest in all primitive verse. But Percy was anxious only for authentic texts. He was enthusiastic for the sublime, the 'forcible Images . . . strong paintings . . . [and] curious display of ancient manners'[3] of the ancient poets. Hearing of Evans's discovery of the *Gododdin*[4]—a poem attributed to Aneirin, the sixth-century poet—Percy noted, 'What a noble field for literary application to rescue such a fine monument of antiquity from that oblivion; to which every revolving year of delay will more certainly consign it, till lost for ever! *Hoc labor! Hoc opus!*'[5] Macpherson, he reported, went on from success to success, 'tho' hardly one reader in ten Believes the specimens already produced to be genuine. How much greater attention would be due to an editor, who rescues the original itself from oblivion, and fixes it's meaning by an accurate version.'

Percy's ideal is that of the scholar. But for the general

[1] *Correspondence of Thomas Percy and Evan Evans*, p. 31. The versions of the Song of Solomon, and the Chinese novel and poetry, were by Percy himself.

[2] Fielding, Introduction to *A Journey from this World to the Next*.

[3] *Percy–Evans Correspondence*, p. 17.

[4] To Lewis Morris this was 'equal at least to the Iliad, Aeneid or Paradise Lost' (quoted in *Percy–Evans*, p. 18 n.).

[5] *Percy–Evans*, p. 19.

reader such authenticity counts for less than the attractiveness of the version presented for his pleasure. Percy could exclaim with delight over the bare Latin gloss of a Norse or Welsh poem; the general reader seems to have ignored his literal versions of *Runic Odes* and Evans's *Specimens of the Poetry of the Antient Welsh Bards* (1764). For Percy, the genuine literalness of

> et Menai absque refluxu ob sanguinis torrentem
> et color virorum sanguinis in salsugine[1]

was enthralling; 'no poet ever hit upon a grander image' was his comment.[2] But the general reader preferred the inventions of Macpherson:

His joy was in the fall of men. Blood to him was a summer stream, that brings joy to the withered vales, from its own mossy rock.[3]

When Percy was corresponding with his publisher about his translation of a Portuguese version of the Chinese novel *Hau Kiou Choaan*, the poet Grainger told him of the publisher's reactions to his letters: 'He wants a pleasing romance, and you talk of a faithful copy'.[4] Percy's passion for accuracy at the outset of his career would have delighted Joseph Ritson, who, twenty years later, was to search for authentic texts in the one publication of Percy's which did not contain them—the *Reliques of Ancient English Poetry* (1765). This was the work that grew out of the plan to print a selection from the Folio MS. During the process of editing, however, the plan changed, largely as a result of the influence of Shenstone. Shenstone had already undermined Percy's scholarly aims, when he commented on the Chinese novel, 'Are you never prejudiced by yᵉ Air of Learning, yᵉ obscurity, yᵉ rarity, and, perhaps, the Difficulty, of your work, to imagine something in it more extraordinary, yⁿ the Publick will perhaps discover?'[5]

From Shenstone, and the lack of public enthusiasm for his authentic versions of primitive poems, Percy learned that it required more than his own enthusiasm and a genuine text

---

[1] A couplet from Evans's Latin gloss of Gwalchmai's ode to Owen Gwynned, translated by Gray as 'The Triumphs of Owen'.
[2] *Percy–Evans*, p. 14.　　　　　　　　[3] *Cath-loda*, Duan iii.
[4] Nichols, *Illustrations*, vii. 249.
[5] Shenstone to Percy, 15 February 1760, in Hecht, p. 31.

to arouse the interest of the poetry-reading public. Shenstone appealed to Percy's own instinct to versify. Percy continued to enthuse to Evans about authentic medieval Welsh poems, such 'productions of Genius' being 'sure to attract the attention of all: Every reader of taste, of whatever country or faction, listens with pleasure'.[1] But at the same time he himself was being urged by Shenstone, 'Let ye Liberties taken by the Translator of the Erse-Fragments be a Precedent for you . . . Many old Pieces without some alteration will do nothing, and with your amendments will be striking.'[2]

The texts which Percy was intending to print from his manuscript did, of course, differ from those in obscure languages whose accurate publication and translation he encouraged. Their authenticity was assured, their language was English, albeit in a form that necessitated a glossary. They were already in verse, and so had an advantage over bald prose translations. But they were, in the Folio MS, often imperfect, partly because the manuscript was damaged, and partly because they had originally been transcribed from debased texts. Except to the trained ear of the scholar, the metre of such early poems was rough and crude, not able to compete with the rhythmical prose of Macpherson. If Percy's texts were to prove popular, some smoothing was essential, and seemed, from the state of the manuscript, justifiable. Macpherson's forgeries inevitably drove out of circulation the rude originals which were in themselves sufficient to excite the scholar. Shenstone, whose taste Percy respected, encouraged him to 'improve' the poems; not to 'plainly contradict Antiquity'— since the antiquity constituted their claim to attention—but to alter a word or two without a qualm, and to print a wholly rewritten line in italic. There was no merit to be gained by a close reproduction of an obviously imperfect and crude text. It was an attitude that died hard, and against which Ritson had to fight all his life. Percy's own sense of uncertainty in matters of public taste led him to accept what proved to be the intelligent assessment of Shenstone,

If I have any talent at Conjecture, All People of Taste thro'out the Kingdom will rejoice to see a judicious, a correct and elegant

---

[1] *Percy–Evans*, p. 16, October 1761.   [2] Hecht, pp. 63 f., September 1761.

collection of such Pieces. For after all, 'tis such Pieces that contain yᵉ true Chemical Spirit or Essence of Poetry, a Little of which properly mingled is sufficient to strengthen and keep alive very considerable Quantities of the kind. 'Tis yᵉ voice of Sentiment rather yⁿ the Language of Reflection, and adapted peculiarly to strike yᵉ Passions, which is the only Merit of Poetry that has obtained my regard of late.[1]

When the *Reliques* appeared in 1765, Percy suggested in his Preface that he had 'endeavoured to be as faithful as the imperfect state of his materials would permit'. He feared that 'the desire of being accurate ha[d] perhaps seduced him into too minute and trifling an exactness'. The trifling exactness probably referred to the introductory note to each poem, where Percy often parades minutiae of literary history, and to the appended essays on ancient minstrels, on the origin of the English stage, on the metre of Piers Plowman, and on the ancient metrical romances. Percy's scholarship in the notes and essays is admirable, full of newly discovered facts, connected by a reasonable argument and plausible conjectures. The scholar interested in medieval literature had a great deal to learn from this material in the *Reliques*. The poets of the next generation, in England and Germany, felt that they could hardly exaggerate their indebtedness to the poems themselves. Percy's correspondence of 1761–5 shows how detailed his enquiries were, and how anxious he was to collate his texts with all other copies. Farmer and Warton were constantly asked to 'be so kind as to collate the enclosed song' with a copy in Cambridge or Oxford. But the texts printed in the *Reliques* were rarely untouched, and the alterations and additions were, until the fourth edition (1794), very slightly indicated. The poems were 'collected, new-modelled, and in many instances . . . composed'[2] by Percy. Thirty years later, after the unpleasant experience of being harried by Ritson, Percy added a paragraph to his Preface explaining his editorial procedure.

These old popular rhimes being many of them copied only from illiterate transcripts, or the imperfect recitation of itinerant balladsingers, have, as might be expected, been handed down to us with

[1] Hecht, p. 46, 10 November 1760.
[2] Wordsworth, Supplement to 1815 Preface, ed. cit., ii. 421.

less care than any other writings in the world. And the old copies whether MS. or printed, were often so defective or corrupted, that a scrupulous adherence to their wretched readings would only have exhibited unintelligible nonsense, or such poor meagre stuff, as neither came from the Bard, nor was worthy the press; when, by a few slight corrections or additions, a most beautiful or interesting sense hath started forth, and this so naturally and easily, that the Editor could seldom prevail on himself to indulge the vanity of making a formal claim to the improvement; but must plead guilty to the charge of concealing his own share in the amendments under some such general title, as a 'Modern Copy', or the like. . . . His object was to please both the judicious Antiquary, and the Reader of Taste; and he hath endeavoured to gratify both without offending either.[1]

In the eyes of Ritson, Percy 'preferred his ingenuity to his fidelity'.[2] In order to make clear his position as an editor, Percy in the fourth edition of the *Reliques* in 1794 printed from his Folio MS the text of *The Marriage of Sir Gawaine*, so that his reader could judge how impossible it would have been for him to print such imperfect and rough material. A comparison shows that no less than forty-six stanzas were entirely composed by Percy, to fill in the gaps in the torn manuscript, and that few stanzas were printed without some verbal alterations in the interests of smoother versification.

Percy's attitude towards the poems in his manuscript is not unlike that of Pope towards the text of Shakespeare. It could never have been the intention of the Bard to perpetrate such crudities; the transmission of the text has, we know, resulted in corruption and debasement; the editor is therefore in the position of the literary executor, unwilling to allow his friend's work to appear in the rough state in which accident has allowed it to survive. There is much to be said for this attitude, but not by the 'mere Antiquarian'. Ritson looked to the *Reliques* for texts that would, in Percy's words, show the 'taste, genius, sentiments, or manners' of our ancestors. He discovered poems like *The Birth of St. George*, announced as 'for the most part modern', which were clearly Percy's compositions. Whenever Percy's Folio MS was said to be the source of a poem,

---

[1] *Reliques* (1794), i. pp. xvi–xvii.   [2] *Ancient Songs and Ballads* (1790), p. xxi.

81

then the text printed departed seriously from any possible original. Commenting on the Folio and *Reliques* texts of *The Marriage of Sir Gawaine*, Ritson summed up the scholar's attitude.

This mode of publishing ancient poetry, displays, it must be confessed, considerable talent and genius, but savours strongly, at the same time, of unfairness and dishonesty. Here are numerous stanzas inserted which are not in the original, and others omitted which are there. The purchasers and perusers of such a collection are deceived and imposed upon; the pleasure they receive is derived from the idea of antiquity, which, in fact, is perfect illusion.[1]

Ritson was unable to appreciate either Percy's position and attitude, or the atmosphere of 1763, when the 'noble pursuit of ascertaining the Dates, and settling the readings of *halfpenny Ballads*'[2] was not likely to be regarded sympathetically outside a narrow circle of antiquaries. Percy had justifiably been nervous on the eve of publication: 'When I consider what strange old stuff I have raked together, I tremble for its reception with the fastidious public. What rare hacking and hewing will there be for Messrs the Reviewers! I fancy I shall afford you fine sport next month.'[3]

As an 'amulet to guard him[self] from every unfavourable censure, for having bestowed any attention on a parcel of Old Ballads' he paraded the names of 'men of learning and character' who had helped and approved—Johnson, Shenstone, Sir David Dalrymple, Thomas Warton, Blakeway and Farmer, Norris and Garrick, Birch and Lye, and hoped that 'he need not be ashamed of having bestowed some of his idle hours on the ancient literature of our own country'.[4]

The *Reliques* bulk large in Percy's correspondence between 1760 and 1765. As early as July 1761, Shenstone was of the opinion that Percy was expending much energy on them,[5] and Percy himself felt the need to explain to both Farmer and Dalrymple that 'it does not engross the whole of my attention'.[6] Percy had 'graver studies', *The Song of Solomon Newly Translated*

---

[1] *Metrical Romanceës* (1802), i. p. cxli. [2] *Percy–Farmer*, p. 31.
[3] *Percy–Farmer*, p. 82. [4] Preface, *Reliques* (1765), i. p. xiv.
[5] Hecht, p. 57, and see p. 51.
[6] *Percy–Farmer*, p. 80; *Percy–Hailes*, pp. 30–1.

(1764) and the *Key to the New Testament* (1764), from which the literary researches were a relaxation. But these researches themselves were formidable. In addition to the *Reliques*, Percy was collecting material for editions of Surrey, Buckingham, the *Spectator*, metrical romances, Spanish ballads, and what he called 'Ancient Fugitive Pieces'. He published his Chinese novel and the *Miscellaneous Pieces relating to the Chinese* (1762) and the *Five Pieces of Runic Poetry* (1763) and supplied in his letters material which Warton included in the second edition of his *Observations on the Faerie Queene* (1762).

During the same period Percy was translating Paul-Henri Mallet's *Introduction à l'Histoire de Dannemarc* (1755) and its supplement, a translation of the *Edda, Monumens de la Mythologie et de la Poésie des Celtes et Particulièrement des Anciens Scandinaves* (1756). These two works illustrate the religion, laws, customs and manners of the Norse people. Since they dealt with the early history of the Germanic peoples, they appealed at once to the growing desire to know more of the origins of the nations of Northern Europe. Mallet's attitude towards history and the sources available to the historian coincided with the interest of Percy and Warton in the narrative poetry of the middle ages.

For why, asked Mallet, should history be only a recital of battles, sieges, intrigues and negotiations? And why should it contain merely a heap of petty facts and dates, rather than a just picture of the opinions, customs, and even inclinations of a people? . . . great light may be thrown on the character and sentiments of a nation, by those very books, whence we can learn nothing exact or connected of their history.[1]

Mallet's work was a vital introduction to the whole new field of study which Percy was himself entering. Offering his translation to the booksellers, he wrote

The subject opens a new field of research which has hitherto been little explored by the generality of the learned, sufficient to awaken the curiosity of anyone, but which must peculiarly interest the English reader, who will here find a faithful picture of his Saxon

---

[1] *Northern Antiquities* (1770), i. 55–6. Original ed. Copenhagen 1755. Mallet is echoing the words of Thomas Bartholin, *De Causis Contemptae mortis* . . . (Copenhagen 1689), sig. bl[v].

Ancestors, as they existed before they left their German forests: Here he will see the seeds of our excellent Gothic constitution and will perceive the original of many of the customs which prevail among us at this day. Here he will find the original of many superstitions, opinions and prejudices which are thought to be of much later date. To instance only one the origin of chivalry ... in this book the reader will find that the ideas of Chivalry were strongly rivetted in the minds of all the northern nations from the remotest ages: ... Here also he will find the original of Dwarfs, Giants and Dragons ... and to complete the subject will meet with the translation of an ancient Islandic Romance that shews the original of that kind of writing which so long captivated all the nations of Europe.[1]

Mallet expressed for the mid-eighteenth century the reasons for the study of Northern Antiquities. He argued that Greek and Roman religion had been exhaustively studied, but that the early religions of the Northern nations, our ancestors, were largely unknown. These were not only interesting in themselves but threw great light on the customs and attitudes of the modern nations of Europe. Modern manners, laws, and government were descended directly from the practices of these early people. Their activities, institutions and beliefs are part of *our* history. Yet it had for long been considered sufficient to dismiss the middle ages as 'barbarous' and to believe that there were inadequate records available for study. Mallet showed that the study of mankind involved more than the study of classical and modern history. 'We must study the language, the books, and the men of every age and country; and draw from these the only true sources of the knowledge of mankind.'[2] The 'ties and bands of connection, which unite together the different nations of Europe' would be more intelligible when traced to their source.

Percy aimed to further the study of Northern antiquities by translating Mallet's work, and by 'adding new notes where necessary', by 'occasionally rectifying some few oversights', and by adding a preface in which he distinguishes between 'Gothic' and 'Celtic' peoples. Mallet, following Cluverius and Pelloutier,[3] regarded the Celts and Goths as originally the same

---

[1] *Percy–Evans*, pp. 84–5.   [2] *Northern Antiquities*, ii. p. xxxviii.

[3] Philip Cluverius, *Introductionis in Universam Geographiam Libri Sex* (Leyden, 1624); Simon Pelloutier, *Histoire des Celtes* (The Hague, 1740–50).

people, 'being ignorant of all the modern branches of the real *Celtic* Language; and very little acquainted with those of Gothic origin'.[1] The distinction between Celtic and Gothic had been drawn as early as 1718 by John Toland, who wrote, 'the Celtic and the Gothic, which have been often taken for each other, are as different as Latin and Arabic'.[2] The poet Gray, who had himself deliberately mingled some Norse mythology in his *Bard*, realized the distinction independently, but argued that a poet might be 'permitted (in that scarcity of Celtic ideas we labour under) to adopt some of these foreign whimsies, dropping however all mention of Woden and his Valkhyrian virgins.'[3]

The mythology of Greece and Rome had long been felt by many critics and writers to be no longer usable in poetry. The mythology of the Northern nations had the advantage of freshness. Mallet's work, translated by Percy, would fulfil the double purpose of furthering a study of the middle ages and of making available to poets an interesting body of mythology. To be a scholar after the school of Percy and Warton was not simply to study 'the manners, genius, and character of our ancestors', but also to 'store the fancy with those sublime and alarming images, which true poetry best delights to display'.[4]

2

The three volumes of the *Reliques* offered 'Old Heroic Ballads, Songs, and other Pieces of our earlier Poets (chiefly of the Lyric kind). Together with some few of later date'. The poems range

[1] *Percy–Evans*, p. 88.

[2] J. Toland, *Critical History of the Celtic Religion and Learning*, n.d. (Lackington and Hughes), p. 47.

[3] Gray to Mason, 13 January 1758.

[4] Warton, *Observations* (1762), ii. 268. Percy began translating Mallet in 1763 (H. Marwell, *Thomas Percy* (Göttingen, 1934), p. 95, and B.M. Add. MS 32336, ff. 42–51). The text of vol. i. was printed by 1765 (*Percy–Evans*, pp. 106, 112, 119–20). In the second edition of the *Reliques* (pub. 3 December 1767) he was able to refer to volume and page of his version. The translation had been completed by John Calder and Thomas Apperley (see Douce's MS note in his copy of *Northern Antiquities* in the Bodleian, and Percy's statement at i. p. ii). It was not published until 1770. In vol. i the following leaves are cancels: A5, A6, A7, A8, E1, F3, H4, N8, P7, U5, 2A8; in vol. ii. 17, L1, S8. A translation of part of Mallet's book appeared in *The Grand Magazine* for 1758 (i. 63 f., 169 f., 228 f., 520 f.). The original was reviewed by Goldsmith (*Monthly Review*, April 1757) and discussed by Gibbon (see *Miscellaneous Works* (1814), iii). Percy's translation became one of Blake's important source books (see Northrop Frye, *Fearful Symmetry*, p. 173).

from the ballads of *Chevy Chase* and *Sir Patrick Spens* to Shenstone's *Jemmy Dawson*, and include lyrics by Suckling, Ralegh, Henry Wotton, Shirley, Grainger, Skelton, Stephen Hawes, Jonson, Mallet and Tickell. 'To atone for the rudeness of the more obsolete poems, each volume concludes with a few modern attempts in the same kind of writing: ... Select ballads in the old Scottish dialect ... are also interspersed among those of our ancient English Minstrels.'[1]

As it turned out, Percy used his Folio MS less than he had expected. He used the Pepys collection at Magdalene College, Cambridge, Anthony Wood's collection in Oxford, the archives of the Society of Antiquaries, and the British Museum. He was interested in poems of 'pleasing simplicity' and 'artless grace', not 'dazzling the imagination' but 'interesting the heart'. In the third volume (originally designed as the first) were ballads devoted to romantic subjects, including *The Boy and the Mantle*, *The Marriage of Sir Gawaine*, *King Ryence's Challenge*, *King Arthur's Death*, and *The Legend of King Arthur*, the poems of 'interesting fable, or romantic wildness'[2] scornfully referred to by Ritson. Percy's interest had been particularly centred on such ballads by his discovery of texts of the medieval romances referred to by Chaucer in his burlesque romance *Sir Thopas*. One of his self-imposed tasks was to collect references to and texts of all the metrical romances, and in this he laid the foundations for all later work on these poems. The work of Hearne had, unfortunately, made the antiquary a figure of fun to many who were considered 'eminent for their taste and genius'. Percy complained that[3]

it has happened unluckily, that the antiquaries who have revived the works of our ancient writers have been for the most part men void of taste and genius, and therefore have always fastidiously rejected the old poetical Romances, because founded on fictions or popular subjects, while they have been careful to grub up every petty fragment of the most dull and insipid rhymist, whose merit it was to deform morality, or obscure true history. Should the public encourage the revival of some of those ancient Epic songs of Chivalry, they would frequently see the rich ore of an Ariosto or a

[1] Preface.
[2] Ritson, Advertisement to *Ancient Songs and Ballads* (1790).
[3] *Reliques* (1765), iii. p. ix. cf. Warton, *History*, i. 209; *Percy–Hailes*, p. 56.

Tasso, though buried it may be among the rubbish and dross of barbarous times.

The romantic ballads in the *Reliques* were a foretaste of the romances which Percy intended to publish. He laboured on the texts, to present them in as palatable a form as possible. His Folio text of *King Arthur's Death*, for example, was so fragmentary that it was necessary to compose four stanzas in order to fill a gap in the narrative. Working from the *Morte Darthur*, Percy succeeded in reconstructing the exact continuity of the text, as now appears from an examination of a perfect copy of the ballad (unknown to Percy) in William Lloyd's *Nine Worthies* of 1584.[1] In addition to Arthurian story, Percy included the ballad summary of *Guy of Warwick*, 'Was ever Knight for ladyes sake So tost in love as I sir Guy', and the account of Guy and Amarant from Samuel Rowlands's version of 1609. In the introduction to these he quotes from Copland's edition of *Guy* to show that the poem to which Chaucer refers in *Sir Thopas* was not lost, and publishes his discovery that the popular prose version of the eighteenth century was but a transprosing of Rowlands's poem.[2] *Bevis of Hamptoun* is introduced also in a note, this time to a ballad doubtless specially composed by Percy as an excuse to display his discovery that 'the story of St. George and the fair Sabra [in Johnson's *Seven Champions of Christendom*] is taken almost verbatim from the old poetical legend of "Syr Bevis of Hampton" '.

Guy and the *Seven Champions* were still, in chapbook form, the popular reading of children, but *Valentine and Orson*, the third favourite romance of childhood, seemed not to have survived in ballad form. Percy therefore composed his own version[3] using the fragmentary *Emperor and Child* in his Folio MS, the common story-book, and, for the episode of the bridge of bells, *Bevis*. He determined also to include the seventeenth-century *Dragon of Wantley*, a 'lively satire on [the] extravagant fictions' of 'old metrical romances and ballads of chivalry', which he believed was directly aimed at *Bevis*.

[1] See C. B. Millican, 'The Original of the Ballad *King: Arthurs Death* in the Percy Folio MS.' *PMLA* xlvi (1931), 1020–4.
[2] See *Percy–Warton*, pp. 57, 64.
[3] He sent it to Warton in 1762, *Percy–Warton*, p. 65.

Evidence that the romances had remained popular reading throughout the sixteenth and seventeenth centuries was often seized on by eighteenth-century scholars as giving respectability to their own interests. *St. George for England*, for example, a ballad of 1612 in the Pepys collection, provided evidence that certain romance heroes were well known at the time—Arthur, Lancelot, Tristan, Valentine and Orson, the Four Sons of Aymon, Huon of Bordeaux, Godfrey of Bulloigne, Bevis, Isenbras, Eglamore, Guy and Richard Coeur de Lyon. But the poem was also interesting to Percy because it burlesqued the style of the romances, particularly 'the rambling transitions and wild accumulation of unconnected parts, so frequent in many of them'.

One other story derived from medieval romance was represented in the *Reliques*, though Percy was unaware of the romance itself. This is *Argentile and Curan*,[1] in the second volume, an extract from Warner's *Albion's England*. Percy thought that the story was Warner's own invention, and instanced its popularity by referring to William Webster's *Curan and Argentile* of 1617, and the degeneration of the original into the 'common Ballad, "of the two young Princes on Salisbury Plain"', which is chiefly composed of Warner's lines'. Warner's poem is, of course, the story of Havelok and Goldeburgh, told with the names used in Gaimar's version—Aldebrict, Edel, Argentille and Curan. The story of Havelok was known to Camden, and is narrated by Gervase Holles (1606–75) in his manuscript collections for Lincolnshire.[2] But the manuscript of the romance, Laud K 60 (now Misc. 108) eluded Warton when he was writing the *History*, probably because it began with lives of the saints and was described as 'Vita Sanctorum' in Bernard's *Catalogue*. Its loss was deplored by Tyrwhitt and Ritson.[3] Like the poems of Minot, and *Sir Gawain and the Green Knight*, it was eventually discovered by accident. But something of the story survived in tradition. Edward Phillips gave a summary of it under the article *Haveloc*

---

[1] William Mason referred to his wife as his 'gentle Argentile' and wrote a play 'Argentile and Curan'.

[2] *The Lay of Havelok the Dane* ed. W. W. Skeat, rev. K. Sisam. (1939), p. xx.

[3] ibid., p. v.

in *The New World of English Words* (1658). Percy's attention was originally called to Warner's poem by *The Muses Library*, that anthology of poetry from Langland to Daniel, which forms the first survey of the history of English poetry. There he found the poem printed,[1] with a comment on Warner's 'Learning, Sense, and Spirit', and on 'the beautiful Incidents, in the Romantick Taste, extreamly affecting, rich in Ornament, wonderfully various in Stile' of this tale. He would have delighted to know the source of *Argentile and Curan*.[2]

To introduce the romantic ballads in the third volume Percy compiled *An Essay on the Ancient Metrical Romances*. Additions and alterations were made to this essay in the second, third and fourth editions. In its original form of 1765, it is the first survey in English of medieval romances and ends with a valuable list of texts known to Percy, on which Warton and Ritson were to build.

Percy's correspondence for the years 1760 to 1765, especially that with Thomas Warton, enables us to watch the growth of his knowledge of the romances. In his first letter to Warton, 28 May 1761, he already shows a wider acquaintance with the texts than any other scholar of the time, though he was at that time largely dependent on the texts in his Folio MS and these were mainly late metrical romances. He had all the eagerness of a young man ploughing a new field but this led him to many conclusions which are no longer acceptable. His particular texts are all too late to support his conclusions about the nature of Chaucer's burlesque in *Sir Thopas*, and it looks somewhat wild now to find him asserting that Malory's *Morte Darthur* was no more than a prose version of 'a hundred Old Ballads, which had been the delight of our Ancestors for many years before'. Percy is too apt also to declare that he has discovered sources, when in fact his texts are only interesting analogues. Thus his ballads of *The Marriage of Sir Gawaine* and *The Boy and the Mantle* are of interest to students of *The Wife of Bath's Tale* and the *Faerie Queene* (IV, v), though neither Chaucer nor Spenser was indebted to them, as Percy assumed. There were inadequate means available to Percy at that time to help in the dating of

---

[1] [Eliz. Cooper] *The Muses Library* (1737), i. 157.
[2] This was pointed out by Ritson, *Metrical Romanceës* (1802), i. p. lxxxvii.

his texts; nor was there any other scholar to whom he could turn for reliable guidance. Warton was quite unable to help even in supplying texts for Percy's intended collection. He told Percy that the Oxford libraries were 'totally destitute of treasures of this sort'. Percy alone had read enough romances to be able to assert that in the fictional representation of Arthur's knights in many different poems, in general the manners and characters of each knight were consistently maintained.

Many points from Percy's early letters were taken over into the second edition of Warton's *Observations*, which was then printing. Percy, for example, discovered in *The Sqyr of Lowe Degre* a specimen of one of those 'prolix and unnecessary enumerations'—in this case a list of trees—which he considered to be characteristic of the digressions found in medieval romances. This provided part of his evidence that *Sir Thopas* was a burlesque of romances of this type, and Warton was glad to include the 'proof' in his volume. Though they recognized the frequency with which such lists appeared in medieval verse, neither Percy nor Warton related the practice to classical rhetorical tradition.[1] But it is not what the early scholars failed to see that interests us. By friendly conversation and co-operation they slowly moved closer to the truth. Thus Warton, in illustrating Spenser's debt to the romances, began by relying on the *Morte Darthur*, *Bevis* and the late sixteenth-century *Seven Champions of Christendom*. It was Farmer who discovered the late date of this last text, and Percy who told Warton of it and who discovered that the text of Part I was closely modelled on *Bevis*.[2] Warton was spurred on by Percy's letters to extend his knowledge of romances. In July 1762 he was still unaware of any manuscript of *Guy of Warwick*, and was dependent on Rowlands's version. But he did discover a collection of printed texts of romances, which he listed in his second volume.[3]

To Percy all signs of a revival of interest in them were pleasing. Hurd's *Letters* and Warton's enlarged *Observations* led

[1] *Observations* (1762), i. 139. Walter Harte, in a note to l. 108 of his translation of Book vi of Statius (1727) gives examples of such lists from Ovid, Claudian, Chaucer, Tasso and Drayton.

[2] *Percy–Warton*, pp. 38–41. See p. 104 below.

[3] *Observations*, ii. 40–1.

him to think that 'a taste for the Old Romances begins to revive (not among the common Readers, where it would do hurt but) amongst our Critics and Poets'.[1] Already he was planning 'a collection of the old ones in metre' and had made a collection of the Spanish romances 'so finely ridicul'd in Don Quixote, most of them original, others in Translations'.[2]

Percy's collection of English metrical romances continued to grow. To those in his Folio MS he was anxious to add those mentioned in *Sir Thopas*. From Garrick's collection of early printed books he transcribed *The Sqyr of Lowe Degre*, *Bevis*, other copies of *Degare*, *Eglamore* and *Triamore*, and the unique Copland edition of *Isenbras*.[3] From Farmer he borrowed a volume of texts from Lincoln Cathedral Library, and collated the texts of *Bevis* and *Ipomydon*.[4] From Bernard's *Catalogi librorum manuscriptorum* (1697) he discovered the existence of a manuscript, which had belonged to Bishop Moore (Moore 690, now Ff. II. 38), in Cambridge University Library. This contained *Guy*, *Bevis*, *Octavian*, *Eglamore*, *Triamore*, *Degare*, *Erle of Toulous*, *Robert of Cisyle*, *Le bone Florence*.[5] *King Horn* he discovered in Harley MS 2253 and *Ippotis* in the Cotton MS Caligula A2. It was not until the fourth edition of the *Reliques* in 1794 that he actually made use of *King Horn*.[6] But even in 1765 he quoted from the Caligula A2 texts of *Titus and Vespasian* and *The Knight of the Swan*[7]; he had collated the Copland *Isenbras* with the Caligula *Isumbras*,[8] and he owned a transcript of the Caligula *Launfal*.[9]

The suggestion in the *Reliques* that 'a judicious collection' of

---

[1] *Percy–Farmer*, pp. 7, 9.

[2] *Percy–Warton*, p. 31. In 1761 he had proposed to the booksellers two volumes of explanatory notes to *Don Quixote* and a revised edition of Shelton's translation. He continued to work on the material until 1767, showed his collection to Boswell in 1772, and finally gave it to John Bowles for his edition in 1781 (*Percy–Warton*, p. 46 n., *Percy–Farmer*, p. 136 and note).

[3] *Percy–Farmer*, p. 21.   [4] ibid., pp. 2–3.

[5] He listed ten romances that he wanted, either from 'old MS. or printed copies', in a letter to Andrew Ducarel (1713–85) in 1764 (Nichols, *Illustrations*, viii. 151).

[6] Note S2 in the notes added to the *Essay on Minstrels*.

[7] *Reliques* (1765), ii. 263.   [8] Prefatory note to Dowsabell, in vol. i.

[9] Warton asked Percy for 'about 40 lines, transcribed as a specimen, of Sir Launfal' for his *History*, in September 1769. See *Percy–Warton*, p. 136; *History*, ii. 102 n. In 1793 Percy asked Samuel Harper for a transcript of the opening lines of *Launfal* from the MS (Nichols, *Illust.*, viii. 293).

metrical romances 'accurately published with proper illustrations, would be an important accession to our stock of ancient English literature'[1] was a statement of one of Percy's projects. 'Such a publication', he went on,

would answer many uses. It would throw new light on the rise and progress of English poetry, the history of which can be but imperfectly understood, if these are neglected. It would also serve to illustrate innumerable passages in our ancient classic poets, which without their help must be for ever obscure. For, not to mention Chaucer and Spenser, who abound with perpetual allusions to them, I shall give an instance or two from Shakespeare, by way of specimen of their use.

As footnote material for editions of Shakespeare, the romances might hope to become respectable. Percy was himself by no means inactive in Shakespeare scholarship, which, as it grew in volume, created an atmosphere more conducive to studies in medieval literature. The year 1760 marked the beginning of a period in which the public grew more favourably disposed to 'works illustrating the history, the poetry, the language, the manners, or the amusements of their ancestors',[2] and Percy naturally hoped to find encouragement for his collection of metrical romances. As he showed in his analysis of *Libius*, the authors of the romances were not always without 'skill in distributing and conducting their fable'. He found *Libius*

as regular in its conduct, as any of the finest poems of classical antiquity. If the execution, particularly as to the diction and sentiments, were but equal to the plan, it would be a capital performance; but this is such as might be expected in rude and ignorant times, and in a barbarous unpolished language.[3]

His enthusiasm for the romances led him to rank them second only to Chaucer in the field of medieval poetry; they had 'a simplicity that makes them be read with less interruption, and be more easily understood; and they are far more spirited and entertaining than the tedious allegories of Gower, or the dull and prolix legends of Lydgate'.[4]

[1] *Reliques*, iii. pp. viii–ix; cf. *Percy–Hailes*, pp. 55–6.
[2] Ritson, Advertisement to *Ancient Songs and Ballads* (1790).
[3] *Reliques*, iii. p. xvi.   [4] ibid., iii. p. ix.

He praised their 'descriptive and inventive powers' and quotes *Richard Coeur de Lyon* to show that the authors 'did not in their fictions neglect the proper means to produce the ends, as was afterwards so childishly done in the prose books of Chivalry'. Only in the fourth edition did he withdraw his comment on the account of Richard's fight with the lion, 'the preceding circumstances are not unworthy the selection of any Epic poet'. *Eger and Grime* he thought 'a well invented tale, scarce inferior to any of Ariosto's'. *Merline*, he noted in the Folio MS itself, is 'more correct and perfect than any in this book. A very curious old Poem, & may be considered as one of the first attempts in Epic Poetry by the English'.[1]

In his quest for texts he visited the Advocates' Library in Edinburgh on 10 October 1765.[2] His visit was so brief that he had no time to examine the Auchinleck MS in detail, but an account of the romances in it was later sent to him by Hugh Blair. In the 1767 edition of the *Reliques* he added to his list of texts of romances some of those in this important manuscript.[3] In his third edition he included a reference to the text of the *King of Tars* in the Vernon MS, and in his fourth edition added *Eger and Grime*, the Ashmole text of the *Erl of Toulous*, and Pinkerton's edition of *Gawan and Gologras* and *Sir Gawan and Sir Galaron* (now called *The Awntyrs of Arthur*).

Percy's surviving transcripts show that he had collected texts of twenty-six metrical romances for his proposed collection.[4] In August 1772 he proposed to print one romance, *The Sqyr of Lowe Degre*, in a collection of *Ancient English and Scottish Poems*.[5] The collection was to have been 'of a more elevated kind than the last; on grave, sublime and moral subjects, not wholly excluding some few Songs or Historial Ballads of superior

---

[1] Hales and Furnivall, *Percy's Folio MS*, i. 477.

[2] See Percy's note in B.M.Addit. MS 32336, f. 75ᵛ.

[3] From the Auchinleck MS he adds *Horn Childe*, *Guy*, *Rembrun*, *Bevis*, *Arthur and Merlin*, *Roland and Vernagu*, *Otuel* and *The King of Tars*. The mutilated texts which he did not identify were of *Amys* and the *Legend of Pope Gregory*. For an account of the MS see pp. 178-9 below.

[4] Percy's transcripts were sold by Sotheby's in 1884; see L. Dennis, in *PMLA*, xlix (1934), 86. The transcript of *Amys* was by Samuel Pegge from his own MS (now Douce MS 326). (See Nichols, *Literary Anecdotes*, viii. 51, and Note T to Percy's Essay on Minstrels in *Reliques* (1794).)

[5] *Percy–Hailes*, p. 122.

Merit'.[1] One section was to have been preceded by an essay 'On the Origin, and Spirit of Chivalry', introducing his romance and *King Hart, The Carle of Carlile, Christ's Kirk* and 'Some of the Songs of King Arthur'.[2]

Like so many of Percy's projects, this was not completed. His appointment as Bishop of Dromore in 1782 turned his attention in a different direction. The attack of Ritson, in his *Observations* on Warton's *History*, in the same year, seems also to have decided him against publication. But he retained his interest, and preserved his collections for his son, and later for his nephew. The death of Ritson at once revived his interest in having his metrical romances published. 'Now all my metrical Romances shall be at the Service of any capable Editor', he wrote to Robert Anderson on 31 October 1803.[3] He offered them to Thomas Park, who, however, refused '... for two very cogent reasons. One is, that I think Ritson's plan injudicious, and his execution of it repulsive; whence his book is likely to prove unsaleable. The other is, that my highly esteemed and respected friend, Mr. George Ellis, is preparing for publication, a general analysis of early English metrical romances.'[4]

Percy's collection did not find an editor. His last attempt to make use of it occurred in 1810, when he read that Weber's *Metrical Romances* was soon to be published. Percy wrote to Anderson that he could furnish Weber 'with some information on the subject which formerly had very much engaged his attention', and he wished to know if Weber had 'entered into any Critical Examination' of Ritson's 'gross mistakes and wilful misrepresentations'.[5] The collection remained in manuscript. It is a witness to Percy's wide first-hand knowledge of romances, and sufficient indication that his list in the *Reliques*, a guide to future scholars, could have developed into the first printed collection of texts.

---

[1] ibid.

[2] See letter to Hailes, on pp. 127, 128 and f., also Vincent H. Ogburn, 'Percy's Unfinished Collection, *Ancient English and Scottish Poems*'. *ELH* iii (1936), 183–9.

[3] Quoted by B. H. Bronson, *Joseph Ritson, Scholar-at-Arms* (Berkeley, 1938), i. 293.

[4] Nichols, *Illustrations*, viii. 377–8, 21 January 1804. Bronson, i. 297.

[5] Bronson, i. 309.

3

No small part of the attraction of the romances and ballads for Percy lay in the figure of the Minstrels whom he imagined to have composed them. Ritson considered Percy's view of them as 'designedly overcharged, for the sake of giving an undue importance to the subject'.[1] Percy excused any errors he might have made in his original account in the *Reliques* (1765) on the ground that the subject was at that time completely new. How new it was may be seen in Ritson's scornful comment that the word Minstrel was referred to in the Vagrancy Act of 1656 and not again '(unless in dictionaries or vagrant acts) till it appeared with such éclat' in the *Reliques*.[2]

Percy conceived the minstrels as the companions of kings, honoured and respected for their recitations, to the accompaniment of the harp, of ballads and heroic lays. The material on which he based his view necessitated a special essay, which opens the first volume of the *Reliques* (he had originally intended to deal with the subject briefly in the Preface). In elaborating his theory, he was obviously influenced by the conception of the minstrels as occupying the same place in the early civilization of the English nation as Homer and his predecessors had held in Greece, as the Bards had filled in Celtic Britain, Ireland and Gaul, and the Scalds throughout Scandinavia. Of the latter he wrote: 'Their skill was considered as something divine; their persons were deemed sacred; their attendence was solicited by kings; and they were everywhere loaded with honours.'

The minstrels of the later middle ages Percy regarded as no longer the historians of the tribe but the most revered of its entertainers. He described them as possessing wild imaginations, unguided by judgement and uncorrected by art. They delighted their gross and ignorant audiences by inventing giants, dragons, witches and enchanters. It was commonly accepted that the 'invention' of such figures was the work of early poets. By 'gross

[1] Scott, *Introductory Remarks on Popular Poetry* (1830) in *Works* (1841), p. 544. The Ritson–Percy controversy is most clearly seen in Ritson's *Ancient Songs* (1790) and Percy's *Reliques* (1794). For modern discussions of Minstrels see E. K. Chambers, *The Medieval Stage* (Oxford, 1903), ch. i–iv, and W. J. Courthope, *History of English Poetry* (1895–1910), i. 426–31; H. B. Wheatley, ed. *Reliques* (1887), i. xiii ff.

[2] *Ancient Songs* (1790), p. xvi.

and ignorant audiences' Percy does not mean the rabble of the nation, but the aristocrats. The evidence for their barbarity was the fact that they had delighted in such narratives as the minstrels provided. But in these very products—such as he believed the older portions of the *Reliques* to be—Percy recognized rudimentary epic qualities. They represented what Scott called 'the National Muse in her cradle'.

Some of his views Percy was later forced to modify. Samuel Pegge's objections led to a revision of the statements about Anglo-Saxon minstrels in the second edition.[1] But Ritson harried him in an attempt to prove him wrong on two main points—that English minstrels were the composers of ballads and romances, and that they were ever received at court in post-Conquest England. Ritson believed that the term 'minstrel' described a performer on a musical instrument. Percy's correspondence with Pinkerton came to an end in September 1794, when the latter wrote that he was convinced that 'minstrel only implied musician, and *was never used for a bard, maker or poet*'.[2] On this issue, Percy and Ritson were nearer than either would concede. Percy modified his statements, to allow for the minstrel's reciting not only his own works but the poems of others. Ritson admitted that in the later middle ages there did exist a body of men who wandered up and down 'chanting romances, and singing songs and ballads to the harp, fiddle, or other more humble and less artificial instrument'.[3] And he admitted that they may have composed some unpolished songs themselves. The minstrel ballad he recognized in the earlier forms of *Chevy Chase* and *Otterburne*, but not in the specimens printed in the *Reliques*.

On the social position of the minstrel there was no compromise. For Ritson it was inconceivable that, the court until the time of Chaucer being French-speaking, any English minstrel should have been received there. The names of French minstrels have survived, those of the English have not. Ritson collected evidence to show that English entertainers must have

---

[1] See Pegge in *Archaeologia*, ii (1773), 100–6 (a paper read to the Society of Antiquaries on 29 May 1766) and iii (1775), 310. Percy had cited the story of Alfred's use of a minstrel disguise in the Danish camp as proof that minstrels were held in high estimation. Pegge showed that the story does not necessarily prove this.

[2] Nichols, *Illustrations*, viii. 149.   [3] Ritson, *Ancient Songs* (1790), p. xvi.

been confined to a vulgar audience. For him the English minstrel was always a degraded figure.

Between them, Percy and Ritson collected a vast amount of evidence about the minstrels, enough to suggest that both had only part of the truth. It is not a subject in which there can be certainty, but it would seem that there were some minstrels who entertained both courtly and popular audiences, others who were attached solely to noble households, and others again whose activities were confined to amusing the common people. Some minstrels probably recited, to the accompaniment of an instrument, ballads and romances composed by others, doubtless debasing the texts in the process. Others probably translated or composed some of the verses they delivered. The term 'minstrel' covered too wide a range of entertainer for either Percy or Ritson alone to be correct in his views. Both modified their positions as the controversy progressed. Percy, for example, was prepared to believe that the longer romances might well be the work of monks. But he was sure that *King Horn* and *The Sqyr of Lowe Degre* were minstrel products. Modern scholars approach such problems of authorship more warily. The particular version of a romance that has survived may suggest that it was delivered by a minstrel. But one cannot know whether it was originally composed by a minstrel, or whether the surviving text simply represents a version adapted from an earlier form by or for a minstrel. The stories told in the English *King Horn* and *Havelock* are to be found in earlier French versions. Yet both these English romances have been considered to be the products of English minstrels of the mid-thirteenth century.[1]

When Percy instanced *King Horn* as a minstrel romance,[2] he was working on the evidence of its opening, which suggested to him that the poem was addressed to a popular audience. He dated the text as mid-twelfth century (about seventy-five years too early) and tried to show that the story was of English origin.

---

[1] See A. C. Baugh (ed.), *A Literary History of England* (1950), p. 177. Other romances are now often stated to be by or for minstrels, e.g. *Athelstone*, *Seege of Troye*, *Sir Tristrem*, *Sir Perceval*, *The Green Knight* (in Percy's Folio MS), see Baugh, pp. 181, 183, 192; R.S. Loomis (ed.) *Arthurian Literature in the Middle Ages* (Oxford, 1959), pp. 482, 497, 511, 516; Baugh, 'The Authorship of the Middle English Romances', *Bulletin of the Modern Humanities Research Association* (1950), pp. 16 ff.

[2] *Reliques* (1794), notes S2 and T added to the 'Essay on Minstrels'.

It did not contain 'any allusions to French or Norman customs, manners, composition, or phraseology', nor any references 'As the Romance seyth' which might suggest that it was a translation. He recognized that the presence of such phrases would not necessarily prove a romance to be a translation, but not that a translator might go so far as to change French names into English ones for his audience. Thus the fact that the names were Northern seemed to him proof that here we had 'exactly such a performance, as one would expect from a Gleeman or Minstrel of the North of England, who had derived his ideas from his Scaldic predecessors there'. Modern scholars accept that the English version was very likely composed in the South Midlands.

Percy recognized a minstrel romance by its ramblingness, which is no sure guide; the presence of references to reading or readers, a more elaborate structure, and a superior style, denoted for him the work of 'sedentary composers'. *Eglamour*, *Ipomydon*, and *Amys* he thought were of this type. Reasonable as his arguments seem, they are not capable of producing conclusions with which modern scholars would agree. His criteria might go some way towards distinguishing a good from a poor romance, but would not determine whether the author was a minstrel.

Although he had 'proved' that *King Horn* was addressed to a popular audience, he still maintained that romances, whether written by minstrels or monks, were intended for noble audiences. Here he seems to be thinking not so much of texts that have survived, as of romances that might be supposed to have existed, in forms more suited to courtly audiences. The oral transmission of these, during a period in which the social position of the minstrel was declining, was for him adequate explanation of the corruption of surviving texts in forms clearly adapted for popular entertainment. His theory of the decline in social status of the minstrel, a theory which is perfectly just, was supported by the evidence of these later versions. But that chivalry was an aristocratic pursuit, suggested to him, quite correctly, that chivalrous romances were of courtly origin.[1] He supplied ample evidence that provision was made for minstrels

---

[1] The opening phrase of some texts, 'Listen Lordlings', he instanced as evidence of a courtly audience. In fact it suggests a popular audience.

in royal and noble households, in particular by Richard I, and by Henry V during the voyage to France in 1415.

Both Percy and Ritson exaggerated aspects of the evidence in order to support their general views. But the importance of the subject lay not only in the realm of medieval scholarship. The minstrel, as Percy represented him, took over some of the associations with which Gray had invested the figure of the Bard. Percy's description 'struck and pleased' James Beattie, who used it for the basis of his poem *The Minstrel*, which tells, in Spenserian stanzas, of a shepherd with a wild and romantic imagination, instructed by a hermit in history, philosophy and music, who, his education complete, follows the profession of a wandering minstrel.[1] It also formed the 'cadre or frame' for Scott's *Lay of the Last Minstrel*. Percy's account of the gradual decline of the minstrels leaves behind an image of the last of these surviving in the 'North Country', composing ballads on Border subjects. Scott, who collected ballads in Scotland, adopted most of Percy's ideas about minstrels, and created the poignant figure—so unlike Ritson's 'beggars, vagabonds and rogues'— of the 'last minstrel'.

> The last of all the bards was he,
> Who sung of Border chivalry;
> For well-a-day! their date was fled,
> His tuneful brethren all were dead, . . .
> No longer courted and caress'd,
> High placed in hall, a welcome guest,
> He pour'd, to lord and lady gay,
> The unpremeditated lay:
> Old times were changed, old manners gone;
> A stranger fill'd the Stuarts' throne;
> The bigots of the iron time
> Had called his harmless art a crime.
> A wandering Harper, scorn'd and poor,
> He begg'd his bread from door to door;
> And tuned, to please a peasant's ear,
> The harp a king had loved to hear.[2]

[1] See Beattie's account in *Correspondence of Thomas Gray*, iii. 1084.

[2] *Lay of the Last Minstrel*, Introduction, ll. 7–26. 'Northern' and 'Scotch' had been used in the sixteenth and seventeenth centuries to mean 'rustic' when applied to songs and ballads. Percy tends to take these words in their literal sense. See J. W. Hales, *Folia Litteraria* (1893), p. 268 n.

CHAPTER IV

THOMAS WARTON

Thomas Warton is not a mere collector of dry and minute
facts, . . . He brings with him the torch of genius, to illustrate
the ruins through which he loves to wander.

Scott, *Life of Horace Walpole*

THOMAS WARTON (1728–90) was the only one of the early
romance scholars to spend his life as a member of a
University. He became a Fellow of Trinity College,
Oxford, in 1751. From 1757 to 1767 he was Professor of
Poetry, and in 1785 he became Professor of History and Poet
Laureate. It is only the scholar who is likely to appreciate the
greatness of Warton. For painstaking accumulation of facts, in
his work on Spenser, on Milton's minor poems, and on the
history of English poetry from the Conquest to 1600, he has few
equals. His knowledge of poetry and his memory for words and
phrases in a large number of poets English and classical was
such that it is hard to remember, when we read his annotations,
that he worked without the aid of concordances. His own
poetry is, like Gray's, a cento of phrases from previous poets,
though, unlike Gray, he rarely achieves a new and original
combination. He was himself attracted to 'fiction and fancy, to
picturesque description, and romantic imagery', so that in his
annotations and comments on Spenser and Milton one of his
main concerns is to illustrate obscurities by reference to
'Romances and fabulous narratives', to 'the treasures of the
Gothic library'.[1]

This 'new line of commentary' he began in his *Observations
on the Faerie Queene* (1754, revised 1762). Here he covers some
of the same ground as Hurd in the *Letters*—the structure of the
Faerie Queene and the survival of chivalry and romance in the
Elizabethan age. But Warton's work is the more crabbed and
detailed work of the scholar; he had read the romances to which

[1] Milton, *Poems upon Several Occasions*, ed. Warton (1785), pp. iii. xx, xxi.

he traced Spenser's debt. It is therefore with Warton, and not with Hurd, that the romances themselves enter the field of historical criticism of literature. But in his first edition Warton showed little enthusiasm for the romances. Spenser is his subject, for Spenser, as Hurd says, 'ranks highest among the Poets; I mean with those who are either come of that house, or have any kindness for it'.[1]

Spenser was 'the poets' poet', as Lamb called him. We have already seen, in the account of Hurd, that the *Faerie Queene* had been the object of editorial labours and critical commentary before Warton wrote his *Observations*. More important was the interest of the poets in Spenser. Not merely his disciples, such as Giles and Phineas Fletcher and William Browne, in the early seventeenth century, but Milton, Cowley and Dryden had venerated him as a great modern poet. In the eighteenth century he was admired by Pope, and his stanza and vocabulary imitated by numerous poets.[2] Gray prepared himself for composing his own verses by reading Spenser,[3] who, more than any other poet, had the power to induce the mood required for imaginative creation and to facilitate a rhythmic flow of language. Above all, his poetry helped a modern poet to escape from the music of the couplet or the harmonies of Miltonic blank verse.

Warton shows, in some of his comments, what it was in Spenser that attracted the numerous imitators of the century. Hurd had tried to explain how the world of 'fine fabling' had been lost, how 'fancy, that had wantoned it so long in the world of fiction, was now constrained, against her will, to ally herself with strict truth'.[4] Warton also explained how, at the end of the seventeenth century, 'imagination gave way to correctness, sublimity of description to delicacy of sentiment, and majestic imagery to conceit and epigram. . . . The muses were debauched at court, and polite life, and familiar manners, became their only themes.'[5]

[1] Hurd, *Letter* xii.   [2] See above, p. 62.
[3] *Correspondence of Thomas Gray*, iii. 1290.   [4] Hurd, *Letter* xii.
[5] *Observations* (1762), ii. 111. In the preface to his edition of Milton's minor poems, Warton characterizes the poetry of the opening of the century in terms of 'wit and rhyme, sentiment and satire, polished numbers, sparkling couplets, and pointed periods'. He sees the 'school of Milton' as rebelling against these qualities.

To free the imagination from such restraints, to restore sublimity and majestic imagery, to escape from themes of polite life and familiar manners, a poet might turn to Spenser, and there absorb 'the careless exuberance of a warm imagination and a strong sensibility'. There he would find a poet whose excess of imagination would help to counteract the prevailing excess of 'good sense' and cautious judgement. Spenser, says Warton, 'did not live in an age of planning'.[1] The modern poet did, and the effect, in the eyes of Warton, was to inhibit the creative imagination.

That Spenser lacked judgement, that his imagination was wildly exuberant, that 'little art or labour was applied' in the formation and disposition of his 'bold and striking images', these are not positions which any modern critic of Spenser would uphold. But Warton wrote at a time when it was expected of a poet that his sense of 'design and uniformity', of 'order and perspicuity',[2] should conform to the ideas held by a body of critics who had derived them from a narrow interpretation of Aristotle and Horace. One half of Warton's mind still approved of these standards. Even when allowing that the *Faerie Queene* should not be judged as a classical epic, he could not divest himself of his preconceptions; he did not take the bold step of searching the poem for quite other principles of organization and design. But if he insisted on retaining the 'great deal of good sense' which had been gained at the expense of 'fine fabling', he also witnessed to the 'graceful and poetic majesty' of Spenser. Always the appeal lay open, from the 'mechanical critics' to the 'transported reader'.

The explanation for Warton's apologetic note in the first edition of the *Observations* (1754) lies partly in his youthfulness. He was only twenty-six. Yet he was already widely read in Elizabethan literature, and provided a considerable amount of original annotation to the *Faerie Queene*. The form in which he presented his information was more like a series of collections from a common-place book than a connected critical commentary. But the modern literary scholar and critic recognizes his book as one of the first major works of English historical scholarship. Its freshness lies in the sustained historical approach

[1] *Observations*, i. 15. [2] ibid., ii. 268.

to Spenser. Warton explained Spenser's choice of Chivalry as a subject, and of a loose romantic structure as the form of his poem, in terms of 'the predominant taste of the times in which he wrote'. Johnson at once recognized the importance of the approach, and wrote to Warton,

You have shewn to all, who shall hereafter attempt the study of our ancient authors, the way to success; by directing them to the perusal of the books which those authors had read. . . . The reason why the authors, which are yet read, of the sixteenth century, are so little understood, is, that they are read alone; and no help is borrowed from those who lived with them, or before them.[1]

Johnson himself hoped to contribute to the removal of such ignorance by the publication of his *Dictionary*.

The 'coeval books' to which Warton directed attention were mainly romances, in particular Malory's *Morte Darthur, Bevis of Southampton*, Richard Johnson's *Seven Champions of Christendom, Arthur of Little Britain*, and *Huon of Bordeaux*. From his wide reading in other sixteenth-century authors he was able to show that the romances were still popular reading when Spenser wrote, and that the renaissance of classical poetry and learning had not driven out the taste for 'unnatural events, machinations of imaginary beings, and adventures entertaining only as they were improbable'.[2] The evidence supported his view that 'Spenser's imagination was entirely possessed with that species of reading, which was the fashion and delight of his age'.[3] It is revealing of the state of contemporary ignorance, that Warton has to explain such terms as 'recreant knight' and 'quest', by reference to the *Morte Darthur*.[4] From the same book he suggests that Spenser derived names such as Tristram, Pelleas, Pellenore and Percival, the circumstances of Tristram's birth, the suggestion for the Blatant Beast, and the story of the mantle trimmed with the beards of knights. He is also able to show that

---

[1] Boswell, *Life of Johnson*, i. 270.
[2] *Observations*, i. 1. His evidence comes from Drayton, Camden, Bacon (*Life of Henry VII*), Drummond's *Conversations*, Ascham's *Scholemaster*, Puttenham, Gascoyne's *Pleasures of Kenilworth Castle*, Jonson's *Prince Henry's Barrier* and *Execration on Vulcan*, Laneham's *Letter*, E.K. on 'the ladies of the lake' in *The Shepeardes Calendar*, and Shakespeare's *Henry IV*, Part 2 (*Observations*, i. 27–52; ii. 124, 138).
[3] *Observations*, i. 65.   [4] ibid., ii. 147, 166.

Spenser's use of 'Faerie' was not unique. 'Faerie' is common in the romances, and does not imply a 'little people'. Malory's Morgan la Fay provided him with an excellent example to prove this point.

In using Johnson's *Seven Champions*, Warton was, in his first edition, unaware that Spenser could only have known it after writing his poem. But, as Warton realized, this did not invalidate his general position. Johnson's compilation was in fact made from earlier romances probably known to Spenser, and uses common romance themes. The false Florimel, for example, is clearly based on the Peninsular-romance theme, which occurs frequently in *Don Quixote*, of the creation of a 'counterfeit similitude' by magicians. It is found in the *Seven Champions* (Part 2, ch. 8) also.[1] The 'doctrine of romance, that a lion will offer no injury to a true virgin',[2] used by Spenser (*F.Q.* I, iii, 5) is found in Johnson's account of St George (Part 1, ch. 11). The story of the Red Cross Knight's birth, and his being stolen, as a babe, by a Faerie (*F.Q.* I, x, 65) is repeated in the first chapter of the *Seven Champions*.[3]

The *Observations* present many details of this kind, building up a picture of Spenser's debt to the romances. Warton's interest is in 'contemplating the chymical energy of true genius',[4] which gave him 'a generous and exalted pleasure'. To trace the 'latent and obscure source, from whence an admired and original author has drawn some favourite and celebrated description' was the function of the book, and gave him a feeling of 'malicious triumph', or, as he had said in the first edition, of 'ill-natured pride and a disingenuous triumph'. Readers who censured his collections as 'both trifling and uninteresting . . . can have no taste for Spenser'[5] since Warton had displayed 'the general cast and colour of his poem'. Such details may not 'improve the judgement' but would 'gratify the curiosity'.

And if there should be any readers, who, disgusted with the ideas of knights, dragons, and enchanters, should, after perusing the FAERIE QUEENE, address the author of it, as cardinal d'Este did Ariosto,

<hr>

[1] ibid., ii. 123–4.
[3] ibid., ii. 137.
[5] ibid., i. 65.

[2] ibid., ii. 128.
[4] ibid., i. 54 (*Observations* (1754), p. 37).

after reading his Orlando, . . . 'Where the Devil did you pick up all these lies?' I beg those gentlemen will look upon this section as a sufficient answer to that question.[1]

The discussion of Spenser's debt, both for details and structure, to the romances, also led Warton to an attempt to trace the origin of romantic fabling, to a dissertation on Gothic architecture, to an account of tapestries and the wall paintings in the Bodleian Library, and to a 'retrospect of english poetry from the age of Spenser'. He also digressed, as Hurd had done, to illustrate Milton's knowledge of romances, commenting on Milton's Latin Elegy on the death of the Bishop of Ely (ll. 59–64),

But these are the ideas of a mind deeply tinctured with romance-reading; to which, perhaps, and to the puritanical cast of the times, which led to religious subjects, we owe the general argument, and most confessedly, many particular descriptions, of the noblest effort of modern poetry, the *Paradise Lost*.[2]

He also notes that both Cervantes and Milton 'express the idea of a prodigious concourse of people' by the same simile from romance.[3]

The *Observations* are thus the first large-scale application of the historical method of criticism. Other writers had urged that the critic and reader should imagine themselves 'exactly situated as the persons for whom the poetry was written, or even as the writers themselves'.[4] Warton applied the method to a poet indebted to the romances of the middle ages, and so helped to direct attention to the sources of Spenser's poem. The *Faerie Queene* had never lacked readers, but the choice of Spenser as the subject of such a series of observations must have been determined by the bent of Warton's own interests in early literature other than Spenser. Like his friend Collins, Warton

[1] *Observations* (1754), p. 44. Omitted in second edition.

[2] *Observations*, ii. 33. Warton also explains many references in the minor poems of Milton from his reading of romances.

[3] *Paradise Lost*, iii. 337–43; *Don Quixote*, Book II, ch. 2 in Motteaux's translation; see Boiardo's *Orlando Innamorato*, i. 10.

[4] Robert Lowth, *Lectures on Hebrew Poetry* (1753), ed. 1787, i. 113. Other quotations from John Husbands (1731), Theobald (1734), Johnson (1745), Joseph Warton (1756), and Gibbon (1761) are included in R. Wellek, *The Rise of English Literary History* (Chapel Hill, 1941), pp. 52–4.

'loved fairies, genii, giants, and monsters; he delighted to rove through the meanders of enchantment'. These delights he found in the romances,

such are their Terrible Graces of magic and enchantment, so magnificently marvellous are their fictions and fablings, that they contribute, in a wonderful degree, to rouse and invigorate all the powers of imagination; to store the fancy with those sublime and alarming images, which true poetry best delights to display.[1]

His evidence for this was not so much the few medieval romances he knew—*Bevis, The Knight of Courtesy, Eglamour, Degare* and *The Sqyr of Lowe Degre*—nor even the *Morte Darthur*, but the fact that Spenser and Milton, Boiardo and Ariosto, had transformed the materials of romance in their own poems. They had shown what could be done.

In his second edition, Warton was emboldened by his reading of Sainte-Palaye and his correspondence with Percy to add a defence of chivalry as an institution. Now he pointed to its 'influence on the manners, policies, and constitutions of antient times'.

It was the school of fortitude, honour and affability . . . inspired the noblest sentiments of heroism. It taught gallantry and civility to a savage and ignorant people, and humanized the native ferocity of the northern nations . . . its magnificent festivals, thronged with noble dames and courteous knights, produced the first efforts of wit and fancy.[2]

This institution, he sees, forms the background to the romances, the 'efforts of wit and fancy' which it produced. The romances preserved 'many curious historical facts, and throw considerable light on the nature of the feudal system. They are the pictures of antient usages and customs; and represent the manners, genius and character of our ancestors.'[3]

Appealing to his reader's interest in the past of his own country, and to the growing admiration for primitive poetry, Warton makes a plea for the romances of the middle ages. His book is thus an important statement not only of the need for an historical approach in literary criticism, but also of the

[1] *Observations,* ii. 268.   [2] ibid., ii. 267.   [3] ibid., ii. 267–8.

need for a study of early English literature as a part of our heritage of English culture. In its more general application it was, like Hurd's *Letters*, a reopening of the critical discussion of the epic. The *Faerie Queene* is not condemned for its failure to reproduce the models of classical epic; Spenser's 'romantic materials claim great liberties', but 'no materials exclude order and perspicuity'. Inconveniences and incongruities might have been avoided by Spenser, by a more studious attention to design and uniformity.[1] The 'use of magical machinery' is not condemned, but is explained 'from the predominant taste of the times in which he wrote'. Warton tried to criticize from the 'judgement' and not from the 'imagination',[2] and his aim was, like Hurd's, to show that Spenser 'copied real manners, no less than Homer'.[3]

2

The 'retrospect of English poetry' that Warton planned when revising his *Observations* was a history up to the end of the seventeenth century. He had 'long been laying in materials for this work',[4] and was encouraged to go on, he told Percy, 'by having such a companion as you'.[5] Gray, having himself planned such a work, was pleased that its execution had fallen to a man of talents, taste and industry,[6] and Warburton welcomed the scheme with the comment that Warton was 'the first Antiquarian of taste and spirit that we have seen since Spelman and Selden'.[7]

Warton was considering also 'a new edition of my favourite Chaucer'[8] in 1762 and doubtless the *History* in its first volume, both in the historical account of poetry up to Chaucer and in the dissertations on romantic fiction and the introduction of

[1] ibid., ii. 268.

[2] *Observations* (1754), p. 310; (1762), ii. 263.

[3] *Observations* (1762), ii. 88.

[4] 'Correspondence of Thomas Warton', *Bodleian Quarterly Record*, vi (1929–31), 303–4, Warton to Hurd, 22 October 1762.

[5] *Percy–Warton Correspondence*, p. 130.   [6] *Correspondence of Thomas Gray*, iii. 1123.

[7] Warburton to Hurd, 7 October 1762, in Nichols, *Literary Anecdotes* (1812–16), v. 653.

[8] *Bodleian Quarterly Record*, vi. 303. The long section on the Arabian learning in the *Squire's Tale* indicates that much of the material in the second Dissertation was originally collected to provide background to Chaucer.

learning into Europe, represented some of his preliminary work on this project. Warton realized how difficult the literature of the middle ages was for a modern reader. It was not simply the barrier of language, about which he was somewhat cavalier. He read on quickly, glossing where he could, with a hit-and-miss accuracy. But he recognized the more profound difficulty, the alien quality of the medieval world. Richard Price, in the Preface to his edition of Warton's *History* in 1824, commented that the modern reader, looking at the middle ages, 'feels like the traveller before the walls of Persepolis, who gazes on the inscriptions of a powerful but extinguished race, without a key to the character recording their deeds'. To understand an author, Warton realized, it was not sufficient simply to have a knowledge of 'all antient classical learning'. One needed to know what classical learning one's author had, and how he interpreted it. Hence the necessity for the dissertation on the introduction of learning into England, where 'learning' meant classical literature and its influence in the period before Chaucer. For Warton it was necessary to know which books, though they were no longer read, were in repute at the time one's author was alive and which he had most likely read.[1] Thus in the dissertation he gave an account of medieval libraries and their contents; of the favourite studies of the time; of the influence of the Church on literacy and on forms of literature; of the way in which the philosophy of Aristotle was developed, and the texts of classical authors studied, explained and imitated. But he was aware that the barrier, though to be penetrated in part by such studies, was yet formidable. Even if we do not think highly of the achievement of the time in gaining an understanding of any past age, yet the principles on which such an understanding must be based are nowhere better expressed than in Warton's words,

In reading the works of a poet who lived in a remote age, it is necessary that we should look back upon the customs and manners which prevailed in that age. We should endeavour to place ourselves in the writer's situation and circumstances. Hence we shall become better enabled to discover, how his turn of thinking and manner of

---

[1] *Observations* (1754), p. 243. Scholars were interested at the same time in Shakespeare's reading, see Charlotte Lennox, *Shakespeare Illustrated* (1754).

composing, were influenced by familiar appearances and established objects, which are utterly different from those with which we are at present surrounded.[1]

To put himself, as the result of great labour and imagination, into the worlds of Chaucer and of Spenser, to read the books they read, in the way they read them, to see in imagination the tilts and tournaments, knights and damsels, the costumes, tapestries, architecture, domestic objects, the orders of the people, their system of government, their food and drink, their manners, ideals, superstitions, their rhetoric, idioms, clichés; this, the noblest ideal of the literary scholar, Warton saw as the necessary path to the understanding of the past.

No wonder that the romances formed the centre of interest for such a scholar, since it was commonly accepted that in them was to be found the clearest picture of the alien world of the middle ages. For Warton, merely to become acquainted with the details of medieval life was sufficiently exciting. He was in no danger of idealizing an age of 'barbarism and superstition'. The audience of the romances was always, to him, 'gross and ignorant'.

Warton's correspondence with Percy was centred on the romances. The Essay in the *Reliques* provided him with a list of texts in manuscripts. Like Percy, he lamented the neglect of romances by former antiquaries, who 'lacked taste and genius', and who were not interested in displaying 'the progress of human manners' and illustrating 'the history of society'.[2] He believed that 'English literature and English poetry' suffered so long as they were neglected, since they preserved 'images of antient customs and institutions not elsewhere to be found or at least not otherwise so strikingly delineated' and preserved the fables which 'formed the taste and awakened the imagination' of earlier poets.[3] In applying this belief to the history of poetry, Warton was committed not merely to an account of the poems, but to a commentary on medieval civilization, 'not a mere gloss upon words, but things, a luminous exposition of whatever had

---

[1] *Observations*, ii. 87.
[2] *History* (1774–81), i. 209. (Unless otherwise stated this is the edition of Warton's *History* to which I shall refer.)
[3] ibid.

changed its character, or grown obsolete in the lapse of time, and which, as it unfolded to the reader's view the forgotten customs of the day, assisted him to live and feel in the spirit of the poet's age.'[1]

For this purpose, as Price pointed out,

it was requisite to enter largely into the domestic and civil economy of our ancestors, their public and private sports, the entertainments of the baronial hall, the martial exercises of the tournament, ... the juggler's dexterity and the necromancer's art; the avocations of the cloister, the *wodecraft* of the feudal lord, and the services of his retainers, ... the occult mysteries of alchemy, ... the popular superstitions of a departed pagan faith, and the legendary marvels of a new religion.[2]

'A longer life than Warton's might have been unequal to the execution of such an extensive project.'[3] But with this in mind we can better understand his attitude to the romances. He does not lose sight of the poems, but often quotes them for reasons other than their own literary quality. The civilizing quality of the imagination is his theme, and the romances represented the means whereby the imagination was aroused. The 'barbarism and superstition' of the middle ages was, for example, exhibited in its tournaments, 'this strange mixture of foppery and ferocity'.[4] But the civilizing influence was there also, in such assemblies, inducing ideas of courtesy and decorum, sentiments of honour and heroism. Schools of philosophy flourished, but were impotent to 'correct and polish the times'; the philosophy was mere sophistry, the religion corrupted with superstition. But for Warton, even learning founded on truth could never civilize and polish a nation. 'For this purpose, the powers of imagination must be awakened and exerted, to teach elegant feelings, and to heighten our natural sensibilities. It is not the head only that must be informed, but the heart must also be moved.'[5]

However much he approved of 'classical taste and judgment' he saw it as at war with imagination. It was for this reason

---

[1] Price, in his Preface to the 1824 edition of the *History*, i. p. (13).

[2] ibid., see for example, Warton's account of the orders of mendicant friars, as preparation for his account of *Pierce the Plowman's Crede*, in Section IX of the *History*.

[3] *History* (1824), i. (12).   [4] *History* (1774), i. 332.   [5] ibid., i. 339–40.

that he did not regret the collapse of the renaissance of letters in the twelfth century—exemplified for him in the work of Giraldus Cambrensis, Alexander Neckam, Roger Bacon, Grossteste and John of Salisbury—and its replacement by the scholastic divinity of Abelard and Peter Lombard. The catholic and the romantic middle ages were one. 'The genius of romance and of popery were the same, . . . The dragons and the castles of the one, were of a piece with the visions and pretended miracles of the other.'[1]

To have chased away the superstition by truth and reason would have destroyed 'those spectres of illusive fancy, so pleasing to the imagination, which delight to hover in the gloom of ignorance and superstition'.[2]

Warton was disappointed in his search for the metrical romances that entertained the Norman barons in England during the eleventh and twelfth centuries. He supposed they had existed, since the Normans were enthusiastic Crusaders and entertained minstrels. But he presumed that their romances, if not lost, existed in modernized, polished and amplified versions in the later metrical tales.[3] The earliest of these, he decided, was *King Horn*, in Harley MS 2253, the first in Percy's list in the *Reliques*,[4] and regarded by Wanley, in the catalogue of the Harley MSS, as the earliest extant English romance. The French version, in Harley MS 527, Warton thought was earlier than the English. When he discussed the romance in the first section of the *History*, it was not the metre and the alliteration which interested him, but 'the force of the story' and the inability of the author to describe 'a delicate situation'. He quotes the opening, the account of Horn's education, and Athulf's impersonation of Horn in Rimenild's bower, supporting his abstract of the story with Sainte-Palaye's description of the education of a page and squire. He is trying to make the past come alive through its literature, so that Rimenild's indelicate behaviour becomes interesting for him not as 'gross and absurd', but as an example of how people really behaved.

[1] ibid., iii. p. xvi.   [2] ibid., i., sig. k4.   [3] ibid., i. 38.
[4] Harley MS 2253 is dated by modern scholars c. 1314–25. Warton dated it c. 1272–1307. *Horn* was written c. 1225, and exists also in two MSS not known to Warton, Camb. U. Lib. Gg, 4, 27.2 (c. 1250–60) and MS Laud Misc. 108, Part II (c. 1300–20). From Percy, Warton also learned of the Auchinleck MS *Horn Child*.

Many of the romances interest him mainly as 'pictures of antient life', the *Sqyr of Lowe Degre*, for instance, because it 'delineates in lively colours the fashionable diversions and usages of antient times'.[1] He devotes a whole section to *Richard Coeur de Lyon*, interspersing his quotations and synopsis with accounts of 'Grecian fire' (a mixture of bitumen, sulphur and naphtha for burning ships), of medieval military machines, moving castles, and Saracen musical instruments, of medieval ignorance of geography, of Richard's reputation among the Saracens, and of the practice of hawking.[2] Much of the information he derived from Du Cange's Latin glossary, but throughout the *History* when illustrating manners and customs he makes use of Froissart and of his favourite romance, *King Alisaunder*, which he discovered in the Laud MS.[3] Quoting a passage from the *Alisaunder* to illustrate 'necromantic operations', he comments, 'it must have formed a puppet-show equal to the most splendid pantomime'.[4]

Warton followed Tanner in attributing this romance to Adam Davie, the author of the religious poems in the first half of the Laud manuscript,[5] and as Adam Davie's *Alisaunder* it attracted the interest later of Park and Ellis. It was while he was preparing an edition of it from the Lincoln manuscript that Ellis realized that it was not by Davie.[6] Warton was delighted with the poem, admiring particularly its descriptions and its lyric passages, and suggesting that it 'deserved to be printed'. He was not usually so enthusiastic about the metrical romances. Some achieve no more than a mention, as *Libius, Octavian, Bevis, Ipotis, The Marriage of Sir Gawaine, The Knight of Courtesy*, and *Sir Gowther*.[7] Some are represented by synopses of the stories, with occasional quotations, as *Guy, The Sqyr of Lowe Degre, Sir Degare, Robert of Sicily, The King of Tars*,

---

[1] *History*, i. 176.

[2] ibid., i. 150–68. He mistranslated 'faucon brode' as 'falcon' (instead of 'falchion') and so was led to describe the practice of hawking.

[3] He also knew of the Lincoln's Inn MS (ibid., ii. 312).

[4] ibid., iii. p. xxxiii.   [5] ibid., i. 214.

[6] Scott, *Letters*, xii. 189, 218 n. Warton dated the Laud MS in the reign of Edward II, Ellis dated the poem as 'as old as 1312'. Modern scholars date the MS (Laud I 74, now Misc. 622) c. 1400 and the poem 1250–1300.

[7] *History*, i. 198 f.; ii. Emendations and Additions, sig. h.3.

Ipomydon, and the *Morte Arthure* in Harley MS 2252.[1] These he treats together as the product of nameless minstrels of the early fourteenth century, though he realized that many of the texts he quoted were of later date.

When he quotes from a romance a passage he admires, it is with some such comment as 'marked with the hand of a master' (of the dragon of *Sir Degare*), 'a curious Gothic picture . . . drawn with some spirit' (of the arming of Richard and the shock of the two necromantic steeds in *Richard Coeur de Lyon*), 'some great outlines of Gothic painting' (of *Ywain and Gawain*), 'touched with the impetuous dashes of a savage and spirited pencil' (of *The Knight's Tale*), 'the warmth of description' is 'not unlike the manner of Chaucer' (of the *King of Tars*).[2] Even where he cannot praise, however, Warton is aware that 'in the infancy of language and composition' there is value even in the most artless rhymer, whose attempts 'contribute to form a style, to teach expression, and to polish his native tongue'.[3] With Percy's analysis of *Libius Disconius* before him, Warton might be expected to be alert to the structure of romances. He shows his awareness by denying that they are all 'incoherent rhapsodies', and asserts that many of them have 'a regular integrity, in which every part contributes to produce an intended end'.[4] As his example he chooses *Sir Degare*,[5] working from the edition of Copland (c. 1550) in Garrick's collection. From this it was easy to show the 'coincidence of events' and 'uniformity of design' since he had stumbled on what is probably an English version of a Breton lai, which presents a more consciously shaped form than most of the romances, as for instance, *Sir Guy*.

The difficulties in discovering the materials for such a vast project as Warton's are well illustrated by the way in which he treats the Breton lai. When he wrote his first volume he knew of the existence of the lais in Harley MS 978,[6] but discovered only from Tyrwhitt's edition of Chaucer in 1775 that they were

[1] ibid., i. 150, 169 f.   [2] ibid., i. 180, 166; iii. 108; i. 360, 197.
[3] ibid., i. 77.   [4] ibid., i. 182.
[5] The earliest MS of this is the Auchinleck (1330–40) but the story was probably composed or translated from the French c. 1300.
[6] ibid., i. sig. a2.

not written by Breton bards under the influence of the Arabs, but by Marie de France. In the Emendations and Additions in his second volume he therefore added a long note to his account of *The Erl of Toulous*, where he describes *Launfal, Emare, Sir Gowther* and *The Franklin's Tale* as Breton lais.[1] He did not, however, recognize the structure he had praised in *Degare* as peculiar to the lai.

Another late discovery, again from Tyrwhitt's *Chaucer*, was of the romance of *Ywain and Gawain*, in the Cotton MS Galba E IX. Tyrwhitt had discovered the poems of Laurence Minot in this manuscript, and directed Warton to it. The romance was clearly too important to omit from the *History*, though Warton had long passed the appropriate chronological section. So, after dealing with Sir Thomas More, Warton digressed to *Ywain*,[2] ostensibly, he assures the reader, to recall his attention to the poetry and language of the previous century. The poems of Minot he quotes in footnotes, for those collecting specimens of alliteration and those interested in the metre of *Sir Thopas*.[3] The double duty of discovering his subject-matter and writing its history inevitably produced examples of such stumbling progression. But in the course of it, Warton was constantly making new finds. While looking at the Cotton MS of *Ywain* he must also have glanced at the most famous of all romance manuscripts, Nero X, and jotted down the opening and lines 1093–1102 of *Pearl*, and lines 601–4 of *Cleanness*. He added them at this late stage in the *History* to his examples of alliteration.[4] The difficult handwriting and what he probably considered the unpromising nature of what he had deciphered, led him to give only a cursory glance at the first half of the manuscript. *Sir Gawain and the Green Knight* was thus left for Richard Price to discover[5] when checking the quotations for the 1824 edition of the *History*. Price at once planned to edit the poem, and quoted the second stanza in the additional note he wrote on *Sir Tristrem*, as an example of what de Brunne meant by

[1] ibid., ii. 103, and Emendations at sig. h2ᵛ; iii. 133 n.

[2] Probably written c. 1300–50; Warton thought the MS, and presumably the poem, were c. 1430.

[3] ibid., iii. 103 n., 106 n.   [4] ibid., iii. 107 n.

[5] Ritson probably checked Warton's quotations from the Nero MS without discovering *Sir Gawain* (*History* (1824), i. p. (17)n.).

'selcouth names'.[1] Warton had unearthed many treasures; from
the seven hundred manuscripts he used, he printed for the first
time, amongst other things, the lyrics of Harley MS 2253, parts
of many romances, passages from the Vernon MS and the Laud
Alisaunder, Gower's *Cinquante Balades*, and *The Kingis Quair*. He
gave the first survey of the Scottish Chaucerians, discovered the
source of *The Knight's Tale* in the *Teseide*, published the first
critical accounts of Gower, Lydgate, Hoccleve and Hawes, and
printed copious extracts from the poetry of the sixteenth
century. But it was reserved for the now almost unknown Richard
Price to discover the greatest metrical romance of the middle
ages.

In quoting *Sir Gawain and the Green Knight* to illustrate what
de Brunne had probably meant by 'selcouth names', Price was
refuting Scott's conjecture that the Auchinleck *Sir Tristrem* was
written by Thomas of Erceldoune.[2] Price did not believe that
de Brunne's mention of a Thomas who composed a romance of
Tristrem could refer to Thomas of Erceldoune, nor that the
language of the Auchinleck poem was 'strange Inglis'.[3]
He was, of course, correct. Warton himself had not known the
Auchinleck *Tristrem*, but he had brought together de Brunne's
reference to Thomas's *Tristrem*, and the poems of Thomas of
Erceldoune,[4] and so provided some of the basis for Scott's later
conjecture.

Malory's *Morte Darthur* was interesting to Warton because it
had been a favourite book in the sixteenth century. He found it
useful for the illustration of the *Faerie Queene*, and to prove the
correctness of the reading in *Hamlet*, 'unhouseled, unanealed'.[5]
But he did not praise it for its literary merits. On the whole,
prose romances, even though telling the same stories as the earlier
metrical ones, did not attract the scholars. They thought of
them as too far removed from the 'true' primitive metrical
versions. Warton read his Malory in the 1634 edition, but also in
some earlier copy which he refers to as 'Caxton's Morte Arthur'
by 'Sir Thomas Maillorie'. He gives his references not to the

---

[1] ibid., i. 187–8. Price's dating of the poem is not clear, though he realized that
the 'selcouth names' were retained in alliterative verse in the fourteenth century.
[2] See below, chapter 7.   [3] *History* (1824), i. 181–98.
[4] *History* (1774), i. 74–7.   [5] ibid., Emendations in ii. sig. kl.

redistributed text of the Stansby edition, but to the books and chapters of Caxton.[1] He asserted that he had examined various 'antient detached histories' from which Malory had literally translated, but offered in support of this only two details— that in disposition it resembled the 1488 edition of the *Histoire de Roy Artur* (2 vols, Rouen and Paris) with its Birth of Arthur, Lancelot, Sangreal, and Death of Arthur; and that one sentence in Book XVII, chapter 23 (on the 'grete bookes' in which the Grail adventures were written) was translated from the end of the Grail section in a British Museum manuscript of *Tristan* (Royal MS 20 D 2).[2] The *History* is rich in hints of this sort, but mention of one more must suffice. In discussing the ending of *Piers Plowman*, Warton conjectures that Langland may have 'had his eye on the old French *Roman d'Antechrist*, a poem written by Huon de Meri, about the year 1228'.[3] Warton's alertness and wide reading are well illustrated by this suggestion, directing attention as it does to the relation of the poem to other allegories and to the medieval 'conjectures and controversies concerning Antichrist'.

When Warton was writing, no distinction was made between French and Anglo-Norman; discussion of such a distinction does not begin until the early years of the next century.[4] Works in French are therefore referred to continental authors. In the early stages of the study of medieval literature this was no great weakness; the important fact is that Warton realized that his task involved a study of French as well as English texts, and a consideration of the problem of priorities. The romance of *Richard Coeur de Lyon*, for example, Warton rightly concluded must be based on a 'French' original, from the evidence of the opening of the Copland edition of the poem, and from Richard's

[1] ibid., ii. Emendations, sigg. c1ᵛ–c4, iii. 119 n., 122 n., 123 n. The long note at the end of Section III in Price's edition (i. 153–61), in which Warton discusses Malory, is from Warton's Emendations and Additions. The Contents in vol. i of the 1840 edition mistakenly attribute it to Price.

[2] ibid., ii. Emendations, sigg. ciᵛ–c4. The sentence occurs in the MSS which Vinaver considers represent Malory's sources (see E. Vinaver, *The Works of Sir Thomas Malory* (Oxford, 1947), iii. 1571).

[3] ibid., i. 285–6. The suggestion is taken up in Dorothy Owen, *Piers Plowman: A comparison with some earlier and contemporary French Allegories* (1912), pp. 81, 91–2, 145–52.

[4] See Isaac D'Israeli, 'The Anglo-Normans' in *Amenities of Literature*.

known patronage of Provençal poets.[1] The realization that most of the French romances were current in England, either in the original or in translations or imitations, committed him to a bibliographical account of the interrelationships, which he arbitrarily attached to the list of romance heroes that he found in the opening of *Richard*.[2] His surveys of the medieval versions of the stories of Troy, Alexander, Bevis and Guy are the first connected accounts of the interdependence of Latin, French and English romances. He often relies for information on Fauchet's *Recueil*, and is often misled. But he is able to trace the Trojan story in Dares Phrygius, Dictys Cretensis, Guido de Colonna, Benoit de Sainte-Maure, Lydgate's *Troy-Book* and Lefevre's *Recuyel*; and the Alexander story from the Pseudo-Callisthenes (which he dates 1070, but which modern scholars date c. A.D. 200) to the French *Roman d'Alexander*. Not having accurately settled the chronology of his many texts, Warton falls into excusable errors. And everywhere he finds 'Oriental imagery' and 'traites of Arabian literature'. Such 'traites' were sure to abound when he had determined that they included brass horses, astronomy, the seven liberal sciences, the magical transformation of characters, speaking birds, magic rings and jewels, giants and dragons.[3]

To the modern scholar reading Warton, it is not his errors in transcripts[4] or dating which attract attention; it is rather the richness of his information, the wealth of documentation, the multitude of his discoveries, his constant alertness to the problems and awareness of the ramifications of his subject. The representation of romance subjects in tapestries, the hints to be gleaned concerning the authors who wrote and the audiences for whom they wrote, evidence for the reciting and reading of romances, changes in style and treatment of subject, all are well documented. Warton has a strong sense of the development

[1] *History*, i. 113 f. Of the seven MSS of the English romance, Warton knew only that in Caius College, Cambridge.

[2] ibid., i. 122 f. The lists in the Vernon MS and the *Cursor Mundi* he used as additional evidence of the popularity of the heroes both in England and in France.

[3] ibid., i. sigg. c1, h3; pp. 126–7; ii. 90.

[4] Warton employed a copyist to transcribe MSS. He was also unwilling to reproduce the 'capricious peculiarities and even ignorance of [the original] transcribers'. (ibid., ii. 220).

of our poetry, and is aware in particular that he is engaged in tracing the poetic ancestry of Spenser. Percy had urged him to look more closely at the metrical romances.[1] The twenty years' labour which resulted in the *History* showed even more thoroughly the heritage of Spenser in romance and allegory.[2] Gothic romance, Italian literature, classical mythology and literary ideals in form and style, the Reformation, and the progress of the 'arts of composition' were traced to the point when 'national credulity, chastened by reason, had produced a sort of civilized superstition, and left a set of traditions, fanciful enough for poetic decoration, and yet not too violent and chimerical for common sense.'[3]

The *History of English Poetry* fills in the background, in elaborate detail, to the *Observations on the Faerie Queene*.

Warton was unaware that he would be followed by generations of painstaking scholars who would tread in his footsteps and examine his every statement. He must have felt of many texts, as he did of the *Pricke of Conscience*, that he would be their last transcriber.[4] In mapping out the history of English poetry he was in part showing not simply what had existed, but what was worthy the attention of the man of taste. 'Anecdotes of the rudiments of a favourite art will always be particularly pleasing. The more early specimens of poetry must ever amuse, in proportion to the pleasure which we receive from its finished production.'[5]

Society, in Warton's time, had developed to the point of the 'highest degree of refinement'. In consequence, the imagination was often most deeply aroused by the contemplation of 'the idea of antiquity', and by the act of tracing the slow gradations which had preceded the attainment of the present state of civility. The present was incapable of exciting the imagination, which quivered into life only when roused by the past, by 'antient remains of English poetry, unexpectedly discovered, and fortunately rescued from long oblivion'. That was why the Rowley poems were at first exciting. Even if they had been

---

[1] *Percy–Warton*, p. 41.
[2] For allegories, see *History*, i. 266–7, 368 f., 457 f.; iii. 233, 498.
[3] ibid., iii. 497. [4] ibid., i. 256.
[5] Warton's Preface to the *History*.

lacking in 'any real or intrinsic excellence' and had been merely crude verses, they would have been 'contemplated with a degree of fond enthusiasm'. For scholars like Warton, it was disappointing to find that they were modern forgeries. However beautiful as poems, they were no longer capable of rousing the imagination, which responded only to what had genuinely survived from the distant past. 'With these pleasures we are unwilling to part',[1] wrote Warton. There could be no substitute for authentic records.

[1] *History*, ii. 164 (Warton's discussion of Chatterton).

CHAPTER V

JOSEPH RITSON

'LET it be remembered to his honour, that, without the encouragement of private patronage, or of public applause; without hopes of gain, and under the certainty of severe critical censure, he has brought forward such a work on national antiquities, as in other countries has been thought worthy of the labour of universities, and the countenance of princes.'

These are the words of Walter Scott,[1] reviewing the collection of romances published by Joseph Ritson. It was Ritson's last publication and Scott's review was not printed until three years after Ritson's suicide. The tribute does well-merited honour to the valuable contributions to English studies of the greatest of the amateur scholars. Ritson (1752–1803), who was born in Stockton-on-Tees, came to London about 1775, took chambers in Gray's Inn, continued his legal studies, and in 1780 set up as a Conveyancer. He was called to the Bar in 1789, but did not practise. His passion, like Warton's and Percy's, was for 'poetical antiquities'. 'A mere antiquarian is a rugged being', wrote Dr Johnson. Ritson seems deliberately to have cultivated the reputation of being rugged. Nothing if not extreme in his views and expression, he shocked his contemporaries by his profession of anti-Christian and anti-clerical sentiments, his uncompromising vegetarianism, his revolutionary politics, his implacable harrying of Warton, his insinuations of Percy's dishonesty, his adherence to his own method of spelling,

[1] *Edinburgh Review*, vii (1806), 395. Ritson was a member of Godwin's circle. Lamb invented an amusing Ritsonian commentary, 'Ritson *versus* John Scott the Quaker', *The London Magazine*, April, 1823. Coleridge quoted from Ritson's collection of romances in the disastrous lectures for the Royal Institution in 1807–8. De Quincey records that the only quotations 'that produced much effect' were 'two or three, which I put ready marked into his hands, among the Metrical Romances edited by Ritson'. (*Reminiscences of the Lake Poets*, ed. 1917, p. 50).

and his crabbed meticulousness in scholarship. 'Fierce, meagre, pale, no commentator's friend',[1] he quarrelled with almost every scholar of his time, seeming always to provoke the breach himself. His life, which ended in insanity, knew little of moderate sentiments or gentler passions. Yet this cavilling, quarrelsome man produced, at the same time as he was violently attacking Warton's *History of English Poetry*, a delightful collection of nursery rhymes.[2] His anthologies of songs, lyrics and ballads, with woodcuts by John and Thomas Bewick and engravings by Blake after designs by Stothard,[3] are sufficient indication of his delight in the beauty of the combined arts of poet, engraver and printer. In personal relationships he was capable of inspiring affection in, and of returning it to those who respected his vegetarian principles and his demand for literal precise statements. His desire for accuracy made him 'disgusted with any loose or inaccurate averment'.[4]

Ritson and George Ellis form the second generation of romance scholars in England. But where Ellis followed the school of Percy, presenting his scholarship in a way which would appeal to the man of general culture, Ritson was regarded as reviving the school of Hearne, the irritable and tasteless lover of antiquity for its own sake. Yet Ritson, like all the scholars of romance, began as a would-be poet, 'fonder of poetry than the law',[5] which was his occupation, and interested in local antiquities and history. As a young man in Stockton-on-Tees, he was a friend of the poet John Cunningham, and of Thomas Holcroft, later to be well known for his novels and plays.[6] As he pursued his legal career in London, however, the love of antiquities and poetry led him to the manuscript collections in the British Museum, in Oxford, and in Cambridge. His new friend at Gray's Inn was John Baynes (1758–87), six

---

[1] T. J. Mathias, *Pursuits of Literature*, Dialogue I, lines 245–6.

[2] *Observations on the three first volumes of the History of English Poetry* (1782), *Gammer Gurton's Garland* (1783–4).

[3] *Pieces of Ancient Popular Poetry* (1791), *Select Collection of English Songs*, 3 vols. (1783), *Robin Hood* (1795).

[4] Scott to R. Surtees, 21 February 1807, in Scott, *Letters*, i. 355.

[5] W. Hazlitt, *Memoirs of Thomas Holcroft* (Oxford, 1926), p. 105.

[6] Holcroft portrayed Ritson, already a vegetarian, as Handford in his first novel *Alwyn, or the Gentleman Comedian* (Hazlitt, pp. 105, 130).

years younger than himself, a Fellow of Trinity College, Cambridge, and not only a member of the Constitutional Society, and so a fellow-revolutionary, but also the owner of a valuable collection of books and manuscripts. It was from a transcript of the Cambridge manuscript made by Baynes that Ritson later printed *The Erl of Toulous*.[1] When Baynes died he left his collection to Ritson. How rich it was in romances may be seen from a list of some of the printed texts that can be identified as belonging to Baynes—*Arthur of Brytayn* printed by Robert Redbone, Ibbitson's edition of *Valentine and Orson* (1549), *Amadis* (1619), *Don Bellianis* (1650), *Palmendos* (1653), *Primaleon* (1619), and *The Seven Champions* (1626, 1639?).[2]

The most important of Baynes's bequests was the fifteenth-century manuscript of *The Awntyrs of Arthur*, now Douce MS 324. Since the hero of this poem is Gawain, Ritson identified it with the *aunter of Gawayn*, said by Dunbar in his *Lament for the Makaris* to have been written by Clerk of Tranent.[3] John Pinkerton, who first printed the poem, gave it the descriptive title *Sir Gawan and Sir Galoran of Galloway*.[4] The printing of this romance by Pinkerton was the occasion of one of Ritson's many quarrels with other scholars, though in this case it is Pinkerton whose behaviour is discreditable. The story illustrates the spirit of competition which marks the romance scholarship of the period. After Baynes's death, and before the manuscript was handed to Ritson, it was transcribed by Francis Douce. The transcript was borrowed by Pinkerton on the understanding that he should not print from it without the permission of the future owner. Although Ritson refused this permission Pinkerton persisted in printing the transcript in his *Scottish Poems* (1792).[5] His behaviour, coupled with his inaccuracies and his

[1] Ritson, *Metrical Romanceës* (1802), iii. 342.

[2] These are described in Ritson's MS Catalogue of Romances, British Museum, Add. MS 10, 285. See also Ritson, *Letters*, 2 vols. (1833), i. 133.

[3] B.M. Add. MS 10, 285, f. 132ᵛ, 311. The MS had belonged to Joseph Ames. Ritson's identification is not correct, see R. S. Loomis, *Arthurian Literature in the Middle Ages* (Oxford, 1959), p. 526.

[4] J. Pinkerton, *Scottish Poems*, 3 vols. (1792), iii. 195–226.

[5] See Douce's note in the MS of the romance, quoted in Bronson, i. 190, and Ritson's accounts in *The Gentleman's Magazine* (1793), p. 32, and B.M. Add. MS 10, 285, foll. 132ᵛ, 311.

forging of the second part of the ballad *Hardyknute*, and thirteen other ballads, marked him out for Ritson's censures.[1]

During the twenty years from 1782 until his death, Ritson published twenty-nine works, and compiled material for many more. Most of his publications were collections of ballads and songs, and included the first collection of Robin Hood ballads (1795), a collection which included all but four of the known poems. His interests were purely scholarly, his aim being to collect and print accurately the material which would illuminate the popular poetry of the middle ages and the sixteenth and seventeenth centuries. In form his works are based on Percy's *Reliques*—elegantly printed and adorned with cuts and designed to appeal both to the antiquary and the man of taste. The annotations are confined to proofs of the source and authenticity of the texts, dates, glosses, illustrations of the historical references from chronicles, and references to other or similar texts. His preliminary dissertations are compilations of facts relating to Minstrelsy and Song, historical anecdotes, and information about his sources, mingled with violent refutations of Warton, Percy and Pinkerton. Though he rarely commented on the literary quality of the texts he published there is sufficient evidence that he enjoyed poetry and was capable of expressing his appreciation. The pleasure he derived from ballads is clearly seen in his letter to Scott, thanking him for the *Border Minstrelsy*: 'I mean, however, to be very chary of it, and by only perusing a single poem, or ballad at a time, extend my gratification which will be exquisite, to the most distant period. Everything is excellent throughout, both in verse and prose.'[2] This, though written at the end of his life, when his health was seriously affected, is Ritson at his most urbane.

He was almost wholly an editor, whose ideal was scholarly accuracy and honesty, a man, in Walter Scott's words, 'of acute observation, profound research, and great labour'.[3] Joseph Walker, the Irish antiquary, described him thus:

---

[1] *Hardyknute* itself is by Lady Wardlaw. On Pinkerton's spurious ballads, see Scott, *Introductory Remarks on Popular Poetry*, prefixed to the 1830 ed. of the *Border Minstrelsy*.

[2] To Scott, 10 June 1802, *Letters of Ritson*, ii. 223.

[3] Scott, *Introductory Remarks on Popular Poetry*.

An enthusiastic lover of historic truth, he sought it with an ardour which often rendered him intemperate. Though the subjects of which he treats generally led him into the bewildering gloom of the gothic ages, he seldom indulged in conjecture; indeed, such was the native integrity of his mind, that he seemed afraid to form an hypothesis, lest he should be seduced into the perversion of truth for its support. As an historian he was rigidly accurate—as a critic, he was uncharitably severe.[1]

Southey described Ritson to Coleridge as 'the oddest, but most honest, of all our antiquaries . . . he abuses Percy and Pinkerton with less mercy than justice'.[2] Though it is impossible to justify Ritson's manner of conducting a controversy—'the petulance and indecency of the manner' as Malone called it[3]—yet '. . . it ought to be said . . . by one who knew him well, that this irritability of disposition was a constitutional and physical infirmity; and that Ritson's extreme attachment to the severity of truth, corresponded to the rigour of his criticisms upon the labours of others.'[4] His constitutional 'irritability of temper', 'disposed him to drive controversies into personal quarrels, by neglecting, in literary debate, the courtesies of ordinary society'; more, it 'induced him to treat antiquarian trifles with the same seriousness which men of the world reserve for matters of importance'.[5]

To Ritson, 'antiquarian trifles' were 'matters of importance'. In an age which had seen many forgeries of literary documents —the poems of Chatterton and Ossian, Ireland's Shakespeare papers, Charles Bertram's *De Situ Britanniae*, attributed to Richard of Cirencester, Pinkerton's second part of *Hardyknute*, and the fragment of that hero's sarcophagus—Ritson was naturally cautious. The proof of an editor's honesty could be manifested only in 'strict adherence to ancient orthography'. I 'can place no confidence whatever', he wrote to J. C. Walker, 'in one who secretly innovates in a single word . . . he begins

---

[1] *Letters of Ritson* (1833), Sir Harris Nicolas' *Memoir of Ritson*, i. lxxvi–lxxvii. Ritson's integrity extended to his legal activities, see i. lxviii.
[2] Southey, *Life and Correspondence* (1850), ii. 203.
[3] Quoted in Bronson, i. 75.
[4] Scott, *Introductory Remarks on Popular Poetry*.
[5] ibid.

with letters & ends in volumes'.[1] If the main interest of the reader was in ancient manners and customs, it was essential that texts be authentic. To look into Percy's *Reliques* 'to be acquainted with the state of ancient poetry' was to be 'miserably disappointed', as Ritson was, or 'fatally misled'.[2]

'Forgery and imposition of every kind, ought to be universally execrated';[3] Percy's impositions seemed to Ritson hypocrisy in a clergyman and prelate. The extent to which he pursued his ideal is seen in his statement, 'I have long entertained an idea that there is a more intimate connection between integrity in literary matters & what one calls common honesty than people in general are aware of. . . .'[4]

The fact, however, that Percy remained to the end of his life interested in every discreditable detail that could be discovered about Ritson, is not to be explained simply on the grounds of Ritson's intemperate complaints about the texts in the *Reliques*. More important was Ritson's disbelief in the existence of the Folio MS 'The Bishop of Dromore says he has it in his FOLIO MS. Did you ever SEE THAT?' he asks Warton.[5] In the introduction to his *Select Collection of English Songs* (1783) and the 'Essay on Minstrels' in *Ancient Songs and Ballads* (1790), Ritson casts doubt on the existence of the MS. In the latter, he lists the number of times that Percy says the manuscript is imperfect whenever he prints from it a text not otherwise available. The list is calculated to sow doubt in the reader's mind. Percy was thus forced to prove the existence of the manuscript, though he was naturally reluctant to allow Ritson to examine it.[6] He described it to J. C. Walker, who wrote to persuade Ritson that it did exist.[7] He left it with the publisher Nichols while the fourth edition of the *Reliques* was at press. In the Advertisement

---

[1] 1 January 1790 (in possession of B. H. Bronson). Quoted in Bronson, ii. 548.

[2] Ritson, *Select Collection of English Songs* (1783), i. xn. cf. *Metrical Romanceës* (1802), i. cxli.

[3] ibid.

[4] Bronson, ii. 548, Ritson to Walker, January 1790.

[5] *Observations on Warton* (1782), p. 11.

[6] Percy to Pinkerton, 28 July 1792, Nichols, *Illustrations*, viii. 144–5. At one time Percy intended to bequeath the MS to Ritson (see Wheatley's ed. of *Reliques* (1887), i. lxxxviii).

[7] Walker to Percy, 22 September 1789, in Nichols, *Illustrations*, vii. 710. Ritson to Walker, 4 November 1789 in Ritson's *Letters* (1833), i. 152.

to that edition he described it, and appealed for corroboration to Daines Barrington, Cracherode, Farmer, Steevens, Malone and Reed. Ritson was satisfied as to the 'mere existence of the MS'. But 'whether it will on a careful examination justify the use Bp. Percy has or pretends to have made of it is a perfectly distinct question'. It had never been shown to a scholar conversant with old manuscripts—Tyrwhitt or Ritson—and might prove to be a forgery.[1] Certainly Percy 'has taken such libertys in his publications from it, that he might as well have had no MS at all. . . .'[2] Ritson went even further, however, in suggesting that Percy was more generally dishonest. Writing to Walker, on 25 January 1793, he says of Percy, 'All are ready to do justice to his taste & genius, but I never met with one that would answer for his morals'.[3]

Ritson was responsible for two discreditable stories about Percy. One, which must have been well known to all his contemporaries, is recorded by Ritson in a letter to Walker of 1 January 1790. In this he tells how a few years earlier Percy had been asked, in a public paper, to account for a manuscript missing from the British Museum, one moreover from which a ballad had been printed in the *Reliques*. As a result, the manuscript had been returned to the Museum on the following day, and was found to contain marks in the hand of Percy.[4]

He further alleged that Percy was responsible for the loss of books from Dulwich College Library. In Ritson's manuscript *Catalogue of Romances*, he notes, in the location of copies of *The Mirror of Knighthood*, that Dulwich had a perfect set which disappeared with certain other things, and adds 'It is also said to have been in the possession of doctor Percy'.[5] In the letter to Walker of 1 January 1790, he offers broad hints to the same effect.[6] Percy's explanation is to be found in a letter to Isaac Reed on 5 April 1794. It would seem that Percy had borrowed some books, a list of which was taken at the time by Mr Swan, a Fellow of Dulwich. They had been saved from the fire in 1780, which destroyed much of Percy's collection,

[1] Ritson to Walker, 25 January 1793 (in possession of Bronson) Bronson, ii. 551.
[2] Bronson, ii. 553. Ritson to Walker, 22 June 1796.
[3] Bronson, ii. 552. [4] Bronson, ii. 548.
[5] B.M. Add. MS 10, 285, fol. 38. [6] Bronson, ii. 548.

and taken to Ireland. All but one had been rebound and returned. The last was sent to Reed, with instructions for rebinding, and a request that Reed should return it in person and ask the Rev. Mr Smith to show him the others, so that he could vindicate Percy from 'any cruel and injurious insinuations which may have been thrown out upon this subject'.[1]

The infirmity of Ritson's temper is not an irrelevance in a study of this kind. The desire not to rouse his ire must have had an effect on the quality of medieval scholarship. But more important were the examples of accuracy he provided. The reviewer of Ritson's *Metrical Romanceës* in the *Annual Review* (1803) speaks of him as 'of all men living the best qualified for the task, and the most trustworthy', and considers his opinions 'with all the attention and deference due to the high and honourable rank which he holds in this department of literature'.[2] This recognition Ritson had won by his labours. He always tried to print with scrupulous fidelity to his source. In his edition of the poems of Laurence Minot (1795), for example, he carefully explains that he has corrected in his text the evident corruptions of the manuscript, but has noted for the reader the manuscript reading. He expands all abbreviations and prints 3 as z. Reviewers were not generally kind to this method of presenting texts. Pinkerton, who had suffered at Ritson's hands, ridiculed his insistence on an accurate text, 'the editor has spared no pains to reject any improvement and to restore [the poems] to error'.[3] The reviewer of the Robin Hood ballads, in *The British Critic*, demanded a more thorough emendation of 'errors'.[4] Ritson would not agree that an editor 'has a right to avoid a disgusting orthography of a common word—at least without affording his readers an opportunity of knowing whether it is disgusting or not. On the contrary', he wrote to J. C. Walker, 'I am persuaded that a strict adherence to ancient orthography, however rude, which I conceive is what you mean by disgusting, is the test of an editor's fidelity'.[5]

---

[1] Nichols, *Illustrations*, viii. 296–7. The Rev. Mr Smith is Thomas Jenyns Smith, Fellow of Dulwich College.

[2] *Annual Review*, ii. (1803), 517, 518. The reviewer was Southey.

[3] Review of Ritson's *Scottish Songs*, 2 vols. (1794), in *The Critical Review*, January 1795, pp. 49 ff.

[4] *British Critic*, January 1797.   [5] Bronson, ii. 548.

Accuracy was a proof of the editor's honesty, not a prerequisite for the study of philology.

In his edition of *Metrical Romanceës*, Ritson describes the method:

> Every article is derived from some ancient manuscript, or old printed copy, of the authenticity of which the reader has all possible satisfaction; and is printed with an accuracy, and adherence to the original, of which the public has had very few examples. The utmost care has been observed in the Glossary, and every necessary or useful information (to the best of the editor's judgement) is given in the Notes.[1]

He admits the necessity of corrections:

> To correct the obvious errors of an illiterate transcriber, to supply irremediable defects, and to make sense of nonsense, are certainly essential duties of an editor of ancient poetry, provided he act with integrity and publicity.[2]

Whenever he emends his source, the manuscript reading is given in the notes,[3] and a list of conjectural emendations is given in volume three.[4] In printing the romances, þ was replaced by 'th', medial and final ȝ by 'gh', and initial ȝ by 'y'. The use of 'z' to represent ȝ 'might have been retained, after the example of respectable editors; but, with the Saxon characters, is sacrificed to public taste or prejudice'.[5] Since the main importance of the retention of þ and ȝ is that these are an indication of the date of the manuscript, Ritson, who always described these graphic peculiarities in his introductions, lost little by not printing them.

Richard Price in his preface to the 1824 edition of Warton's *History*, witnesses to the influence of Ritson on scholarly practice. 'The example and authority of Mr. Ritson have ... established as an indispensable law', a careful attention to the orthography of manuscripts.[6] His precept and example over twenty years had been 'scrupulously adhered to by his

---

[1] *Metrical Romanceës* (1802), i. iii.
[2] ibid., i. cix.   [3] ibid., iii. 219–24.
[4] ibid., iii. 442–3. Errata in the text are corrected at iii. 437–41.
[5] ibid., iii. 264.   [6] Warton, *History* (1824), i. (103).

disciples', and the laxity of Warton's times had disappeared. Price tries to combat Ritson's ideal, by arguing that the reproduction of the chaotic spellings of the scribes merely serves to perpetuate the belief, shared by Mitford and Sharon Turner, that the English language 'fell into confusion' as a result of the political and social upheaval following the Norman conquest.[1] There is, of course, an element of truth in this notion, but Price is concerned to refute those who hold to it in its most naïve form. He cannot accept that political changes can produce a breakdown of grammatical usage. He is more interested in the then recent discovery that the English language can be shown to have undergone a steady grammatical development that would have been exactly the same had there never been a Norman conquest. This fact, he felt, had not been recognized by Ritson, and its discovery had, if anything, been delayed by Ritson's insistence on reproducing the often chaotic spellings of his manuscript sources. The grammatical development would, he thought, emerge more clearly if all spellings were 'normalized', in the way that editors of Greek and Latin texts normalized the spellings found in their manuscripts. The actual spellings found in medieval manuscripts could only be the result of an ignorant scribe, or of an attempt to produce a phonetic spelling. Though Price wrote only twenty years after Ritson's death, it is clear that Ritson would have found the context of his remarks strange. Ritson was an accurate reproducer of manuscripts, because only thus could he prove the authenticity of what he printed. Price has passed beyond this; he is interested in the development of the language; authenticity he can take for granted.[2] But this was largely the result of Ritson's influence, seen in the greater accuracy of the quotations in Price's edition of Warton's *History*.

Ritson's interest in romances dates from some period before 1782, when he published his *Observations* on Warton's *History*. In this he already shows enough knowledge of Middle English to

---

[1] ibid., p. (106).

[2] ibid., p. (110). Price understood Old English grammar and the principles of alliteration in Old English verse so well that he could recognize a mistranscription in the printed text of *Beowulf*, and correct it, without recourse to the manuscript. He corrected the reading 'Fyrstne anbidan' to 'fyrst Nean bidan'.

be able to correct some of Warton's more doubtful glosses, and he gives evidence of a wide reading of romances. He took issue with Warton and Warburton on the question of the origin of romances, preferring a Celtic to any Arabian or Gothic theory. His reading in Spanish romances was already sufficient to enable him to refute Warton's wilder assertions. Ritson selected a hundred and sixteen errors in Warton's three volumes to illustrate the unreliability of the work. He exposed the inaccuracies in the transcript of *Launfal*, which Percy had sent to Warton; he corrected Warton's confusion of *Robert the Devil* and *Robert of Sicily*; he showed the real reason for the inclusion of *Ywain and Gawain* so late in the *History*; and he compared the early printed texts of *Guy*, *Bevis* and *Richard* with manuscript versions to show that Warton was wrong in his conjecture that they had been modernized by the printers.[1] Occasionally Ritson himself was in error. In one case, however, the error is itself interesting. Warton had assigned the stanzaic *Morte Arthur* in Harley MS 2252 to the early fourteenth century, in spite of Wanley's dating of the manuscript as early sixteenth century. Though modern scholars date the manuscript late fifteenth century, the poem was probably composed about 1400. Ritson, however, insisted on dating both poem and manuscript as early sixteenth century. But he did realize that there was a close relationship between this poem and Books xx and xxi of Malory's *Morte Darthur*. He was led by this to assert that the poem was a versification of these two books, a judgement that the earlier dating of the poem has reversed.[2] But Ritson must have known both the poem and Malory's work in detail in order to make such a claim.

It was not only the romances that interested him, though these were the main works of any length which he considered worth reviving. He knew the alliterative fragment of *Alexander and Dindimus* (in Bodley MS 264), for example, sufficiently well to be able to deny Warton's assumption that it was an imitation of the style and manner of *Piers Plowman*. But though he was correct here, he went on to question Langland's authorship of

[1] Ritson, *Observations* (1782), pp. 16, 28, 33, 35.
[2] ibid., p. 10; *Metrical Romanceës* (1802), i. cv–vi; see Vinaver, *Works of Malory.* (Oxford, 1947), iii. 1600 f.

Piers Plowman.[1] As his knowledge grew in later years he realized that the poem existed in at least two versions, though he still preferred the version as printed by Crowley (a form of Skeat's B text), and called the author 'Robert' Langland.[2] But in the unprinted *Catalogue of Romances* he followed Tyrwhitt in describing the author as 'William'. He did not think the poem worth reprinting, but admired the satirical passages for their poetical merit and the 'insight they afford into the manners and customs of those times'.[3] It was again the now almost unknown Richard Price who first realized that there were three versions of *Piers Plowman*.[4]

Few of Warton's contemporaries could have detected the errors, or had read widely enough to be able to question many of the conjectures in the *History*. But Ritson's tone in his pamphlet was indefensible. An error, to him, was a crime. When Warton glosses 'faucon brode' as a 'falcon', Ritson writes, 'such unparalleled ignorance, such matchless effrontery, is not, Mr. Warton, in my humble opinion, worthy of anything but castigation or contempt'.[5] When Warton writes that Marlowe's mortal wound was in the bosom, Ritson is astonished: 'Your propensity to corruption and falsehood seems so natural, that I have been sometimes tempted to believe, you often substitute a lye in the place of a fact without knowing it.'[6] He had, as he avowed, no personal motive in publishing what he acknowledged to be 'his scurrilous libel against Tom Warton'.[7] He was anxious only for accuracy. The *Observations* and the resulting controversy brought him, at the age of thirty, to the notice of a wide public and established his reputation as a learned,

---

[1] *Observations*, p. 12.

[2] Ritson, *Bibliographia* (1802), pp. 26–31. Ritson is following Bale, Crowley and Hearne in calling him 'Robert'.

[3] Add. ms 10285, fo. 248ᵛ; Tyrwhitt, *The Canterbury Tales* (1775), iv. 74.

[4] Warton, *History* (1824), ii. 482. Price discovered two mss of the A text, an early incomplete version (Harley ms 875) and a later one (Harley ms 6041). He rightly concluded that 'a third version was once in circulation'. Skeat, who rediscovered this fact, refers to Price's perception, in the Preface to his edition in three parallel texts (Oxford, 1886), ii. p. vii.

[5] *Observations*, p. 9.   [6] ibid., p. 42.

[7] ibid., p. 1; Ritson, *Letters*, i. 61. The *Observations* produced a controversy in *The Gentleman's Magazine* (vols. 52 and 53), see the account in Bronson, and Douce's copy of the *Observations* in Bodley, Douce RR. 165.

widely-read antiquary, but petty and waspish, of the tradition of Hearne, and not of Warton and Percy.

In the midst of his legal studies and his practice as a conveyancer, Ritson undertook vast projects in literary antiquities. One of the largest was the compilation of a bibliography of romances in French, Italian, Spanish and English, to include all printed editions before 1660 of those in English, before 1600 of the rest, with appendixes listing manuscripts of French and English texts. Two sheets of this were printed in the same year as the attack on Warton, but the complete work, listing about fifteen hundred romances in three thousand entries, is still in manuscript.[1] The basis for the catalogue was the library of the Rev. Thomas Croft, Chancellor of Peterborough, a collection rich in French romances. But Ritson also described copies in the British Museum, the Bodleian, Cambridge University Library and the Advocates' Library, as well as books in the possession of Baynes, Douce, Farmer and Steevens. He continued to work on the catalogue until the end of his life, though in 1799 he realized that he would never live to publish it, or even complete it.[2] Its very existence shows how important the romances were to Ritson, though by romance he seems to mean fiction in general. Thus he includes the works of Spenser, Lodge, Anthony Munday, Greene, Dante, Kenelm Digby, Samuel Rowlands, Richard Johnson and Langland. For most of the works he gives a bibliographical account—title, colophon, imprint, date, format, type, location of copies, description of contents, and where possible a reference to the Stationers' Register and to Ames' *Typographical Antiquities*. The appendix in which he lists manuscripts of English romances includes forty-four titles.[3] It is an impressive addition to the knowledge of medieval romances and well indicates the extent of Ritson's researches.

The closeness of his attention to manuscripts can be seen in his study of the Auchinleck MS, where in 1792 he discovered *Orfeo, Lai le Freine, Floris* and *Tristrem*. He transcribed some of

---

[1] B.M. Add. MS 10, 283–5.

[2] Ritson, *Letters*, ii. 180, 207. Croft died in 1781. For his library see *Bibliotheca Croftsiana* (1783), drawn up by Samuel Paterson (Nichols, *Anecdotes*, viii. 482–3).

[3] See Appendix 2.

the texts, and compiled a description of the manuscript and a list of contents.[1] He did not, however, transcribe *Sir Orfeo*; when he came to edit the poem he depended on Scott's transcript, sent in April 1802.[2] He cannot have read more than the opening of *Lai le Freine*, since, from the similarity of the prologue to that of the Harley text of *Orfeo*, he concluded that this was but another text of *Orfeo*.[3] The Auchinleck *Tristrem* he must have transcribed, since he quoted from it in the glossary to his edition of Minot in 1795. In his unpublished *Bibliotheca Scotica*, a catalogue of Scottish authors and their works completed by 1801, he collected many of the references to Thomas of Erceldoune, to whom he attributed the poem. If he planned an edition, he resigned the task willingly to Scott, who had the benefit of Ritson's notes in the *Bibliotheca*.[4]

Ritson's brief friendship with Scott is one of the happier episodes in his life. Scott sent him notes for the glossary to the edition of romances, a metrical translation of the *Recollections of the Chatelain*, and, rather surprisingly, the Maitland manuscript.[5] Ritson replied with transcripts of *The Wee Man* and Geoffrey of Monmouth's life of Merlin.[6] Scott introduced him to Ballantyne, who undertook to print an edition of the *Pistill of Susane* from the Vernon MS. This work was interrupted by Ritson's death, but before then the printer was groaning 'over the peculiarities of his type & orthography'. 'Pity it is', wrote Scott, 'that such labour and research should be rendered useless & ridiculous by the infirmity of his temper.'[7] Ritson, perhaps fortunately, did not live to examine the *Border Minstrelsy* with care. Had he done so he would have concluded

---

[1] See H. M. Smyser, 'The List of Norman Names in the Auchinleck MS', in *Medieval Studies in Honor of J. D. M. Ford* (Harvard, 1948), p. 261.

[2] Ritson, *Letters*, ii. 217–19.

[3] ibid. He exchanged with Scott a transcript of Marie's original for one of the Auchinleck *Lai le Freine*.

[4] Bronson, i. 229; Bronson, 'Ritson's *Bibliotheca Scotica*', *PMLA*, lii (1937), 122–59.

[5] Ritson, *Letters*, ii. 226; Scott, *Letters*, i. 199–203; xii. 219. Scott's translation of the *Chatelain* is printed in W. C. Hazlitt's edition of Ritson's *Ancient Songs* (1877), pp. 135 f.

[6] Ritson, *Letters*, ii. 219.

[7] Scott, *Letters*, xii. 220–1, 228; Bronson, 'The Caledonian Muse', *PMLA*, xlvi (1931), 1208–11.

that Scott too was of the school of Percy, and he alone the upholder of scrupulous accuracy and honesty. The 'scalping knife' would, as Scott feared,[1] have been resumed, and that friendship also broken.

Ritson always moved on the fringe of the circle of friendly scholars who were interested in the romances, men like Richard Heber, Thomas Park, George Ellis, Francis Douce, and Scott. Scott's assistant, John Leyden, Ritson loved 'with a love surpassing the love of women' for his 'multifarious and many-tongued lore'.[2] But Ritson quarrelled even with Francis Douce, whom he had known since 1787 and who had also been a friend of Baynes. Douce contributed to the 'Catalogue of Romances', and, with his customary generosity, allowed Ritson to use his extensive collection of books and manuscripts.[3] According to a manuscript note in Douce's copy of Ritson's *Ancient Engleish Metrical Romanceës*, it was from Douce that Ritson learned of the existence of the Havelock story in Gaimar's *L'Estoire des Engles* in the Royal MS 13, A, xxi.[4] Douce was himself not of the easiest temperament, but when the break came in September, 1801, he was shocked by Ritson's declaration that 'he would never taste another drop of tea in Douce's house; never commune with him in the Museum reading room, never even exchange with him the common forms of civility'.[5] Yet after Ritson's death Douce wrote, 'I really loved the man to an extent that he little dreamt of'.[6] Scott also loved Ritson, and had found him kind and indulgent, with an honesty of principle that was respectable.[7] He praised his profound researches, his care and taste, his zeal and industry, his accuracy as transcriber and editor, while deprecating his severity and

[1] Scott, *Letters*, xii. 197–8.

[2] ibid., xii. 197, 231.

[3] These are now in the Bodleian Library.

[4] See Douce's copy in Bodley, Douce RR 37, I, lxxxviii. Ritson could have discovered this from Tyrwhitt, *Canterbury Tales* (1775), iv. 62, or de la Rue (*Archaeologia*, xii (1796), 307–12).

[5] Scott, *Letters*, xii. 197 n.; Bronson, i. 267. Ritson's vegetarianism was the basis of the quarrel. Douce's account is in a letter to Ellis in B.M. Add. MS 28099, fo. 41.

[6] Bronson, i. 311. This, with many other letters and notes, is bound in the British Museum copy of Joseph Haslewood's *Account of Ritson* (1824), G. 13123.

[7] Scott, *Letters*, i. 355; ii. 316.

irritability.[1] 'I wish we had his like at present', he wrote in 1810 to Ritson's friend, Robert Surtees.

Ritson's fight for standards of accuracy in literary researches seemed to most of his contemporaries a manifestation of his insanity, for there was as yet no audience demanding such standards. Ritson was therefore anxious to establish them by being the first to edit texts of the romances, before the adherents to Percy's methods debased this branch of literature also. He was uneasy, as his edition progressed, to find that Thomas Park and George Ellis,[2] who had also come to literary research by way of an indulgence in writing poetry, were preparing an edition of 'Adam Davie's *King Alisaunder*'. Ellis had already printed a romance, *Launfal*, in Gregory Lewis Way's second volume of translations from Le Grand's *Fabliaux* (1800), and on the evidence of this Ritson concluded him to be of the school of Percy, 'a very flippant and hastey writer'.[3] But Ellis had promised not to precede Ritson in printing, and had persuaded Nicol to publish Ritson's work.[4] Throughout 1801 Ritson saw himself as constantly threatened by Park and Ellis's edition of *Alisaunder*; in the event the poem was not printed until 1810, when Scott's German protegé, Henry Weber, published it in his edition of *Metrical Romances*. Ritson's volumes were delayed in 1802, from May to October, by the alarm of the publisher at the 'enormous portion of blasphemy' that Ritson had 'contrived to insert into his dissertation and notes'. With the help of Heber, the offending passages were cut and nine cancel leaves inserted.[5] The first collection of metrical romances

[1] Scott, *Introductory Remarks on Popular Poetry*, prefixed to 1830 edition of *Border Minstrelsy*.

[2] For Ellis, see chapter 6. Park abandoned a career as engraver in 1797 to pursue literary antiquities. His poems (*Sonnets*, 1797) were corrected by Anna Seward, and published on the recommendation of Cowper. He helped Ritson with his *Bibliographia Poetica* and *Bibliotheca Scotica* and began a new edition of Warton's *History*. His library was catalogued by A. F. Griffith, *Bibliotheca Anglo-Poetica* (1815).

[3] Bronson, i. 243. Ellis's errors are noted in Ritson's edition of *Launfal*.

[4] Bronson, i. 242, 248, 257.

[5] For the cancelled passages, see H. F. Burd, *Joseph Ritson* (Madison, 1916), pp. 206–8, and Douce's copy of *Ancient Engleish Metrical Romanceës* in Bodley, Douce RR, 37. Cancel leaves are vol. i. a5, c7, d6, el, k2; vol. iii, Q7, R4, Y1, Z7. The blasphemies had also to be cut out of Ritson's *Essay on Abstinence from Animal Food*, published at the same time. For Heber's part, see Scott, *Letters*, xii. 228 n.

was then offered to the public 'with cold indifference, expecting little favour, and less profit; but certain . . . to be insulted by . . . a base and prostitute gang of lurking assassins, who stab in the dark'.[1]

2

The *Metrical Romanceës* were prefixed by a lengthy dissertation on romance and minstrelsy. This reminded Scott of 'a heap of rubbish which had either turned out unfit for the architect's purpose, or beyond his skill to make use of'.[2] One of the main differences between Ritson and the rest of the romance scholars was the propensity of all but Ritson to indulge in conjectures, to build persuasive pictures of medieval life. Ritson assembled facts and quotations, believing that the state of knowledge was as yet insufficient to warrant the sort of deductions that other scholars made. Like a true Baconian, he realized that the collection of facts was less likely to harm the advance of learning than systems too hurriedly embraced. Thus his facts are best used in demolishing the theories of Percy and Warton. Yet, of course, even the listing of facts depends on some presuppositions, if only the belief that an existing theory is wrong. Each of the four topics that Ritson chooses for discussion depends on a supposition. The first, on the origin of romance, assumes that romance and fiction in verse are synonymous. It is then easy for Ritson to assert that classical epic and romance need not be distinguished. Elaborate theories of origin are rendered unnecessary, and instead the topic becomes one of tracing the developing meanings of the word 'romance' in the middle ages to show how, from being 'a book in the vernacular', a 'romance' became a book of chivalry. Presumably as part of his thesis, Ritson then gives an account of French romances from the (then) lost *Chanson de Roland* to Chrétien de Troyes. If the term 'romance' is French, then to seek the origin of romance was to trace the development of French romances.

The second and third sections are built on the assumption that English romances are invariably later than the French. Ritson's evidence is therefore arranged to show that the language

---

[1] Ritson, Preface to *Metrical Romanceës* (1802), i. p. iv.
[2] Scott, *Letters* i. 205.

spoken by the Saxons was corrupted by the Danes, infected by the Normans, confined to the vulgar after the Conquest, and despised by the learned. The English language that developed from this mixture was used by Layamon and developed by Chaucer and Gower. Ritson's purpose is to collect references to the language spoken by the kings of England and to suggest that English was too poor a medium for any French poet to wish to borrow romances from it. It was, of course, Percy who had suggested the interchange of romance between England and France. By stressing the ignorance and illiteracy of the Anglo-Saxons, Ritson is also denying Warton's contention that the tales of the Scandinavian scalds were known to the Anglo-Saxons. Ritson's knowledge of Anglo-Saxon must have been small, as small as Warton's. The existence of the Saxon romance *Apollonius of Tyre*, because it is in prose and a translation from Latin, he does not consider relevant to his general argument. The first English romance that he recognizes is Layamon's *Brut*, a version of Wace's poem.[1] But this, being in 'a mixture of Saxon and Norman' is passed over for the first real metrical romance in 'English', *King Horn*. Ritson knew this only in the latest manuscript, Harley 2253, and dated the poem early fourteenth century.[2] The Anglo-Norman or, as he called it, French version in Harley MS 527 suggested that the English was not the original, though the French text does not use the same names as the English. Ritson therefore conjectured the existence of another French version. Both he and Tyrwhitt thought that all English romances before Chaucer were translations from the French.[3] Tyrwhitt, however, believed that *Horn*, *Bevis* and *Guy* were written in French in England, and perhaps by Englishmen.[4] Ritson, with a preference for things French rather than English which was perhaps a relic of his revolutionary politics,

[1] Ritson correctly dates the Caligula A. ix manuscript of Layamon early thirteenth century, and the composition of the poem in the reigns of Henry II or Richard I. But he makes two mistakes—in describing the MS as Claudius (for Caligula) and in stating that the other MS, Otto C. xiii, was destroyed by fire; it was damaged in 1731, but still contains 23,590 lines.

[2] Two earlier MSS are Camb. Univ. Lib. Gg. 4, 27, 2 (c. 1250) and MS Laud Misc. 108 Part II (1300–20). The poem is now dated c. 1225.

[3] Tyrwhitt, *Canterbury Tales* (1775), iv. 68; Ritson, *Metrical Romanceës* (1802), i. xcvii.

[4] Tyrwhitt, iv. 61. A point that was important to Scott later.

was prepared to assert that the metre was 'Norman' and that the poem must be of French origin. The reviewer of the *Metrical Romanceës* in the *Annual Review* for 1803 suggested a Scandinavian origin for the story. Richard Price thought it older than the Conquest; Scott tried to add this poem to the works of Thomas of Erceldoune. The controversy on the origin of this story was thus beginning almost as soon as the manuscript was printed.[1] In his notes on the romance, Ritson printed the Auchinleck *Horn Child*, and started the long discussion of the identity of the lands of Estnesse, Westnesse and Sudene.[2] He also quoted from de Worde's edition of *Ponthus and Sydoyne* (1511), to give a parallel to Horn's exchange of clothing with the palmer, but seems not to have realized that this was a version of the Horn story. Why Ritson enjoyed this romance he does not say, but the reviewer in the *Annual Review* thought that if it were 'told in the sweet verse of Spenser, nothing in romance would be more beautiful'.

Ritson, like Percy and Warton, thus begins with *King Horn*. His account of English romances after this is a narrative version of his catalogue, with dates, lists of manuscripts, information about probable French originals, and all that he could collect relevant to the stories. It is here that, for the first time, references to the Havelock story in Gaimar, Camden and Warner are collected. But he devotes a great deal of space to displaying, on evidence provided by Percy in the fourth edition of the *Reliques*, the alterations and additions made by Percy in the text of *The Marriage of Sir Gawaine*.

The fourth section of the dissertation is also aimed at Percy, this time at his views on minstrels. It was Percy who had brought the minstrels into prominence, as the supposed composers and reciters of the exploits of romance heroes. Ritson in irritation compiled an astonishing list of anecdotes and quotations to show the varied activities of popular entertainers, but insists that minstrels were musicians who performed on

[1] *Annual Review*, ii. (1803), 528; Warton, *History* (1824), i. 46 n; for Scott, see below, p. 184. On the localizing of the legend in Roxburghshire, see *PMLA* xlvi (1931), 102–14 and xviii (1903), 1–84.

[2] He identifies Estnesse as England, Westnesse as Ireland, but realizes that in the poem Westnesse is sometimes England. Scott printed a letter from Ritson about this in *Border Minstrelsy*, 3rd. edn. (1806), iii. 13.

instruments, occasionally reciting stories. French minstrels he will allow to have composed romances, but he will not assign any English romance to a minstrel's pen; they 'were too ignorant and vulgar to translate pieces of several thousand lines'. The only 'romance' he will concede to an English minstrel—thus contradicting himself—is *The battayle of Egyngecourt*, and this, of course, is not a romance, but a poem in celebration of the victory. On the social status of the English minstrel, however, Ritson does not compromise. Percy's insistence on the minstrel as the companion of kings irritated him too much. With a sweeping array of quotations from Langland's 'Activa Vita' to Stubbe's *Anatomie of Abuses* he shows the minstrels to be 'a parcel of drunken sockets and baudy parasites'.

> Beggars they are with one consent,
> And rogues by act of Parliament.

If Percy went too far in one direction, Ritson, with an equally impressive show of learning, went too far in the other. Without the impetus to refute Percy, Ritson might have held a more balanced view. But he could then hardly have justified the attention he paid to the romances. He offers only Percy's words to explain the value of his edition, that the romances are epics in embryo and shed light on the history of poetry and on our ancient classical poets.[1] There is a place for the scholar who collects facts and edits texts, as Ritson did. But the desire to know the facts and read the texts must be inspired by a scholar of a different order, one who, like Percy, 'doth not only show the way, but giveth so sweet a prospect into the way, as will entice any man to enter into it'. These qualities Scott and Ellis had in common with Percy and Warton. Ritson was born almost a century too early.

Accurate editing is never wasted work, and Ritson's edition of twelve romances is still read by scholars. It is particularly useful as a compendious collection of texts for a reader without access to more recent editions of the separate romances.[2] Ritson alone

---

[1] *Metrical Romanceës*, i. pp. i–ii; *Reliques* (1765), iii. pp. viii–ix.
[2] The only modern collection of romances is that by French and Hale, *Middle English Metrical Romances* (New York, 1930).

of the scholars did all his own transcribing. He was probably too poor to pay a copyist. But he never mastered the difficulties of manuscript-reading sufficiently to know, for example, when a word or letter was expuncted, or to understand a final contraction, particularly after *n* or *h*. He does not always reproduce accurately *u*, *v*, and *i*, *j*, and occasionally joins or separates words incorrectly. Nor is his glossing always faultless. He is quite capable of glossing *roun* (whisper) as 'run'.[1] Where he had more than one manuscript of a text, he produced an eclectic text, in the main reproducing a single manuscript (as in *Orfeo* and *The King of Tars*), recording the main variations, but correcting corruption and supplying omitted passages in his copy-text by reference to the second. All his dealings with any text are, however, carefully noted.

As an annotator it is perhaps natural that 'to show his learning was his sole endeavour'. It is learning designed to show the interrelationship between a French and English text, the presence of similar episodes in other romances, the various skills of knights and ladies, the variations in different texts of the same romance. Ritson carefully notes the places at which he has conflated the Harley and Auchinleck MSS readings in *Sir Orfeo*,[2] and prints from the Auchinleck MS the passages not found in the Harley MS. He remarks on the different ways of telling the Constance story, found in Chaucer, Gower and the poet of *Emare*. His note on *Termagant*[3] is a good example of his detailed learning. He corrects Percy, who had believed the French *Tervagan(t)* to be a corruption of the English *Termagant*, by showing that the reverse is true, and offers a conjectural etymology—*ter vagans*. In support of this he quotes the *Metamorphoses* to show that turning thrice round was a magical incantation, and the *Aeneid* to show that 'three had some mystic signification with the ancients'. Hickes in the *Thesaurus* and Lye in his Saxon dictionary provide evidence that *Tyr* was a Saxon deity, and a name sometimes applied to a prince or to

[1] See F. Maddan in *The Gentleman's Magazine*, 103 (1833), pp. 307–8; W. W. Skeat in *Notes and Queries*, Series 8, ii, (1892), 3. For a collation of Ritson's text of *Emare* with the MS see E. Kölbing, *Englische Studien*, xv. 248.

[2] *Sir Orfeo*, ll. 39–40. *Metrical Romanceës* (1802), iii. 335. A similar note points to the insertion of ll. 115–20 in *Kyng of Tars* from the Auchinleck MS.

[3] Note to *Lybeaus*, l. 1301, iii. 257–262.

God. Ariosto and Tasso are quoted as using the French form, and Bale's *Acts of English Votaries* is used to show that there was a stage character *Termagant*. Had Percy not discussed the word at length in the *Reliques*,[1] Ritson might not have collected his valuable list of references with which to correct him.

3

Ritson's selection of romances 'from a pretty general acquaintance', exhibits his taste in this branch of literature. Pride of place, and the most thorough annotation is given to *Ywain and Gawain*, in a collection which includes *Launfal*, *Libeaus*, *King Horn*, *King of Tars*, *Emare*, *Orfeo*, *Le bone Florence*, *Erl of Toulous*, *Sqyr of Lowe Degre*, and *The Knight of Courtesy*. *Ywain* is a condensed version of Chrétien de Troyes' masterpiece, *Ywain, ou Le Chevalier au Lion*. One might judge Ritson's sureness of taste by his obvious admiration for this romance, for it is one of the most successful of its *genre*. 'It has no moments of tedium, and no shortcomings as a romance', is the comment of a modern critic.[2] Here 'the modern *idea* of the romance is fulfilled', a fantastic subject is treated with great artistic sensitivity. Ritson offers no literary comment on the poem, but the care with which he edited it suggests that his choice of it to open his collection was no accident.

In the annotations, Ritson gives lengthy accounts of Ywain, Gawain, Arthur and Guenevere, drawing on Malory, but also on Carte's *History*, John Lewis' *History of Great Britain* (1729), and on William Owen [-Pughe], *The Heroic Elegies and other Pieces of Llywarch Hên. With a Literal Translation* (1792). The Welsh historians, or as Ritson calls them 'the literary Welsh idiots . . . [of] the eighteenth century' provide information about Owen and Urien, whom Ritson accepts as historical persons.[3] William of Malmesbury is the chief source of his information on Gawain. In discussing Arthur (he was preparing his *Life of King Arthur* at the time), Ritson refers to 'authentic history', William of Malmesbury, Henry of Huntingdon,

---

[1] In a note to *King Estmere* in vol. i. Percy provided the reference to Bale; he has others to Alleyn's letters, *Hamlet* and La Fontaine.

[2] George Kane, *Middle English Literature* (1951), p. 78.

[3] *Metrical Romanceës* (1802), iii. 225–8.

Nennius, the *Vita S. Gildae* in Royal MS 13 B VII, and Carte. These, he believes, show that Arthur was a 'brave warrior, and, in all probability, a petty king'.[1] Geoffrey of Monmouth's *Historia* is dismissed as 'fabulous and romantic', but is dated accurately as 1138, following William Lloyd, Bishop of St Asaph (1680–92).[2] The account of Guenevere[3] is taken from Malory, and from the *Life of St Gildas* attributed to Caradoc of Llancarvan. The latter had been used by Usher in the seventeenth century, but it is significant that its value for Arthurian studies did not escape Ritson.[4]

Other Arthurian material is used in the notes to Thomas Chestre's translation of the lai by Marie de France, *Launfal*. The name Marie de France had been given by Claude Fauchet, in his *Recueil* (1581) to the authoress of the *Fables*. The existence of the lais was noticed by Warton,[5] but their attribution to Marie was the work of Tyrwhitt.[6] The Abbé de la Rue contributed a *Dissertation on the Life and Writings of Mary, an Anglo-Norman Poetess of the 13th. Century* to the Society of Antiquaries on 12 January 1797. In this he surveyed all the known works, and identified 'le cunte Willame' as William Longsword, natural son of Henry II.[7] Ritson insisted on believing that 'Breton' signified not Armorica but Britain.[8] His evidence is drawn from the place names in the lais—*Kardoel* (*Lanval* 1.8) as Carlisle,[9] *Carwent* (*Yonec* 1.13) as *Venta Silurum*, Chepstow.[10] The identification of *Kardoel* with Carlisle is

[1] ibid., p. 232. He is combating Pinkerton's view that Arthur was Aurelius Ambrosius (Pinkerton's *Enquiry into the History of Scotland* (Edinburgh 1790), i. 76). See Ritson, *Life of King Arthur* (1825), pp. xli f, and A. B. Hopkins, 'Ritson's Life of King Arthur', *PMLA*, xliii (1928), 253–4.

[2] In a letter to Thomas Price, printed in Nicholas Owen, *British Remains* (1777), p. 84.

[3] Note to *Ywain*, l. 49. *Metrical Romanceës* (1802), iii. 235.

[4] Hopkins, op. cit., pp. 280, 284. It was also used by Leland, see T. D. Kendrick, *British Antiquity* (1950), p. 93.

[5] See pp. 113–14 above.   [6] Tyrwhitt's *Chaucer* (1775), iv. 165.

[7] De la Rue, *Archaeologia* (1800), xiii. 46. This is the view of Sir John Fox, see *Marie de France, Lais*, ed. A. Ewart (Oxford, 1947), pp. viii–ix.

[8] Note to *Emare*, l. 1030, *Metrical Romanceës* (1802), iii. *328. (Sheet Y in vol. iii has a leaf inserted before Y3, paged *327, *328.)

[9] *Metrical Romanceës* (1802), iii. 244.

[10] ibid., p. 331. Ewart, op. cit., identifies with Caerwent in Monmouthshire. Ritson, in the next paragraph, refers to Caerwent, the correct identification. Caerwent is four and a half miles wsw of Chepstow.

accepted by later scholars, and seems to have been arrived at by Ritson from Usher's *Britannicarum ecclesiarum antiquitates* and the entry under the year 1092 in the Saxon Chronicle.[1] Other Northern connections of the Arthurian story he derives from the references to Tarn Wadling in *The Awntyrs of Arthur* and in Percy's *The Marriage of Sir Gawaine*.[2] The other annotations to *Launfal* are mainly accounts of Merlin, Lancelot, Percival, Ban and Ryence, drawn from Malory and the French *Merlin* and *Lancelot*. There are also indications wherever the English text departs from Marie's original.

Material from the *Life of King Arthur* was used to provide one of the notes to *Libeaus Desconus*. Here, in a note to l.11, Ritson summarizes his views on the round-table, quoting Wace

> Fist Arthur la ronde table,
> Dunt Breton dient meinte fable.

as the first writer to mention it.[3] He did not discover Layamon's account of the origin of the round table, but quoted the accounts in Malory and the French prose *Merlin*, which described it as originally the property of Leodegrance, King of Kamelard, and made by Merlin in token of the roundness of the world, or in imitation of one made by Joseph of Arimathea in the form of that used at the Last Supper.

Ritson's reading in French romances was extensive, if we may judge by his quotations from them in the *Metrical Romanceës*. But he was equally widely read in all the literature that related to Arthur, and drew on this for many of his notes. The fruit of this reading he presented in his *Life of King Arthur*, finished just before his death,[4] but not published until 1825. In this he anticipated many of the conclusions of later scholars.[5] He successfully identified the Walter, Archdeacon of Oxford, from

---

[1] Hopkins, op. cit., p. 269.

[2] *Metrical Romanceës* (1802), iii. 244; *Life of King Arthur*, pp. 90 f.

[3] *Metrical Romanceës* (1802), iii. 255; *King Arthur*, pp. xvi f.

[4] Ritson, *Letters* (1833), ii. 238 (to Scott, 2 July 1803); ii. 247 (to Joseph Frank, 16 August 1803). Ellis, who saw the MS in 1804, told Scott that it contained 'very few anecdotes of Arthur'. Scott, *Letters*, xii. 258 n. He did, however, use, with acknowledgement, some of Ritson's material, in the Introduction to his *Specimens of Early English Metrical Romances*.

[5] For a thorough study, see A. B. Hopkins, 'Ritson's *Life of King Arthur*', *PMLA* xliii (1928), 251–87, to which I am indebted.

whom Geoffrey of Monmouth states that he received 'a certain most ancient book of the British language', as Walter Calenius, i.e. of Wallingford, and ended the tradition, derived from Leland, of identifying him with Walter Mapes.[1]

Ritson was prepared to believe in the possibility of a British source for Geoffrey, but not that any of the Welsh manuscripts of the *Historia* were earlier than Geoffrey's Chronicle. Some of the probable sources he did recognize—Caesar's *Commentaries*, Bede, Gildas, Nennius and Saints' legends.[2] Of the material in such legends, he used the *Life of Gildas*, referred to above, and also printed in an appendix the Arthurian anecdotes in a manuscript (Cotton, Vespasian A.xiv) containing lives of Welsh saints.[3] He discovered this manuscript, and dated it accurately (thirteenth century), but regarded the anecdotes as post-Geoffrey forgeries, instead of possibly independent evidence of the survival of Arthurian stories.

Ritson is equally in advance of all the scholars of his day, in refusing to recognize two Merlins—Ambrosius and Sylvestris. He was the first scholar to make use of a discovery which had been made by Edward Lhwyd, Evan Evans, John Leyden and John Whitaker. This was that the Romano-British leader Ambrosius Aurelianus, in the account of Gildas, had been confused with the sixth-century Welsh bard Myrddin, to produce Merlinus the prophet, Ambrosius Merlinus in Geoffrey of Monmouth. Merlin had thus become identified with this Myrddin-Ambrosius figure. From the confusion Giraldus Cambrensis[4] had extricated two Merlins—Ambrosius, author of the prophecies in Book VII of Geoffrey's *Historia*, and subject of the *Vita Merlini*, and Silvestris, sometimes called 'The Wild', author of the poems attributed to Myrddin.

In tracing the geography of Arthur's domains, Ritson used

[1] Hopkins, op. cit., p. 257. Ritson was preceded in this identification by Camden, White Kennet and Le Neve.

[2] *Life of King Arthur* (1825), p. xv.

[3] ibid., pp. 143 f. see W. J. Rees, *The Lives of the Cambro-British Saints* (1853), pp. 23 f, 97 f, 149 f, 158 f, 188 f. Hopkins, op. cit., p. 284. E. K. Chambers, *Arthur of Britain* (1927), pp. 243–9, prints the passages from the MS and discusses them at pp. 80–5.

[4] Hopkins, op. cit., pp. 262–3; *Life of King Arthur*, pp. xix n, ch. xiii, 'Of Ambrose Aurelian', pp. 47 f.; E. K. Chambers, op. cit., pp. 95–9.

all the available sources—Caradoc's *Life of Gildas*, Gildas, Nennius, Bede, the *Saxon Chronicle*, William of Malmesbury, Henry of Huntingdon, Leland and Dugdale—to establish that Cornwall and Somerset were traditionally associated with Arthur,[1] and Froissart, *Awntyrs of Arthur*, and *Launfal*, to establish the Karduel-Carlisle identification.[2] The Welsh *Triads* he regarded as later than Geoffrey, deriving his information from William Owen [-Pughe], *The Cambrian Biography* (1803).[3] The accounts of the discovery of Arthur's tomb at Glastonbury, by Giraldus Cambrensis and William of Malmesbury, are carefully examined, and the portions in William of Malmesbury's *De Antiquitate Glastoniensis Ecclesiae* which deal with the discovery are rightly suspected of being later interpolations.[4]

Ritson was also the first scholar to realize that the passage in Nennius (ch. 56) which mentions Arthur, has, in some texts, an interpolation which states that Arthur was called Mab Uter because he was cruel from his boyhood; the first to state that Geoffrey was responsible for making Arthur the son of Uther Pendragon; to explain Pendragon literally as 'dragon's head', and in its figurative use as 'leader' from the use of a dragon as a crest; and the first to interpret Mab Uther as meaning 'son of Uther'.[5] He was similarly the first to collect a number of references to the expectation of Arthur's return from Avalon.[6]

As a collection of documents which throw light on the historical problems connected with Arthurian study, the *Life of King Arthur* was far in advance of its time. Even when published in 1825, there were few scholars prepared for such a work, and by the time that similar studies were engaging the attention of medieval romance scholars, Ritson's book was forgotten. The chapters (xiv–xxvii) dealing with the birth, achievements, death and place of burial of Arthur, contain the first thoroughly documented discussion of most of the problems of Arthurian scholarship. Most of his sources were in manuscript, and those that were printed required to be checked and interpreted

---

[1] *Life of King Arthur*, ch. xiv, pp. 51 f., 78 f.

[2] ibid., ch. xxii, pp. 90 f.

[3] ibid., pp. 55 n, 59. He does quote on p. 107 from Harley MS 4181, a MS of the *Triads*.

[4] *Life of King Arthur*, pp. 85, 98 f., 126 f. E. K. Chambers, op. cit., pp. 112–27.

[5] *Life of King Arthur*, pp. 53–5.   [6] ibid., p. xxvi.

critically. For example, he could read Nennius in Thomas Gale's *Historiae Britannicae Scriptores* (1691), but, not content with this, he examined other manuscripts of the work, and noted the variants of the place-names[1] and the existence in some manuscripts of marginal references to Beulan and Samuel.[2]

The conscientiousness and attention to detail of Ritson's work here was to some extent spoilt by the method in which it was presented. Like all his publications it is full of acrimonious references to Percy, Pinkerton and Warton. It suffers also from an almost complete lack of connecting narrative. It failed to appeal to any reader. The early nineteenth century regarded it, along with the *Metrical Romanceës*, as a failure on account of its arid unreadableness. But later nineteenth-century scholars discussed as though for the first time the matters with which it dealt and unwittingly confirmed many of Ritson's conclusions.

The *Metrical Romanceës* were, says Scott, neglected.[3] The *British Critic* and the *Critical Review* gave no more than accounts of the contents and comments on Ritson's dullness. The latter admitted that romances illustrated the manners and customs of former times, and occasionally told interesting adventures, but condemned them for their improbability, their style and their immoral tales of unchastity, murder and robbery.[4] Scott failed even to review them in the *Edinburgh Review* until January 1806, when he made amends by praising Ritson's industry, fidelity to his sources, and wide knowledge, and he seized the opportunity to praise the romances also. *Ywain and Gawain* he thought 'the most interesting [romance] which now exists'; the study of the romances generally had taught us more of the domestic habits, language and character of our ancestors 'during the dark, warlike and romantic period of the middle ages', than Leland and Hearne could discover from 'monastic annals'. Ritson's achievement, without patronage, without public applause, was amply recognized by Scott. If we look elsewhere for enthusiasm we find it only in Southey, whose response to Ritson's *Romanceës* echoes that of Shenstone, Percy and Warton in the previous generation to the ballads in

[1] ibid., pp. 71 f. [2] ibid., p. 115.
[3] Reviewing Ritson and Ellis's *Specimens* in *Edinburgh Review*, vii (1806), 390.
[4] *British Critic*, xxiv (1804), 231–43; *Critical Review*, xxxix (1803), 179 f.

the *Reliques* and to the romances. They are 'a treasure of true old poetry', 'fine studies for a poet'; 'there has rarely, if ever, appeared in this country a publication so valuable to the antiquary, the philologist, and the poet'.[1] But Ritson was not to read the praise of either Southey or Scott. His life ended in madness and suicide on 23 September 1803. His three volumes of metrical romances have won the esteem of scholars and even today are not entirely superseded.

[1] *Annual Review*, ii (1803), 533, and C. Southey, *Life and Correspondence of R. Southey* (1850), ii. 203, 213. Southey's contributions to the *Annual Review* are preserved in the British Museum, 11824, w, 10.

CHAPTER VI

GEORGE ELLIS

> Others dug deeper for materials; but he alone gave vivacity to antiquities, and diffused those graces of literature and society, which were peculiarly his own, over the rudest remains of barbarism.
>
> *Gentleman's Magazine*, lxxxv (1815), 372

OF George Ellis (1753–1815) it was said that 'no man of his time better united the character of a gentleman and a man of letters'.[1] He was educated at Eton a generation earlier than two men who were later to be his friends, George Canning and John Hookham Frere. He came to antiquarian studies late in life, and until 1800 was better known for his light verses, *Bath; Its Beauties and Amusements* (1777) and *Poetical Tales of Gregory Gander* (1778), and for his contributions to the *Rolliad* and the *Anti-Jacobin*. He went on a diplomatic mission to The Hague, in 1784, and was member of Parliament for Seaford in 1796.[2] Until his death he remained active on the fringe of political life, but for a short period, until about 1805, his main energies were devoted to literary antiquarianism. Scott described him as

a wonderful man who through the life of a politician and statesman, conversing with princes, wits, fine ladies, and fine gentlemen, and acquainted with all the intrigues and tracasseries of the cabinets and ruelles of foreign courts has yet retained all warm and kindly feelings which render a man amiable in society and the darling of his friends.[3]

[1] *Gentleman's Magazine*, lxxxv (1815), 371.

[2] In addition, Ellis was a member of the club founded by Johnson, being elected in 1801. He was a Fellow both of the Royal Society and of the Society of Antiquaries. He reviewed in the *Edinburgh* and *Quarterly Reviews*, especially Scott and Byron. As a member of the Alfred Club he was known to Byron (see Byron, *Works*, ed. R. E. Prothero, ii (1898), 86 n, 322). In 1802 he married the daughter of Sir Peter Parker.

[3] Scott, *Letters*, iii. 60–1.

In personality and in his background of affluence and polite society Ellis could hardly present a greater contrast with Ritson. Yet both men shared a deep attachment to 'poetical archaeology', and worked in the same field of medieval romance and poetry. To Ritson, Ellis must have seemed much as he did to the professional writer, Southey, 'a little too much of the air of high life, a little too much of the conversationalist, eyes too small, a face too long, and something in his manner which showed, or seemed to show, that it was a condescension in him to be a man of letters.'[1]

Like the other scholars, he began as a practising poet, and as the witty originator of the *Rolliad* and contributor to the *Anti-Jacobin* is assured of a place in the history of parody and burlesque.[2]

His first venture into the history of poetry was an anthology of 'all the most beautiful small poems that had been published in this country during the sixteenth and seventeenth centuries'.[3] This collection, from Wyatt to Dryden, offers a combination of poetic commonplace book and history of lyric poetry. In the preface Ellis noted that he had adopted modern orthography, and occasionally omitted passages from the poems. As a specimen of book production, it is a handsome volume. Ellis aimed to win readers for the poems. But the 'mutilation' of some of the texts was not universally approved. Sir Egerton Brydges, for example, complained of Ellis's attitude to the texts.[4] Ellis, however, was under no illusion about the nature of his audience. 'A library is like a butcher's shop', he wrote to Scott, 'it contains plenty of meat, but it is all raw; no person living . . . can find a meal in it'. The editor is like a good cook who says, 'Sir, I see by your looks that you are hungry; I know your taste—be patient for a moment, and you shall be satisfied that you have an excellent appetite'.[5] Thus Ellis approved of Scott's

[1] J. W. Robberds, *Memoir of William Taylor* (1843), ii. 131. Southey had been attacked in the *Anti-Jacobin*. Ritson's politics were all that Ellis hated.

[2] See G. Kitchin, *Survey of Burlesque and Parody in English* (Edinburgh, 1931), pp. 12, 143–8, 176–93; O. E. Holloway, 'George Ellis, *The Anti-Jacobin* and the *Quarterly Review*', *R.E.S.* x (1934), 58 f.

[3] *Specimens of the Early English Poets* (1790), p. i.

[4] In his edition of Edward Phillips, *Theatrum Poetarum Anglicanorum* (Canterbury, 1800), p. lxxii.

[5] Quoted in Lockhart, *Life of Scott*, ch. xiv.

'improvements' in the *Border Minstrelsy*.[1] He advised Scott, when editing Dryden, to suppress 'whatever is in point of expression vulgar—whatever disgusts the taste—whatever might have been written by any fool, and is therefore unworthy of Dryden'. For Wordsworth 'a correct text is the first object of an editor'; Ellis would have agreed, but he did not consider a complete text necessary for an 'editor who should be disposed to make an appeal to the public taste'.[2] He knew the taste of his audience. He 'alone gave vivacity to antiquities'; his contemporaries found him 'a critic of most elegant taste, and a man whose sagacity is as uncommon, as his knowledge is various'.[3]

This early volume of *Specimens* was, in 1801, expanded to three volumes.[4] In its enlarged form it is an anthology based on Warton's *History*, aiming to exhibit, by means of specimens, the rise and progress of the English language and poetry from the tenth to the seventeenth centuries. Over a third of the work is taken up by an introduction which recounts as a connected narrative the history of poetry from the Anglo-Saxons to Skelton, David Lindsay and John Heywood, including the Scottish Chaucerians. Accounts of, and extracts from, twenty-five poets are given, with critical and biographical commentary. Anglo-Saxon poetry is represented by *The Battle of Brunanburgh*, which is given in the original, in a literal translation, and in a version in Middle English composed by Frere. It is followed by an account of Norman poets in England, Wace's *Brut*, Gaimar, Benoit and Samson de Nanteuil, drawn from articles by l'Abbé Gervais de la Rue.[5] Ellis thought that a copious selection from these poets was worth publishing, for the details to be found there of medieval dress, customs, occupations, arts and learning.

Ellis found Layamon's *Brut* (c. 1185) interesting because it seemed to him to illustrate the curious mingling of Saxon and

---

[1] Scott, *Letters*, i. 137 n. Anna Seward also approved (ibid., p. 145).

[2] Lockhart, ch. xiv.   [3] *The British Critic*, xxiv (1804), 234.

[4] It was reprinted in 1803, 1811, 1845, and 1851.

[5] *Archaeologia*, xii (1796), 50–79 (Wace); 297–326 (Samson, Gaimar, etc.); xiii (1800), 230–250 (Samson, etc.); 35–67 (Marie de France). de la Rue (1751–1835) was later Professor of History in the University of Caen. He took refuge in England during the French Revolution. His chief work is *Essais Historiques sur les Bardes, les Jongleurs, et les Trouveurs normands et anglo-normands*, 3 vols., 1834. See Scott, *Letters*, xii, 430.

Norman which produced the English language. He could not imagine that it would ever be printed in full, but quoted extracts in the orthography of the manuscript, to show the 'rudeness' of the language at that time.[1] One poem which attracted him was the thirteenth-century *The Land of Cockayne*. It is humorous and satiric, like Ellis's own poems, and was admired for its 'elegance' and 'refined irony'. Ellis printed it in full. He saw the intermingling of Saxon and Norman as completed by about 1216, and the English language as developing steadily until the fourteenth century, with ecclesiastics writing chronicles and lives of saints, and minstrels composing love songs and satires. But after 1300 he detected a new influx of French words, the result, he thought, of a hasty series of translations by both clerics and minstrels, of French romances. Ellis's view of the English minstrels is drawn from Percy, and he also considered that they were descended from the scalds, but patronized, while French was in the ascendancy at court, by rich English merchants. Thus the English imitated the Norman barons, and 'laid the foundation of a native minstrelsy on the French model'.[2] The romances, derived from Geoffrey of Monmouth, the Pseudo-Turpin Chronicle, Benoit's story of Troy, and the medieval Alexander legends, are briefly described, with lengthy extracts from 'Davy's' *Alisaunder* and the *Sqyr of Lowe Degre*. *King Horn*, which he had intended to print in full, was held back in deference to Ritson's proposed edition.[3] The rest of the introduction describes the poetry of Minot, Langland, Chaucer, Gower, Lydgate, the Scottish Chaucerians, and ends with Skelton and Lindsay. It draws heavily on Warton and Tyrwhitt, but presents the information in a more attractive form and style. Southey thought it contained more 'pertinent matter' than Warton's *History*.[4]

The revised *Specimens* were welcomed by Scott as

a work, to which our predecessors and our posterity are alike obliged; the former for the preservation of the best selected examples of their poetical taste; and the latter, for a history of the English

---

[1] *Specimens of the Early English Poets* (1801), i. 61–73. The transcript was made by Douce (B.M. Add. MS 28099, f. 18).
[2] *Specimens* (1801), i. 130.   [3] ibid., i. 106 n.
[4] *Annual Review*, ii (1804), 538.

language, which will only cease to be interesting with the existence of our mother-tongue, and all that genius and learning have recorded in it.[1]

They established Ellis as 'the hope of poetic archaeology',[2] and the welcome given to them showed, thought Scott, that 'good taste & learning' were still 'struggling amid the inundations of German *anomalies* with which we have been lately overwhelmed'.[3] Ellis himself reported that his work had diffused a taste 'or at least an affectation of taste' for 'literary antiquity'. His aim was 'to make it a really useful assistant to young Poets by diffusing among them just and rational opinions about the merit of their ancestors'.[4]

The romances, at this time the centre of attraction for the scholars, were reserved for a volume of abstracts which Ellis intended to publish. The idea of this method of presenting the texts to a wider audience than Ritson could hope to reach grew while he was working with Gregory Lewis Way[5] on two volumes of verse translations of *Fabliaux or Tales* (1796, 1800). Way had selected his fabliaux from a collection published in 1779 and 1781 by Pierre-Jean-Baptiste Le Grand D'Aussy,[6] and had translated them into verse, adopting the general cast of his diction from the Authorized Version of the Bible and from Spenser.[7] By making the stories attractive to modern readers, by giving them all the 'graces of language and versification' which in the original they lacked, Way hoped to extend the audience for medieval literature. He had intended to print Lydgate's *Lay of the Little Bird*, to illustrate 'that it was impossible to adopt, in a publication intended for readers of the present day,

[1] *Minstrelsy of the Scottish Border* (Edinburgh, 1806), iii. 213–14.
[2] *Critical Review*, iii (1804), 51.   [3] Scott, *Letters*, xii. 187.
[4] National Library of Scotland, MS 873, f. 11ᵛ: (Ellis to Scott, 18 July 1801). By 15 September 1801 about 600 copies had been sold and a second edition planned (ibid., f. 22ᵛ).
[5] G. L. Way (1756–99). For biographical information, see *Notes and Queries*, Series ix, ix. 195, and *Fabliaux or Tales* (1800), ii. 292–6.
[6] *Fabliaux ou Contes du xiiᵉ et du xiiiᵉ siècles*, 3 vols. (Paris, 1779); *Contes dévots, Fables et Romans anciens* (Paris, 1781). In 1795 Le Grand became keeper of manuscripts in the Bibliothèque Nationale. See *Nouvelle Biographie Générale* (Paris, 1859), xix. 429–30.
[7] *Fabliaux or Tales* (1796, 1800), i. p.v, ii. 292. William Stewart Rose modelled his metrical version of Book I of *Amadis of Gaul* (1803) on Way's *Fabliaux*.

a phraseology so very obsolete as that of Lydgate'.[1] But Ellis substituted the text of *Launfal*, from Cotton Caligula A II as more 'amusing' in itself and just as obsolete in language. The difficulties of Middle English were well exemplified; Charles Burney, in the *Monthly Review*, agreed that *Launfal* was '*too far gone* to be read with pleasure', though he added that, if it were modernized in the style of Dryden in the *Fables*, it would be a valuable present to lovers of 'our old national poetry'.[2]

Way's two volumes of *Fabliaux* are still a collector's piece, with their vignettes by Thomas and John Bewick of twelfth- and thirteenth-century costumes.[3] Mrs Scott thought them 'the most elegant and amusing present she ever received',[4] and Scott himself regarded the translations as almost worthy of Dryden. The stories included *Aucassin and Nicolette, Lanval, Gruélan, Gugemar, The Land of Cokaigne, Hueline and Eglantine*, and *The Countess of Vergy*. The attraction of the stories themselves did not depend on the beauty of presentation, however. Before Way's version appeared, a selection in English prose, *Tales of the Twelfth and Thirteenth Centuries*, was published in 1786, reprinted as *Norman Tales* in 1789, and again as *Tales of the Minstrels* in an undated 'fourth' edition. Some of these tales were adapted for the stage as farces. For example Stephen Storace's musical farce, *No Song, No Supper* was adapted from *The Poor Scholar*.[5] Way showed how the material of the middle ages could be used by the serious poet.

The notes and introduction to Way's volumes were provided by Ellis. Here he described the rise and fall of chivalry, and gave information about armour, weapons, shields, helmets, castle architecture, costume, social classes, courts of love, judicial combats, and the knights of the Round Table. For his information he drew on Malory (in the 1634 edition), Froissart, Aaron Thompson's translation of Geoffrey of Monmouth (1718), Evan Evans's *Dissertatio de Bardis* and *Specimens of the Poetry*

---

[1] ibid., ii. 296–7.   [2] *Monthly Review*, xxxvi (1801), 278.

[3] *Fabliaux or Tales*, vol. i, 1796, vol. ii, 1800; reprinted 1815. Reviewed in *Critical Review*, xxx (1800), 413–17; *Monthly Magazine*, x (1801), 609; *Monthly Review*, xxiii (1797), 174–6 (by William Taylor), xxxvi (1801), 276–8 (by Charles Burney).

[4] Scott, *Letters*, xii. 166.

[5] See the preface to *Tales of the Minstrels* (n.d.).

of the Ancient Welsh Bards (1764), Edward Jones's *Musical and Poetical Relics of the Welsh Bards* (1784, 1794) and William Owen's notes to his edition of the poems of Dafydd ap Gwilym (1789). Ellis's notes were the most attractive part of the work for Scott, not simply for their wealth of information, but also for their 'lightness and elegance'. As annotation they formed the ideal to which Scott tried to approximate in his own works. When praising the notes that Rose provided to *Amadis* (1803) Scott compared them with those of Ellis.[1] Scott's praise of Ellis as 'the purest & most classical of our modern English writers'[2] is repeated in the obituary notice in *The Gentleman's Magazine* (perhaps by Scott himself) where the preface and notes to Way's *Fabliaux* are said to contain 'some of the purest and most classical passages of Addisonian composition which this age has produced'.[3]

In preparing the second volume of Way's *Fabliaux* for the press,[4] Ellis's interest in the romances and the possibilities of finding a wider audience for them, developed rapidly. Among Way's papers were some metrical translations of the verses quoted by de Tressan in his *Corps d'Extraits de Romans de Chevalerie*. De Tressan had given prose abstracts of many medieval romances, occasionally quoting in the midst of an abstract some of 'those natural and simple passages' of his original.[5] Way had intended to give metrical translations of the shortest of de Tressan's abstracts, and had begun by versifying some of the passages of Old French poetry from the originals introduced by de Tressan in *Tristan* and *Floris*. Ellis printed these,[6] with brief synopses of the stories. He commented on de Tressan's method of presenting the romances:

By thus happily contrasting the elegance and perspicuity of modern language with the quaint simplicity of the *Norman Romance*, he has been able to give such variety to his style, that the attention of the reader is kept awake through a series of events often disgusting by their improbability, tiresome by their sameness and by their number,

---

[1] *Edinburgh Review*, iii (1803), 136.   [2] Scott, *Letters*, xii. 252.
[3] *Gentleman's Magazine*, lxxxv (1815), 372.
[4] Way died in 1799.
[5] *Fabliaux* (1800), ii. 273. See Louis Elisabeth de la Vergne, Comte de Tressan (1705–83), *Oeuvres Choisies*, 12 vols. (Paris, 1787).
[6] *Fabliaux* (1800), ii. 274–86.

GEORGE ELLIS

and so unconnected as to bid defiance to all the resources of method and arrangement.[1]

In a letter to Francis Douce he described his intended work as 'similar to that of M. de Tressan', that is 'a faithful abstract of the fables . . . with extracts from the metrical originals: selecting such extracts either on account of their poetical merit, or their singularity of expression, or their allusion to ancient manners and customs'.[2] Here then was the origin of Ellis's treatment of English romances in his *Specimens of Early English Metrical Romances* (1805), the work that earned for him the title of 'the Tressan of England', as his account of chivalry in Way's *Fabliaux* earned him the title 'the Sainte-Palaye of England'.[3] Both Ellis and de Tressan were men of rank and fashion, whose styles were formed by reading the best books and frequenting the best company. In undertaking to rewrite the romances for a modern sophisticated audience neither was able to suppress his sense of what was ludicrous in them. Both had the gift of enlivening the dull or absurd details of the romances by presenting them with vigour and wit.[4]

Ellis's work on the abstracts of romances was delayed for a time by the assistance which he gave to Thomas Park in preparing an edition of *Kyng Alisaunder* from the Laud MS. In July 1801 Park was busy compiling a glossary from the notes provided by Ellis and Douce.[5] Douce (1757–1834) was a wealthy and erudite amateur scholar, with a large collection of books and manuscripts which he generously allowed his friends to use. He was 'a perfect gentleman of the old school', reserved at first, but 'easy, affable and kind'.[6] In scholarship he was not easily satisfied, but he watched Ellis's progress with delight and praised the work on the glossary of *Alisaunder* as showing Ellis's 'wonted and miraculous industry'. Scott offered to send a transcript of the single leaf of the poem in the

---

[1] ibid., 273–4.
[2] Ellis to Douce, 29 January 1801, Bodley MS Douce d. 34, f. 3ᵛ.
[3] *Gentleman's Magazine*, lxxxv (1815), 372.
[4] Scott, *Edinburgh Review*, vii (1806), 412.
[5] National Library of Scotland, MS 873, f. 11.
[6] *Gentleman's Magazine*, August 1834, p. 215. For Douce see *Bodleian Quarterly Record*, Nos. 74, 75, 81.

Auchinleck MS[1] for Park's use. But, like many of Park's projects, the edition of *Alisaunder* came to nothing. He was deterred from printing by the failure of Ritson's *Metrical Romanceës*.[2]

Before we consider Ellis's major contribution to Romance scholarship, however, there is one other activity of his that claims attention. This was his encouragement of William Owen (later Owen-Pughe) in the preparation of a translation of the *Mabinogion*. Percy had been interested in Welsh stories of Arthur, but what he had gleaned from Evan Evans about them had not inspired him to pursue the subject. Since they were in prose, Percy assumed they must be later than English metrical romances. To English scholars of the time, the difficulty of the Welsh language proved an insuperable barrier, and they had no means of disproving the patriotic claims of Welsh scholars that Welsh literature existed which had been written in the sixth century. Only Sharon Turner, who had learned Welsh, was prepared to support them.[3] In order to win acceptance for the authenticity of the *Mabinogion* and encourage support for an English edition, it was essential to gain the confidence of English scholars.

Owen was the sort of scholar who inspired such confidence. He had edited the poems of Dafydd ap Gwilym, edited and translated Llywarch Hên (1792), edited the first 'learned' Welsh periodical, *The Cambrian Register* (1796, 1799, 1818), edited the texts of early Welsh literature in the *Myvyrian Archaiology* (1801–7), compiled a biographical dictionary of Welsh authors and characters, *The Cambrian Biography* (1803), and a Welsh Dictionary (1803). He called attention to the *Mabinogion* and his intended translation in a paper to the Society of Antiquaries in January 1802, representing it as the earliest romance-writing in Europe.[4] In July Scott wrote to him for information about the Bardic tradition concerning Tristram, and the ensuing correspondence resulted in Owen's being introduced to Leyden, Ellis and Heber.[5] At the same time Southey

[1] Scott, *Letters*, xii. 189.
[2] National Library of Scotland MS 873, f. 74ᵛ.
[3] Sharon Turner, *Vindication of the Genuineness of the Ancient British Poems* (1803).
[4] *Archaeologia*, xiv (1803), 219.
[5] For an account of Owen and the *Mabinogion* see the present writer's article in *National Library of Wales Journal*, x (1958), 323–8.

and Coleridge were preparing to learn Welsh in order to co-
operate with Sharon Turner and Owen on the history of Welsh
literature for the proposed *Bibliotheca Britannica*.[1] Ellis (who also
began to learn Welsh), Scott and Southey were excited by the
prospect of an authentic version of the *Mabinogion*.[2] Already
they had a foretaste in the translation of the first part of *Pwyll*
in the *Cambrian Register* for 1795. Ellis saw some of the work in
manuscript, and suggested that, to ensure its success with the
public, it would be necessary to adopt 'a less servile mode of
translation; to remove carefully all the obscurities; and to
render the whole ... easy and flowing in point of stile'. He
predicted that the stories would be as popular as the *Arabian
Nights*, or as Macpherson's Ossian.[3] Douce was persuaded of the
authenticity of the tales 'being unable to resist the strong
internal evidence', and Southey wrote to John Rickmann,
Coleridge, Williams Wynn and William Taylor about the
'Three parts of the Mabinogion' that he had read.[4] Ellis
offered to write a preface and to advise on the presentation of
the finished book; Southey was ready to help Sharon Turner
correct Owen's grammar. Ellis was excited by the 'Asiatic'
quality of the tales, and thought that these were the prototypes
that the Normans tried to imitate in their romances; Southey
thought they were so unlike all other romances that so far from
explaining the origin of romance, they simply posed another
problem.

For the solving of problems connected with Arthurian romance, the tales were regarded as vital. Ritson had turned to
Owen's *Cambrian Biography* for information about the *Triads*,[5]
but in general he distrusted Welsh scholars. One piece of information about Arthur in that work he quickly demolished. This
was the account of the mythological and historical Arthurs.
The former Owen described as son of Uther Bendragon (or

[1] Southey, *Life and Correspondence*, ed. C. C. Southey (1850), ii. 218, 222.

[2] See Southey in *Annual Review*, ii (1803), 523.

[3] National Library of Wales, MS 13221, p. 163 (Ellis to Owen, 31 March 1803);
Nat. Lib. Wales MS 13223, p. 909 (Ellis to Owen, 4 March 1804).

[4] National Library of Scotland, MS 873, f. 61; Southey, *Life*, ed. C. C. Southey
(1850), ii. 289, 293, and *Letters*, ed. J. W. Warter (1856), i. 278; Robberds, *Memoir
of William Taylor* (1843), i. 511; ii. 130, 198.

[5] Ritson, *Life of King Arthur* (1825), pp. 55 n, 58–9, 83 n.

'Wonder the supreme leader') and Eigyr ('the generating power'). This figure, called Arcturus, the Great Bear, the pro-prietor of the constellation Lyra, Owen found 'obscurely figured' in *Culhwch and Olwen*, a story which he thought had a common origin with that of Hercules and the Argonauts. The quest for a common origin for all myths, which attracted Jacob Bryant, Edward Davies and William Blake, led Owen to con-jecture that Olwen represented the fecundity of nature, while the Menw of the Culhwch story he associated with the character of that name in Indian mythology.[1] Ellis put forward these views tentatively in his *Specimens of Romances*, but cautiously waited until Owen should publish *Culhwch* before accepting them.

This type of speculation, in more elaborate forms, fills Edward Davies's *Celtic Researches* of 1804, and was used by Blake as the basis of his account of the picture of the Ancient Britons.[2] Davies, in *The Mythology and Rites of British Druids* (1809), even gave an account of the Auchinleck *Tristrem* in terms of Druidism. Ellis was partly carried away by such speculations, and was almost persuaded by Owen's version of *Manawydan* that the 'style and turn of adventure' was so truly 'Asiatic' that speculations about the Asiatic origins of the Britons were not entirely without foundation.[3]

The co-operation between Owen and Ellis, and the encouragement of Scott, Southey and Sharon Turner, which would have produced a translation of the *Mabinogion* thirty years before Lady Charlotte Guest's, came to nothing. Scott was anxious that Owen should be kept to 'something that is rational—I mean to *iron horses*, and *magic cauldrons*, and *Bran the Blessed* . . . to something more pleasing and profitable than old apophthegms, triads, and "blessed burdens of the womb of the

[1] See *Cambrian Biography* (1803), pp. 15 f. cf. Ellis, *Specimens of Romances* (1805), i. 97–100 and Warton, *History* (1824), i. (83) n.; Scott, *Letters*, i. 166 n.

[2] Ellis praised Davies's *Celtic Researches* (Scott, *Letters*, xii. 248). Blake's rough translation of the Welsh triad on which he based his paintings was probably obtained from Owen (Blake, *Descriptive Catalogue of Pictures* (1809), No. iv). The triad, on the three Britons who escaped from the battle of Camlan, was first printed in translation in *The Cambro-Briton*, ii. (1821), 385. On the mingling of Celtic and Hindu mythology, see *Cambro-Briton*, i. 128; ii. 389; iii. 269, and for Blake's use of it, see D. Saurat, *Blake and Modern Thought* (1929), pp. 56 f.

[3] Ellis to Owen, 4 March [1804], Nat. Lib. of Wales MS 13223, p. 909.

isle of Britain"'.[1] But, though Owen had translated *Pwyll*, *Branwen*, *Manawydan* and *Math* by November 1805, and later completed the other contents of the Red Book of Hergest, the translation was never printed.[2] Until 1816 his attention was occupied by the management of his inherited estates in Wales, and by his activities as one of the Elders of Joanna Southcote. The excitement which Ellis predicted in 1803 was eventually aroused in 1839 when Lady Guest's version began to appear, in such a style as Ellis would have approved. What was known of the *Mabinogion*, however, in 1803, gave greater hopes of attracting public interest to the romances than any other text.

While the work on the *Mabinogion* was progressing fitfully, Ellis began to transcribe manuscripts of romances for his volume of abstracts. So far he had not ventured far 'into the land of MSS. & of unexplored authorities',[3] and in January 1801 he began by experimenting with *Sir Triamour*,[4] using Copland's edition that had been in Garrick's collection. How he planned to make the romances interesting may be seen in a short extract. Quoting a stanza in which Aradas, King of Arragon, makes a vow to go to the Holy Land in order to encourage Heaven to give him an heir, Ellis continues

This sudden and unexpected resolution, when communicated to the queen, filled her with horror and dismay. Though not less anxious than her husband for the completion of their mutual wishes, she doubted the efficacy of the means: her piety suggested to her, that Heaven might possibly be irritated by a vow evidently dictated by impatience; and her affection represented in frightful colours the dangers to which Aradas would be exposed, while employed in slaughtering the crowds of Saracens whose death might be required as the purchase of an heir to the crown of Arragon. But neither the length of the voyage, the hazards of the sea, the dangers of an

[1] Scott, *Letters*, i. 203. The 'blessed burdens' Scott remembered from Owen's *Llywarch Hên* (1792), p. xi n.

[2] Some pieces did appear in periodicals, and the manuscript was used by T. Crofton Croker for his *Fairy Tales and Legends of the South of Ireland* (1827) and by W. Gunn for his edition of *Nennius' Historia Brittonum* (1819). The manuscript is now Nat. Lib. of Wales MSS 13242–4.

[3] Scott, *Letters*, xii. 199.

[4] Ellis to Douce, 29 January 1801, in Bodley, Douce MS d. 34, f. 3ᵛ.

ungenial climate, nor the multitude and ferocity of the un-
believers, could arrest for a moment the impetuosity of the king:
he assumed the cross, assembled an army, and was soon ready to
depart.[1]

This, from *Sir Triamour*, was submitted to Francis Douce, who
approved it, provided that Ellis used 'the old metal without
adulteration', that is, without the sort of embroidery that de
Tressan added. One might have thought that here was embroidery enough, since almost the whole of this paragraph is
Ellis's amused invention of details to fill out his bare original.
But Douce was satisfied; 'any new arrangement of the legends
on this sort of coin, may be entirely at your own discretion',
he wrote, 'and it will issue from your mint with additional
beauty of impression'.[2]

In selecting romances to re-tell, Ellis excluded those edited
by Ritson, and relied to a great extent on texts provided by
Douce and Scott.[3] In addition to lending manuscripts and
books, Douce wrote an analysis of *Alphonsus de Clericali Dis-
ciplina*, a collection of Eastern stories of the early twelfth century,
which Ellis printed in an appendix. The romance of *Sir Eger*,
which Ellis himself analysed, had been known only in the
inaccessible Percy Folio MS. But in September 1801 Douce
bought a printed copy and at once lent it to Ellis. The latter
immediately set his future wife to transcribe it for Scott.[4] A
common interest in the romances drew these three scholars, of
different ages and backgrounds, together, and their co-operation was marked by generosity. Before he began to corre-
spond with Scott in March 1801, Ellis intended to include
an abstract, with copious quotations, of the Auchinleck

[1] *Specimens of Romances* (1805), iii. 177.
[2] Douce to Ellis, 1 February 1801, in B.M. Add. MS 28099, f. 30ᵛ.
[3] From Douce he borrowed four MSS—*Arthur and Merlin* (Douce MS 236, early
fifteenth century); *Richard Coeur de Lyon* (Douce MS 228); *The Sowdone of Babylone*
(called by Ellis *Sir Ferumbras*, Douce MS 175, a transcript by George Steevens of a MS
owned by Farmer and later by Phillipps and J. E. A. Fenwick); and *Amys and
Amiloun* (Douce MS 326, once owned by Samuel Pegge); and three printed
texts— *Sir Eger* (1711), *Roswall and Lillian* (n.d.) and *Bevis* (Pynson, n.d. S.T.C.
1988).
[4] Scott, *Letters*, xii. 196. The MS is now in the Abbotsford collection. See J. G.
Cochrane, *Catalogue of the Library at Abbotsford* (Edinburgh, 1838), p. 103.

Tristrem[1], but Scott's eagerness that it should first appear in Edinburgh as the earliest piece of 'Scottish' poetry to be reprinted, led him to resign this text to his new friend.

The friendship with Scott blossomed rapidly and within a few weeks Scott was sending transcripts from the Auchinleck manuscript. John Leyden, under Scott's supervision at first, transcribed *Arthur and Merlin, Guy, Richard, Roland and Vernagu, Otuel*[2], *The Seven Wise Masters, Floris and Blanchefleur* and *Lai le Freine*, all of which were used by Ellis. The Auchinleck *Guy* and *Bevis* interested Ellis as 'if not the very originals to which Chaucer alludes [i.e. in *Sir Thopas*], at least unadulterated versions of the same period'.[3] A strongly supported modern view that Chaucer did in fact know the Auchinleck manuscript[4] would have delighted him.

Another discovery that Ellis and Scott between them were on the verge of making, concerns the Auchinleck *Roland and Vernagu* and the Fillingham manuscript of *Otuel and Roland*. Ellis used both, and was the only scholar to use the Fillingham manuscript, until it was acquired by the British Museum in 1907.[5] Ellis had intended to include in the *Specimens* an abstract of the Pseudo-Turpin Chronicle, so often referred to by romance scholars but not easily available to their readers. Scott discovered that the Auchinleck *Roland* 'was a versified edition of a chapter of Turpin's chronicle entitled de bello Ferracuti giganti. . . . The Latin version and the poem resemble each other even in the minute particulars', and added that Otuel was referred to in Turpin. Ellis, having abstracted both romances from the two manuscripts, realized that he had in fact provided a version of the Pseudo-Turpin Chronicle, with a long account of Otuel in the middle.[6] Modern scholarship has

---

[1] Ellis to Douce, 29 January 1801, in Bodley Douce MS d. 34, f. 3ᵛ. Douce to Ellis, 1 February 1801, in B.M. Add. MS 28099, f. 30ᵛ.

[2] Leyden's transcript of Otuel is now Douce MS 376.

[3] Nat. Lib. of Scotland MS 873, f. 20 (Ellis to Scott, 2 October 1801).

[4] See L. H. Loomis, 'Chaucer and the Auchinleck MS', in *Essays in Honor of Carleton Brown* (New York, 1940), pp. 111–28.

[5] It is now Add. MS 37492, see *Firumbras and Otuel and Roland*, ed. M. I. O'Sullivan, E.E.T.S. O.S. 198 (1935), pp. xi–xiii.

[6] Scott, *Letters*, xii. 202, 206 n., 207; Ellis, *Specimens of Romances* (1805), ii. 291, 313, 356.

confirmed this,[1] though Ellis's anticipation of the discovery has not hitherto been noticed.

Scott poured information into Ellis's *Specimens*. He provided the material in Ellis's introduction to *Richard Coeur de Lion* on the satanic properties of Richard's mother from Gervase of Tilbury and Fordun's *Scotichronicon*,[2] and also the meaning of 'Dissawar', the name assumed by Roswal, which he found in David Macpherson's edition of Wynton's *Chronicle* (1795).[3] The Northern localities associated with Arthur were described by Scott in various letters, and many more texts offered than Ellis could use. Ellis, at the same time, gave considerable assistance with the edition of *Sir Tristrem*. It was, as Scott described it, 'even as iron sharpeneth iron'.[4]

Ellis did not depend solely on Scott and Douce. He also used books and manuscripts in the British Museum, Lincoln's Inn Library, and at Caius College, Cambridge.[5] The resulting three volumes were intended as a more detailed treatment of the progress of our language and poetry in the late thirteenth and early fourteenth centuries. In the long introduction Ellis traced the rise and progress of romantic composition in France and England, laying before his readers his 'whole stock of materials'. This is the most masterly survey of the subject. He uses all that previous scholars had contributed to the discussion, with a fine power of selection and clarity of presentation. Unable to avoid the topic of theories of origin of romance, he reasonably suggests that many scenes and characters were borrowed from the Bretons or the Welsh, some of the colouring and some of the adventures from the Scandinavians, and occasional episodes and machinery from the East. But he also wished to believe that romances originated in the reworking of Celtic material by Anglo-Norman and English poets—by

[1] H. M. Smyser, '*Charlemagne and Roland* and the Auchinleck MS', *Speculum* xxi (1946), 275 f. and R. N. Walpole, 'The Source MS of *Charlemagne and Roland* and the Auchinleck Bookshop', *Modern Language Notes*, lx (1945), 22–6.

[2] Scott, *Letters*, xii. 221–7, 234; Ellis, *Specimens*, ii. 176–9.

[3] Scott, xii. 219; Ellis (1811), iii. 386 n (not in first edition).

[4] Scott, *Letters*, i. 115. Canto V of *Marmion* is addressed to Ellis, who was also privileged to hear the beginning of the *Lay of the Last Minstrel* (Lockhart, ch. xi).

[5] For texts of *Arthur and Merlin*, *Le Morte Arthur*, *Ipomydon*, *Roberd of Cicyle*, *The Seven Wise Masters*, *Bevis*, *Richard*, *Isumbras*, *Eglamore*, *Degare*, *Triamore* and Marie's *Lais*.

Anglo-Norman poets for the English court (which is a reasonable supposition if one does not think of such romances as the 'first'), and by English poets for Scottish barons (which is fantastic).

In his introduction Ellis undertakes to demonstrate the reasonableness of this position. He begins with a survey of the development of the Romance language. Using the evidence collected by Ritson and de la Rue, he shows that the 'Romance of the year 842, which very nearly resembled the present Provençal, was the general language of France, and not a southern dialect',[1] that the lack of 'an easy and constant intercourse' between the various departments of France, after the Danish invasions of 845, produced a variety of dialects,[2] and that Norman French was not employed as a written language till very near the time of the Conquest.[3] From the available information these are just conclusions. With equal justice Ellis concludes that Anglo-Norman literature, before the middle of the twelfth century, was mainly metrical lives of saints, scientific treatises, chronicles, devotional and moral tracts, war songs (the *Chanson de Roland*), satirical songs, encomiastic songs, and historical ballads.[4]

But it may be safely affirmed, that no trace of a professed work of fiction; no semblance of an epic fable; in short, no specimen of what we should now call a romance, is to be found before the middle of the twelfth century; indeed, this period might, perhaps, be still further extended.[5]

Ellis admits that many works may now be lost. These may only have been current in the repertoires of the minstrels, who were generally considered to be the authors of the earliest fictions. Here Ellis follows Percy in thinking it probable that the Normans brought with them from Denmark their 'domestic bards'.[6] The skill in poetry of these entertainers must be presumed to have declined, when they were forced to use the undeveloped language of Romance, and only to have revived again after the Crusades. With the beginning of these expeditions, the clergy found themselves 'interested in opening to the

[1] *Specimens of Romances*, i. 4.　　　[2] ibid., i. 6.
[3] ibid., i. 12.　　　　　　　　　　　[4] ibid., i. 12–13.
[5] ibid., i. 14.　　　　　　　　　　　[6] ibid., i. 16.

illiterate, through the medium of the vulgar tongue, those stores of literature to which they alone had access'[1], as a means of exciting a spirit of enthusiasm. Thus Ellis is led by a series of rational conjectures, to conclude that the earliest works of fiction were the invention of the clergy, and not of the minstrels, since fiction is 'a species of composition which may be termed the luxury of literature, usually growing out of and indicating a large previous stock of necessary and useful learning'.[2]

The view that fiction is the 'luxury of literature' stems from the assumptions (made, for example, by Huet, Caylus, and Percy, as well as Ellis) about primitive societies—that the necessity of providing the bare requirements of life would leave little leisure, that such an economy would support few 'entertainers', and that these few would be required to record the 'history' of the tribe. Huet, as we have seen,[3] explained the transmission of romantic fabling in terms of the development of pleasure-loving societies. The truly primitive society, theorizers about the origin of romance assumed, would be interested only in the recording of fact. Once the art of writing had been invented, facts could be more permanently recorded, and poets would have leisure for invention. In holding such views, neither Huet nor Ellis was deterred by the absence of early written records of pure fact, nor by the knowledge that, in all known primitive societies, there exist fictitious narratives which are recounted for entertainment. Both seem to have thought of primitive man as an eighteenth-century rationalist cast away on a desert island and faced with the task of keeping himself alive. To write, or to read, novels would indeed be a luxury. In the history of Europe after the fall of Rome, therefore, it seemed clear that fiction must be a late development.

In Ellis's view, the minstrels, who had skill in 'extemporaneous composition' but who had never had leisure or learning sufficient to invent elaborate fictions of non-existent characters, were supplied with the necessary stories by the clergy some time in the twelfth century. These they then developed into the romances as we now know them. But as the number of readers increased, the status of the minstrel declined, and the same

---

[1] ibid., i. 18.   [2] ibid., i. 19.   [3] See p. 16 above.

stories came to be written at even greater length in prose. It is surprising that the coolly logical mind which entertained such notions of the development of fiction should also have found attraction in William Owen's and Edward Davies's theories about comparative mythology. Their theories, which in the light of later knowledge seem so wild, did, however, suggest new approaches to the old problem of the origin of fiction. The study of comparative mythology and of folk-lore in time overthrew the assumptions about the development of fiction on which Ellis based his conjectures. The first English scholar to use the new materials and methods was Richard Price, in his preface to the 1824 edition of Warton's *History*. There the works of Creuzer, the Grimm brothers and Brand, of Frederic Schlegel and Schelling, were used to transform what had become a tired subject—the origin and development of fiction—into an exciting study of particular motifs.

Where Ellis has material provided by writers who had made a close study of particular texts, he is able to make the sort of deduction with which modern scholars would agree. For example on the evidence compiled by de la Rue,[1] de la Ravalière[2] and de Tressan[3] he shows that many works hitherto believed to have been written for the French court, were in fact composed for the Norman kings of England. Benoit de Sainte-Maure, Wace and Gaimar wrote their metrical chronicles, the earliest forms of romance, for the Norman court,[4] which was richer and more powerful than the French.

Ellis discusses his subject in a chronological sequence, but sees the problems he is facing imaginatively. Thus he is led to imagine the gradual settling of the Norman kings in England, the growing attachment of themselves and their followers to the

---

[1] See above p. 150.

[2] Pierre-Alexandre Levesque de la Ravalière (1697–1762), *Poésies du roi de Navarre*, 2 vols. (Paris, 1742). Contains a preliminary dissertation on 'La langue française depuis Charlemagne jusqu'à St. Louis'.

[3] Preface to 'La Fleur des Batailles' in *Corps d'Extraits de Romans de Chevalerie* (Evreux, 1796), viii. 3–4.

[4] *Specimens of Romances*, i. 38–41. Though de la Rue wrote of Marie de France as 'an Anglo-Norman poetess', and is the first scholar to use this term, Ellis uses 'Anglo-Norman' to mean 'English' and 'Norman French' to mean 'Anglo-Norman', see Scott, *Letters* xii. 200 n, 206 n., 218 n. *Specimens of Poets* (1801), iii. 417.

wealthy island which contained their property, and the beginning, about the reign of Stephen, of an interest in 'the history and antiquities of a country which they henceforth considered as their own'.[1] Though this method has its dangers, it produces a vivid picture of the events, and enables Ellis to explain the development of an interest in British history. Norman scholars of the early twelfth century, seeking for the history of the island, found accounts in Gildas, Nennius, Bede and the Saxon chronicle, and a living body of Wesh traditions, which were gathered by Walter Calenius, Archdeacon of Oxford, 'during his travels in Armorica', and were translated into Latin by Geoffrey of Monmouth. Thus the pro-British prejudice of the Normans led to the collecting of materials for the British history of Geoffrey, one of the foundations of romance in that it inspired an interest in the exploits of Arthur. Geoffrey's *Historia* and *Vita Merlini* are summarized by Ellis as part of his introduction. He is inclined to believe that Geoffrey would have taken more pains to make his story credible had he been the inventor of it,[2] and that his assertion of the existence of an Armorican book as his source, though it *may* be false, is not improbable, since before dismissing it, one should first consider whether 'a series of fables, intended to give an exaggerated opinion of British greatness, is more likely to have been forged in the twelfth century, than during the ignorance and credulity of some antecedent period'.[3] Ellis points out that Nennius, in the ninth century, has accounts of Brutus and Merlin very similar to those of Geoffrey, and William of Malmesbury and Gaimar refer to the existence of Arthurian traditions not found in Geoffrey. The 'Breton lais' suggest that Armorica possessed traditional stories, some connected with Arthur. Alanus de Insulis, in the twelfth century, witnesses to the vitality in Armorica of the tradition that Arthur still lived.[4] On this evidence, Ellis is prepared to accept that Geoffrey's *Historia* is based on slowly accumulated traditions 'raised on the foundation of the history attributed to Nennius'.[5]

[1] *Specimens of Romances*, i. 42. For an account of Geoffrey of Monmouth's *Historia* see *Loomis* (ed.) *Arthurian Literature in the Middle Ages* (Oxford, 1959), pp. 72–93.
[2] *Specimens of Romances*, i. 87.   [3] ibid., i. 89.
[4] ibid., i. 93. See E. K. Chambers, *Arthur of Britain* (1927), pp. 110, 265.
[5] *Specimens of Romances*, i. 94.

For the Arthurian stories in saints' lives, Ellis goes to Sir John Price, the contemporary of Leland, and one of the visitors of the monasteries appointed by Henry VIII. Price,[1] in the *Historiae Britannicae Defensio* (1573), says that he had seen accounts of Arthur similar to that in Geoffrey, but of earlier date, in manuscript lives of saints David and Dubricius written in both British and Latin. In addition, Ellis uses some of the information in Ritson's manuscript *Life of Arthur*,[2]—the *Life of St Gildas*, and of *St Gundlei* and *St Patern* (*Padarn*).[3] These, he suggests, would have provided embellishments for Geoffrey. Their existence certainly suggests that Geoffrey's *Historia* was not his invention, but rather the embodiment of traditions. The effect of Geoffrey's work was 'to stamp the names of Arthur, Merlin, Kay and Gawain with the character of historical veracity', and to authorize the collection of all the fables concerning them and their companions—Lancelot, Tristrem, Ywain, Joseph of Arimathea—the Grail adventures, and the Round Table. These, though not mentioned by Geoffrey, were 'additions apparently derived from the same source'.[4]

The inundation of Europe by 'the nursery-tales of Wales and Armorica', at a time when the Welsh were themselves confined to the western extremities of the British Isles and France, is explained by Ellis on two grounds. First, the Normans had already, in Normandy, imbibed from the Armoricans a taste for Celtic legends. Secondly, the political intrigue between the Norman barons and the Welsh chieftains,—in which the barons were concerned to maintain the independence of Wales, 'as a place of refuge to fugitives from arbitrary power',[5] and as a supplier of troops and allies—provided conditions favourable to the 'exchange of literary materials'.[6] The theory that the earliest metrical romances in English had been written in Scotland, which had attracted Scott, but which had been originally Ellis's suggestion,[7] still remained to be explained. Its 'proof' depended on the evidence collected by Scott in the

---

[1] For Price, see T. D. Kendrick, *British Antiquity* (1950), pp. 88 f.; Ellis, *Specimens of Romances*, i. 95.

[2] Ellis saw this in 1804. See Scott, *Letters*, xii. 258 n.

[3] See E. K. Chambers, op. cit., pp. 262, 248; Ellis, *Specimens of Romances*, i. 96.

[4] ibid., i. 102.   [5] ibid., i. 114.

[6] ibid., i. 116.   [7] Scott, *Letters*, i. 113.

introduction to his edition of *Sir Tristrem,* and this evidence consisted mainly of an account of the Northern associations of Arthur [1]—the identification of Carduel as Carlisle, Joyous Garde as Berwick, the Castle Orgueilleux as Bamborough, and references to Arthur's 'seat' in Edinburgh and the grave of Merlin at Drummelzier near Peebles. Ellis summarized the argument, and left it as 'probable' and 'deserving of attention'. The theory is an interesting relic of Scott's imagination at work on the problem of the origin of romance.

Ellis is a much more entertaining writer than Percy, Warton or Ritson. His long introduction presents an elaborate argument with ease and charm, and is often imaginative to good purpose. The learning it displays is, for its time, excellent. And in the midst of his discourse, Ellis offered his reader a valuable synopsis of Geoffrey of Monmouth's *Historia.* This provided the 'common reader' with the sort of information that would enable him to understand the discussions of Warton and Ritson. [2] If the findings of scholars are to be presented for more general readers, Ellis has few peers in the performance of this task.

In presenting his abstracts of twenty romances, Ellis divided his selection into six groups—Arthurian, Saxon, Anglo-Norman, Charlemagne, Oriental and Miscellaneous. He is the first scholar to attempt to group the romances according to the nature or source of their subject-matter—the method now used in bibliographies and in most discussions of romances. His Arthurian romances are *Merlin* and the stanzaic *Morte Arthur.* To the latter he prefixed a synopsis of Chrétien's *Lancelot* taken from the *Bibliothèque des Romans* for April 1777. His Saxon romances are *Guy of Warwick* and *Bevis;* his Anglo-Norman example is *Richard Coeur de Lion.* [3] He prints these in an order which follows naturally from his abstracts of Geoffrey's *Historia* and *Vita Merlini,* first the romances of Celtic origin, derived

---

[1] See below, ch. 7, and Scott, *Letters,* i. 113, 133; xii. 213, 253–60; Ellis, *Specimens of Romances,* i. 123 f.

[2] The *Historia* had been translated into English by Aaron Thompson in 1718. This was reprinted in 1842.

[3] For *Merlin* he used the Lincoln's Inn and Auchinleck MSS; the stanzaic *Morte Arthur* is in Harley MS 2252; for *Guy* he used Caius College MS 107 and the Auchinleck MS; for *Bevis,* Caius College MS 175, supplemented by Douce's copy of Pynson's edition.

from the same sources as Geoffrey, then the stories based on
Saxon heroes, followed by *Richard*, a romance elaborated by the
Normans in England on the exploits of a Norman king. The
Charlemagne romances are preceded by a dissertation on the
Pseudo-Turpin chronicle,, which was always regarded as their
basis. The relationship between the metrical romances and both
Geoffrey's *Historia* and the Pseudo-Turpin chronicle appeared
much more simple and direct to eighteenth-century scholars
than it does to modern students. Though Warton believed that
the elements of romance originated in the East, most of the
scholars wrote as though the metrical romances had been
systematically invented. They saw their authors as either
naively believing in their own fantastic compositions, or as
deliberately setting out to 'abuse the credulity of the public'.
Even Ellis, who appreciated Dryden's treatment of the supernatural in *Theodore and Honoria*, makes few discriminating
comments on the various romances. He does not distinguish
between those which merely recount wonders and those in
which an attempt is made to make the marvellous credible.

As an Oriental romance, Ellis chose *The Seven Wise Masters*
and in his comments on this he shows his awareness of the
ancient origin and wide dispersion of many of the stories in the
collection.[1] His Miscellaneous group includes *Floris, Robert of
Cysille, Isumbras, Triamour, Ipomydon, Eglamour, Lai le Freine, Sir
Eger, Degare, Roswall and Lillian* and *Amys*. The texts printed by
Ritson, *Sir Tristrem* and *Alisaunder* were for various reasons
excluded. Ellis's aim was to supplement Ritson's collection, and
to afford the general reader interested in medieval literature a
means of becoming acquainted with the romance stories. He
is in the tradition of Dryden as a modernizer of medieval
literature, but his attitude towards the romances is one of
amusement and detachment. Primarily he was a dilettante,
who, in correspondence with Scott and Douce, shows an interest
in all the details of medieval scholarship—palaeography,
etymology, chronology, careful transcription of manuscripts, the
relationships between different texts, and the sources of the

---

[1] For his abstract Ellis used the Auchinleck MS and MS Cotton Galba E IX. The
survey of versions of the stories in Hebrew, Greek, Latin, French, and English, up
to Kirkman's *Prince Erastus* (1674) was based on material supplied by Douce.

stories. This interest is to some extent reflected in his introductions and notes. But in his presentation of the romances themselves he has no sympathy with the ideals of chivalry, the extravagances of the adventures, the rambling structures of the narratives and the strange simplicity of the diction. Thus his abstracts are not written to give the reader the atmosphere and tone of the originals. They are the work rather of a highly-cultured eighteenth-century man of letters, to whom the romances were, as literature, primitive without being sublime, and the middle ages of historical interest without being in any way worthy of admiration. The intervening four hundred years of progress made it difficult to see the fourteenth century, its language, literature and ideals, as an age which merited consideration as a finely organized civilization.

As an illustration of Ellis's style of recounting the stories, I choose a passage from *The Sultan of Babylon*, called by Ellis *Sir Ferumbras*. In the central episode of the romance, Ferumbras, son to the Sultan, has been captured by the French under Charlemagne, while Roland and Oliver are taken by the Saracens. The Sultan, on the advice of his daughter Floripas, orders the two Christian knights to be cast into a dungeon, as hostages for his son.[1] The romance continues:

> Tho were thay cast in prison depe.
> Every tyde the see came inne,
> Thay myght not see, so was it myrke;
> The water wente to her chynne.
> The salte watir hem greved sore;
> Here woundis sore did smerte.[2]

Ellis renders this

It may be necessary to observe, that the walls of Laban's palace were in part washed by the sea; that within these walls was a garden, and beneath this garden were the cells of the dungeon, which, therefore, at high tides were nearly filled with water.[3]

This makes clear not only the situation of the dungeon, but also of the garden, from which Floripas hears the knights'

---

[1] *Specimens of Romances*, ii. 379; W. O. French and C. B. Hale, *Middle English Metrical Romances* (New York, 1930), p. 240, ll. 1511–38.
[2] French and Hale, p. 241, ll. 1539–44.   [3] *Specimens of Romances*, ii. 379.

complaints, and of the tower from which she pushes Marigounde for refusing to assist in their relief. This is simply abstracting the story. But, having described the murder of Marigounde and of Britomarte the jailer, and the release of the knights,[1] Ellis is faced with the sudden transition to the scene in the camp of Charlemagne. He exploits this by a humorous summary of the recent activities of Floripas:

Thus had the gentle Floripas, in the course of a few hours, kicked her governess out of window, knocked out the brains of a jailer, and cheated her father, for the purpose of saving from destruction two of his most inveterate enemies. It was an eventful day; and scarcely more so at the court of Laban than at that of Charlemagne . . .[2]

Ellis cannot take seriously the sudden change in the behaviour of Floripas, the heroine of the romance, or her practical brutality in achieving her ends. The mocking tone which he adopts in such an episode is maintained throughout most of the abstracts. But, as Southey admitted, 'it is difficult to relate absurdities without seeming to perceive them'.[3] Ellis comments frequently on the situations he is describing. When Arthur captures the sword, Marandoise, of King Ryence, Ellis writes:

As Escalibore was certainly the best sword in the world, Arthur seems to have had little occasion for Marandoise; but there is perhaps a pleasure in cutting off infidel heads with an infidel weapon; and in this pleasure Arthur indulged himself so long as his horse was able to carry him.[4]

Arthur's dream before the last battle with Modred, as described in the Harley MS 2252 *Morte Arthur*, is quoted in full from the manuscript, but is introduced in a manner which destroys the sense of impending catastrophe:

But on the eve of the intended battle he had a dreadful *sweven* (dream); and as the dreams of Arthur were often more to the purpose than his waking thoughts, the reader will be pleased to see this in the words of the original.[5]

---

[1] ll. 1551–1664 are reduced to 30 lines of prose and 16 lines of quotation from the text.

[2] *Specimens of Romances*, ii. 381–2.

[3] Reviewing the *Specimens* in *Annual Review*, iv (1805), 544. This review is included in Southey's collection of his reviews for the *Annual* in B.M. 11824. w. 10.

[4] *Specimens of Romances*, i. 304.   [5] ibid., i. 373.

The 'ponderous facetiousness', the superiority which can describe the deaths of Guenevere and Lancelot as 'these melancholy events', is not redeemed by the quotation of Malory's encomium on Lancelot as the conclusion to the abstract of the stanzaic *Morte Arthur*.

Southey would have preferred the abstracts to have been written 'in the manner of an old chronicler'.[1] Scott thought that the humorous touches occurred too often, and felt them to be irreverent—it 'looks as if the jest were levelled at once against the reader, the editor, and the original minstrel'.[2] Nevertheless his 'sides were sorely agitated at the ludicrous turn' given to the dullest romance, and Mrs Scott,

to whom of course the narrative as well as the manner is altogether new, can scarcely persuade herself that the lively & delightful tales wt. which she is so much charmed have sprung out of the old *Rums* which she heard occasionally discussed at Sunninghill. The transformation of a grub into a butterfly is scarcely more wonderful.[3]

Lockhart Muirhead, librarian of the University of Glasgow, in his review in the *Monthly Review*, regarded the *Specimens* as completely adequate to gratify a laudable curiosity, admitted the taste and diligence of Ellis, but wished that he had reserved his 'playful remarks and witticisms' for the annotations, and not blended them with the narrative.[4]

The other aspect of Ellis's work, the quotation, in modern orthography, of 'such passages of the originals as appeared to him worth preserving, either from their poetical merit,—from their representing correct pictures of antient manners,—or from their being characteristic of the author's feelings, or of those of the nation'[5] was little noticed by the reviewers. Yet, of the twenty romances analysed, 5380 lines are quoted from the originals. The longest single quotation is one of twenty-three twelve-line stanzas, from the Auchinleck *Sir Guy*, recounting Guy's fight with Colbrand.[6] This, Ellis thought, showed 'a

---

[1] *Annual Review*, iv (1805), 544.

[2] *Edinburgh Review*, vii (1806), 412. Scott himself was not above glossing the Sangreal as 'blessed tureen' in a note to Fytte 3. stanza 91 of *Tristrem*.

[3] Scott, *Letters*, xii. 274. *Rums*, i.e. old and unsaleable books.

[4] *Monthly Review* v (1806), 287.   [5] *Specimens of Romances*, i. p. iv.

[6] ibid., ii. 70–82.

degree of spirit and animation which formed a striking contrast with the usual monotony of the minstrel compositions'.[1] He considered the Auchinleck *Lai le Freine* of greater merit than any other poem of its period 'in point of language and versification',[2] and quoted 242 of its 340 lines, including a single quotation of 202 lines, the episode from the exposing of Le Freine to the arrival of her sister as bride of Sir Guroun.[3] In the *Seven Wise Masters*, the story of the Magpie is given complete in the original, from the Auchinleck MS, probably because, being brief (106 lines) and easily intelligible with a few words glossed, it illustrated the manner and style of the poem.

The abstracts are sufficiently faithful to the details of the romances to enable the reader to appreciate the structure of the tales. Ellis himself comments on the broken structure of *Sir Guy* when, after Guy's return and marriage to Felice, he introduces the later adventures of Guy in the Holy Land and the fight with Colbrand, with—'Here, therefore, the reader will naturally expect a termination of this long-winded story'.[4]

Only in *Sir Eger* does Ellis embellish his original, and here his copy did not give a clear account of the end of the story.[5] Scott suggested that Sir Graham fell in a tournament 'by the lance of his friend Sir Eger without their knowing each other'.[6] Ellis makes the death a natural one.[7] The text from which he worked describes preparations for a tournament, and then suddenly passes to an account of Eger sending far and wide for Bishops, Abbots, Monks and Friars

> Four hundred in procession,
> That were men of Religion,
> Singing for him devotion.
> When he was dead and laid in grave,
> Sir Eger lov'd him by the lave . . .

The corruption of the end of *Sir Eger* is such as to make Ellis's inventions necessary.

In spite of Ellis's humorous treatment of the romances, they

[1] ibid., ii. 6.
[2] ibid., iii. 282.
[3] ibid., iii. 287–296.
[4] *Specimens of Romances*, ii. 59.
[5] ibid., iii. 299.
[6] Scott, *Letters*, xii. 226. 29 November 1802.
[7] *Specimens of Romances*, iii. 345. See *Eger and Grime* ed. J. R. Caldwell (Cambridge, Mass. 1933), p. 349, ll. 2770–2785.

did not achieve a wide popularity, and he was unwilling to continue his abstracting as Scott urged.

I do not think that Ritson's publication which has fallen dead from the press should be any reason against your extracting the pith and marrow of Ywain & Gawain, Hornchilde, Libius Desconius & others the most interesting of his collection. In fact your doing so would rather serve his publication . . . since it would make it more generally known to antiquaries.[1]

Ellis did not respond to this, possibly being too sure of his audience to believe that a second collection would succeed, and certainly being 'a martyr to the liver' and heavily engaged with articles for the new *Quarterly Review*.[2] The *Specimens of Romances* were not quite so popular as the *Specimens of Early Poets*,[3] though Ballantyne printed a second edition for Longman in 1811, the year in which the earlier *Specimens* reached their fourth edition. Southey, like Scott, hoped that Ellis would publish more abstracts, though he preferred the printing of complete texts.[4] Scott praised the wit and elegance of his friend's summaries, which would 'encourage many a gentle reader to attempt the originals, who would before as soon thought of wearing the dress, as of studying the poems of his ancestors'.[5]

Yet of the second edition Henry Crabb Robinson wrote that it was 'better qualified to instruct than give immediate pleasure'.[6] It is probable that for the general reader the *Specimens* were too scholarly, and for the new generation of scholars they were not a substitute for accurately printed texts. Only the exuberant Weber believed that they had aroused a desire for a collection of original texts, and he with his German thoroughness seemed to Douce, 'to meditate the publication of all the romances in the world'.[7]

---

[1] Scott, *Letters*, xii. 275.

[2] O. E. Holloway, 'George Ellis, *The Anti-Jacobin* and the *Quarterly Review*'. *RES* x (1934), 58 f.

[3] Scott to Leyden, 5 July 1806, *Letters*, i. 309.

[4] *Annual Review*, lv (1805), 544. cf. Scott in *Edinburgh Review*, vii (1806), 413.

[5] *Edinburgh Review*, vii (1806), 395.

[6] F. J. Morley, *H. C. Robinson on Books and their Writers* (1938), iii. 848.

[7] Douce to Ellis 5 February 1810. B.M. Add. MS 28099, f. 56. J. J. Conybeare, with more modesty, composed a translation *à la Ellis*, of the French version of *Octavian*, which he submitted to Douce in 1808, see B.M. Add. MS 28099, f. 47ᵛ. It was published as *The Romance of Octavian* (Oxford, 1809).

Percy, Warton, Ritson, Ellis, Scott and Heber were more interested in the romances than in any other type of medieval literature. They entertained high hopes of the benefits to be derived from 'a judicious collection of them accurately published with proper illustrations'. These hopes were rational, and had not varied since they were first expressed by Percy. From the texts we should learn more about the customs and manners of our ancestors; we should see the English language in an early state; we should find interesting stories, sometimes told by authors with a sense of structure; we should have examples of the early stages of fiction; our knowledge of the development of English poetry would be increased, and we should be better able to understand passages in the works of Chaucer, Spenser, Shakespeare and Milton. Pitched somewhat higher was the hope that modern poets would benefit from reading narratives written by authors who were not afraid of wonders and marvels. As Dryden had transformed the prose of Boccaccio into superb narrative poems, so, more than one writer hoped, a modern poet might be able to use the stories of Arthur, Tristrem or Ywain.

There were, however, other writers, especially those who had come in contact with German criticism and the medieval revival in Germany, whose hopes were more elevated. One of these, William Taylor of Norwich, strikes the note of aspiration common in German criticism at the time. In a review of Scott's *Sir Tristrem* he works up from the more humble views of the English scholars to a final expression of the effects that the romances might be expected to have on the national character.

The philologer, the poet, and the antiquarian have much, the historian, the statesman, and the philosopher have some, profit to expect from attending to these infantine lispings of the epic Muse. They serve to endear by association those indigenous spots and ancient halls, the supposed scenes of celebrated events. They respect the stock of fablery, out of which may best be derived the substance of future epopoeias. They illustrate the manners of remote ages, record the inter-marriages of eminent families, and attach pedigrees, as it were, to the gods. They nourish and preserve a complacence in courage, generosity, independence; and, by aggrandising our forefathers, invigorate our own emulation.[1]

In a more persuasive form this note is found in the 'philosopher' of chivalry, Kenelm Henry Digby, whose *Broadstone of Honour* is an exposition of the ideals of chivalry. Digby transforms the middle ages from an 'age of barbarism and superstition' to the 'Age of Faith'. For Digby, the students of 'the history and literature of chivalry serve their country by adorning its peculiar traditions . . . preserving alive in the memories of men, the magnanimity and greatness of ages that are gone by'. But Digby does not look back to the English scholars with any pleasure. Inevitably he quotes Frederick Schlegel in support of his view:

Such national recollections, the noblest inheritance which a people can possess, bestow an advantage which no other riches can supply; for when a people are exalted in their feelings, and enobled in their own estimation by the consciousness that they have been illustrious in ages that are gone by . . . in a word, that they have a national poetry of their own, we are willing to acknowledge, that their pride is reasonable.[2]

Digby's idealization of chivalry and the middle ages is made to serve in the propagation of Roman Catholicism in England. He attempts to restore men to the ideals which he finds in the ages of chivalry and faith.[3] His book represents one of the ways in which the romance scholarship that stems from Percy began to exert an influence outside the narrow group of scholars. Warton had written that 'the genius of romance and popery were the same'. The attempt to 'popularise a sort of reading that was once too popular' was beginning to produce results that Percy, Warton, Ritson and Ellis could not have foreseen and would not have welcomed.

---

[1] *The Critical Review*, third series, September 1804, iii. 47. The emphasis on the power of the stories to foster courage is common in the prefaces to the prose versions of romances in the seventeenth century, see p. 31 above.

[2] K. H. Digby, *The Broadstone of Honour, Godefridus* (1829), pp. 10–11.

[3] J. C. Hare admired Digby's book in its earlier version, but not in its later form when it became a polemic in favour of Catholicism, see *Guesses at Truth*, first series, where Hare comments in all three editions (1827, 1838, 1847), modifying his original view. *The Broadstone* was admired by Wordsworth (Morley, *Henry Crabb Robinson on Books and their Writers* (1938), i. 357) and Ruskin (*Works*, ed. E. T. Cook and A. Wedderburn (1903–12), vii. 361 n.).

CHAPTER VII

WALTER SCOTT

> For this good old gentleman had, from his antiquarian researches, acquired a delight in building theories out of premisses which were often far from affording sufficient grounds for them.
>
> *The Antiquary*, ch. xiv

WITH Scott (1771–1832) we reach the third generation of romance scholars. Like Southey he had absorbed in childhood and youth the romantic stories that were the common reading of children of his time, and of the preceding century. They were for him, as for Wordsworth and Coleridge, the necessary food of his young imagination. 'Of ballads and romances I think I have held a longer acquaintance than have I with any other kind of learning', he wrote.[1] Fairy tales, eastern tales, Ossian, Spenser, Hoole's translation of Tasso, 'everything that touched on knight-errantry', de Tressan's abstracts of medieval romances and those in the *Bibliothèque Bleue*, were 'read or heard as a favourite, and sometimes as an exclusive, gratification'. The discovery of Percy's *Reliques*, at the age of thirteen, was a memorable occasion. Looking back on the experience, Scott declared that the delight came not simply from the sudden addition to his stock of ballad poetry, but from the realization that this material was not despised by the editor, a man of obvious poetical genius who considered such works as worthy of 'sober research, grave commentary, and apt illustration'. Scott's response underlines Percy's originality in treating the ballads with the seriousness of scholarship.

The attraction of ballads and knight-errantry for the young is well illustrated by Scott's passion. Composing interminable adventures of knights-errant gave way to the writing of a romantic poem on *The Conquest of Granada*, and then to a

---

[1] Scott, *Letters*, i. 7. Scott gives an account of his early reading in the 1829 Preface to *Waverley* and in the opening of his Autobiography, written in 1808.

rewriting of some of the ballads. When he first fell in love, at sixteen, he sent modernized versions of 'When the nightingale sings the woods waxen green' and 'Blow northern wind' to the lady. But for Scott himself, even at this age, they lost 'much of their grace by being deprived of their antique garment'. In one of the notebooks which he began to keep in 1792, when he was twenty-one, there is evidence of his developing interest in medieval literature, in the Old Norse *Vegtams Kvitha*, in an account of the death of Balder, in the verses of Canute on passing Ely, etymologies from Du Cange, notes on Malory, and extracts from *Guerin de Montglave*.

This 'odd lumber of the brain, especially that which was connected with the recondite parts of history'[1], was the very material he turned to his advantage, first in annotating the *Border Minstrelsy* and *Sir Tristrem*, and later in his own metrical romances and novels. It was the material that had delighted Percy, Warton, Ritson and Ellis. Scott's tenacious but selective memory responded whenever his imagination was caught. And it was caught in particular where natural beauty was 'combined with ancient ruins, or remains of our fathers' piety or splendour'. The ballads were alive for him in the scenes of the country he knew. His imagination recreated from the stores of memory the history the ballads recounted and the society for whom the minstrels recited. As we look back on Scott, it seems almost inevitable that he should have edited the Auchinleck *Sir Tristrem*. From Warton's *History*, not only Scott but Ritson and Ellis deduced that Thomas of Erceldoune had written a famous romance of Tristrem. The discovery of the only English romance on this hero, in a manuscript in the Advocates' Library in Edinburgh, made it plausible to assume that here was Thomas's poem. But Scott had grown to consciousness in the very spot associated with Thomas of Erceldoune. From his grandfather's house at Sandy-Knowe he could see 'the purple peaks of Eildon, the traditional scene of Thomas the Rhymer's interview with the Queen of Faerie; . . . and the blasted peel which the seer of Erceldoune himself inhabited'.[2] Scott, at an

---

[1] Autobiography in Lockhart, *Life of Scott*, ch. i. During this period he transcribed *Sir Guy* from the Auchinleck MS (*Letters*, xii. 198, 201).

[2] Lockhart, ch. ii.

early age, called himself 'the Rymour'; the prophecies
attributed to Thomas were still known, some of them being
applied during the rebellion of 1745; the ruins of the tower
were still shown to visitors in 1800.[1] Scott's interest in the
Auchinleck text was more than that of a mere antiquary. It
was for him the literary counterpart of the 'blasted peel'
which dominated the scene where his childhood was spent.

From 1789 to 1800 Scott enjoyed the use of the Auchinleck
MS in his own home, and in 1801 he again borrowed it from the
Library of the Faculty of Advocates,[2] to which it had been given
in 1744 by Alexander Boswell of Auchinleck, the father of
Johnson's biographer. Boswell had rescued it in 1740 from a
professor of Aberdeen University who had been tearing out
leaves to make covers for notebooks.[3] Originally it had contained fifty-seven items. The forty-four remaining include
eighteen romances, two from the Matter of France, five from
the Matter of Britain, six of English heroes, four of Eastern
interest, and one didactic romance. Only four extant manuscripts containing English romances are older.[4] Recent work
has shown that it was possibly known to Chaucer, and used by
him during the composition of *Sir Thopas*. It was compiled in
London, between 1330 and 1340, by six scribes working under
editorial supervision. Some of the French texts from which they
made their metrical translations have been identified. The
romance of Tristrem which interested Scott is a version of the
French poem by Thomas of Brittany, an unfortunate coincidence, since it encouraged Scott to identify the Thomas
mentioned by de Brunne with Thomas of Erceldoune. Scott
believed that the text preserved no more than a southern
minstrel's version of the northern Thomas's original.[5] The
whole manuscript is written in a Southern dialect.

[1] *Letters*, i. 7; *Border Minstrelsy* (ed. 1806), iii. 166 f.

[2] *Letters*, xii. 168, 174.

[3] David Laing recovered four leaves (see D. Laing, ed. *A Penni worth of Witte*,
1857, Preface); two other leaves have been found (see G. V. Smithers, 'Two newly-
discovered Fragments from the Auchinleck MS.' *Medium Aevum*, xviii (1949), 1–11).

[4] These are Cambridge Univ. MS. Gg. 4.27.2 (*Horn, Floris and Blanchefleur*); Cotton
Vitellius D. III (*Floris*); Harley 2253 (*Horn*); and Laud Misc. 108 (*Horn, Havelock*).

[5] *Letters*, i. 112; Lockhart, ch. xii. In this Scott was supported by nineteenth-
century scholars like R. Garnett (in Warton, *History* (1840), i. 110) and F. Madden
(*Gentleman's Magazine*, ciii (1833), 308).

Scott was anxious that *Sir Tristrem* 'make his appearance first in Edinburgh', 'for the honour of Scotland',[1] showing the same sense of proprietary right in a romance that Ritson was exhibiting at this time. George Ellis therefore abandoned his plan to include it in his abstracts, though Scott was prepared to assist Ritson in editing it. The rumour of Ritson's owning a printed text, from which he was about to publish, proved false, and John Leyden began to prepare an edition under Scott's supervision. Leyden, however, refused to put his name to the work when he found, after transcribing over a thousand lines, that it became 'too free and easy', that is, he found a stanza containing the word 'queynt'. Douce, Ellis and Scott were not abashed. The ears of antiquaries are 'like those of Confessors', Douce suggested; 'the extreme antiquity of the language is a complete fig-leaf', Scott thought.[2] As a result, Scott himself undertook the edition, finally publishing it with the offending line omitted, except in twelve copies, destined for his scholarly friends.

The whole process of Scott's editing can be traced in detail in the correspondence with George Ellis. The most notable characteristic of the edition is the attention paid to the presentation of the text. It is the first adequate edition of a single romance, and though the text is not long, the elaborate presentation results in a large volume. It was Ellis who urged that Scott write a long introduction, provide a glossary, number the lines or stanzas, punctuate the text carefully, especially distinguishing the speeches, and divide the text into sections prefacing each with an abstract of the contents. This is what Ellis had done with the intended edition of *Alisaunder*.[3] In addition he suggested that Scott make a metrical version, in Middle English, of the end of the story, that was wanting in the manuscript, after the fashion of Frere's version of the *Battle of*

[1] Scott to Richard Heber, 10 March 1801 (*Letters*, xii. 174).

[2] See Scott to Ellis, 27 March 1801 (*Letters*, i. 110; xii. 175) and Ellis's reply in Nat. Lib. Scotland MS 873, f. 2ᵛ. The Duke of Roxburghe advocated retaining any indelicacies, but refused to allow the work to be dedicated to him (Partington, *Sir Walter's Post-Bag* (1932), p. 13).

[3] Ellis to Scott, 2 April 1801 (Nat. Lib. of Scotland MS 873, f. 1ᵛ), and 12 November 1801 (ibid., f. 28). Ballantyne, the printer, also urged a long introduction and glossary, to swell the book to thirty shillings (Partington, p. 13).

Brunanburgh. This conclusion, the composing of a poem in Middle English, 'with the assistance of "Bidene", "Of yore", "In lede", "I wot & nou3t at werre" and all the legitimate crutches which prop the hobbling stanza of the Minstrels',[1] was Scott's first attempt to create a poem from a body of antiquarian lore. In the *Lay of the Last Minstrel* he used the same method, the notes exist for the text, the text to whet the appetite for the notes. As Jonathan Oldbuck explained, 'good notes may very probably help off an indifferent text'. When *Sir Tristrem* appeared, Frere learned Scott's conclusion by heart, and thought it 'the best imitation of old English at present existing'.[2] Ellis, complaining that the edition was only of a hundred and fifty copies, thought that a much larger number would have been sold 'for the sake of the introduction, the notes, and the epitome of the story'.[3] It would seem that it was from the experience of writing the conclusion that Scott decided to write poems in modern English on historical subjects with supporting annotation. The attraction of the middle ages for scholars was not shared by ordinary readers. Scott realized this even more strongly when he supplied a conclusion for Joseph Strutt's unfinished romance *Queen-Hoo-Hall* in 1808. From his experience he learned to avoid an antiquated language, and to set his stories in a period later than the medieval; 'the manners of the middle ages did not possess the interest' which he had imagined.[4]

The edition of *Sir Tristrem* was the work on which Scott 'put out his strength as an antiquary'.[5] Within five months the text was ready for the printer. On 25 August 1801 the first Fytte, with an analysis of each stanza, was sent to Ballantyne. He had discarded the þ but retained the 3. Later he cancelled the first sheet, at the instigation of Ellis and Ritson, and discarded the 3 also. The text was printed by October 1802.[6]

The introduction and notes continued to occupy his attention. The difficulty in explaining the hunting terms was

---

[1] Scott, *Letters*, xii. 187.   [2] ibid., xii. 271 n.
[3] ibid., i. 230 n. cf. *Edinburgh Review*, iv (1804), 427; *British Critic*, xxv (1804), 368; *Critical Review*, iii (1804), 52.
[4] Preface (1829) to *Waverley*.
[5] Scott to Jacob Grimm, 29 April 1814 (*Letters*, iii. 438).
[6] *Letters*, xii. 190, 195, 221.

solved by Ellis's loan of Lady Juliana Berners' *Boke of St. Albans*. In his attempt to date the manuscript, Scott was warned by Ellis that 'Ritson will tell you that the antiquity of *each piece* must rest on its own individual proofs; and that *of the volume* on the *orthography & mode of writing*'.[1] But Ritson arrived in Scotland in September 1801 in time to confirm Scott's dating of c. 1330, from both the orthography and the 'circumstance of its containing no Poem which can be proved to be of later origin'. With this settled, Scott turned to the most interesting problem, the relationship between *Tristrem* and two French fragments in a manuscript owned by Francis Douce (Bodley, Douce MS d.6).

Douce's manuscript is of the mid-thirteenth century and contains two fragments. The first is lines 1268–3087 of the twelfth-century poem on Tristan by 'Thomas of Brittany', from which the Auchinleck poem is derived. This fragment corresponds to the stanzas following number 78, Fytte 3, in Scott's text. The second fragment is a version of the *Folie Tristan* (c. 1175–1200) in which Tristan, disguised as a fool, recounts to Mark and Ysolt his previous history.[2] Scott used abstracts of these, made by Ellis, and found that incidents treated at length in the French were barely hinted at in the English, and that the transitions were sometimes obscure as a result. He hoped to be able to make the story clear by reference to the Douce fragment, and to show, if possible, 'from one or two parallel passages that the *woof* if not the *warp* of the two poems was nearly the same'.[3] Ellis undertook to compare the text of the Auchinleck poem with the Douce manuscript, and point out verbal similarities. But he found none. All that Scott could show in his notes was that the English poem is closer to the Douce fragment than to the French prose *Tristan*. Ellis's abstracts of the two French texts he printed in his edition.

A sense of patriotism encouraged Scott to believe that the English romance was the original version of the Tristrem story,

[1] ibid., xii. 193 n.

[2] See Joseph Bédier, *Le Roman de Tristan* (Paris, 1902–5) and *La Folie Tristan* (Paris, 1907). Douce's manuscript was first edited by Francisque Michel, *Poetical Romances of Tristan* (1835). For discussion of the Auchinleck *Tristrem* see R. S. Loomis (ed.), *Arthurian Literature in the Middle Ages* (Oxford, 1959), pp. 514–16.

[3] *Letters*, xii. 202–4.

considerably expanded later by the French author or authors. Douce urged that the French texts were older than the English. Scott argued that the English represented Thomas of Erceldoune's poem, written about 1250, while the French manuscript on Douce's showing was late thirteenth-century. References to Tristrem by Chrétien de Troyes and the King of Navarre, Scott dismissed as allusions to the popular legend, not to any existing French poem which would antedate that of Thomas of Erceldoune. All Scott's ingenuity was exercised to maintain his position. Tristrem was a Celtic hero; his adventures would therefore most likely be written down in an area in which Celtic traditions survived, that is in the kingdom of Ystrad Clwyd, or, as Scott called it, Strathclwyd, which had been a Welsh kingdom until the year 850. Thomas of Erceldoune, who died between 1286 and 1299, had lived in this area. Robert de Brunne recorded that a poet called Thomas had written a *Tristrem* which was often not accurately reproduced, because of its 'quaint English' and difficult stanza form.[1] The Auchinleck *Tristrem* is certainly written in an awkward stanza. The 'quaint English', Scott thought, could refer to the brevity and obscurity of the style of narration. Above all, the poem itself began

> I was [at Erceldoune]
> With Thomas spak Y thare.[2]

The identification of the author with Thomas of Erceldoune seemed complete—allowing for the poet's affectation of speaking of himself in the third person, and for the surviving text being a late redaction by a southern minstrel of the original poem. The French in Douce's manuscript could thus well be older than the English in the Auchinleck.

For help in establishing the Celtic origin of Tristrem, Scott turned to William Owen, asking in particular for the names used in Welsh versions. The transmission of the story from the Welsh to a Border Minstrel in the thirteenth century could have been effected by one of two routes—directly via the Celtic

[1] See p. 115 above.
[2] The vital statement 'at Erceldoune' is missing in the text, the MS being damaged, but it is preserved in the catchword at the foot of the preceding page.

traditions in southern Scotland, or indirectly via the Normans in England who had brought the story from Brittany.[1] Both Scott and Ellis favoured the first alternative. The origin of some romances at least should be given to Scotland; the existence of many northern localities connected with Arthurian story made it a plausible theory. Owen supplied for the edition a text and translation of the Welsh dialogue between Trystan and Gwalchmai, but was unable to give more help. More useful was Ellis's suggestion, based on de Tressan and de la Rue, that the earliest French romances on Arthurian themes were composed by Norman minstrels for the Anglo-Norman court in England.[2] Scott immediately imagined the southern English nobles being entertained by romances in French, while in southern Scotland poets like Thomas the Rhymer of Erceldoune, Kendal, and 'Hutcheson of the Awle Royal' were writing down the local Celtic legends in English verse. Once the idea had been accepted, Scott threw caution to the wind. Recollecting that the names and setting in *King Horn* were northern, and that in the French version of the poem there is a mention of a Thomas, Scott added *King Horn* to the list of Thomas the Rhymer's productions.[3] To accommodate this poem he made his Thomas 'dress backwards for ten years', dated *Tristrem* 1250, and suggested that the French version was produced very shortly after the English original.[4] By assuming that the French used in England 'remained stationary, or was retrograde', he extricated himself from the difficulty that the French of both Douce's fragments of *Tristram* and of *King Horn* were earlier than the English of the supposed originals.[5]

To the flourishing school of lowland Scots romance writers of the thirteenth century, invented by Scott, he attributed *Gawen and Gologras*, *Galoran of Galoway*, *Sir Eger*, and the lost romance of Wade mentioned by Chaucer (since tradition

---

[1] *Letters*, i. 148, 167. On this see R. S. Loomis, 'The Oral Diffusion of the Arthurian Legend', in R. S. Loomis (ed.), *Arthurian Literature in the Middle Ages* (Oxford, 1959), pp. 52–63.

[2] *Letters*, xii. 206 n.

[3] Scott used a transcript of Douce's MS (No. 132) of the French *Horn*, not the British Museum copy, see *Letters*, i. 215–16 and Douce's copy of *Sir Tristrem* (1804) [in Bodley Douce E. 264], p. lvii.

[4] *Letters*, i. 215.   [5] *Sir Tristrem*, p. xliv.

identified Wade's castle as being near the Roman Wall). Most of these conjectures occurred to him only five weeks before the publication of the edition on 2 May 1804, and during that period he was 'chiefly engaged in travelling backwards and forwards to Selkirkshire upon little fidgetty pieces of business'.[1] But they were added to the Introduction. There was no small element of local patriotism in Scott's claims. But the whole system of theories had the merit for him of simplicity and uniformity. There was a great attraction in being able to write, 'In one word, the early romances of England were written in French, those of Scotland were written in English',[2] and in contemplating the surprise of antiquaries in finding a French and an English romance 'upon the same subject & composed about the same early period throwing light upon each other'.[3]

Scott had originally intended to print *Sir Tristrem* in the third volume of the *Border Minstrelsy*, but he realized that it would 'hang heavy on its skirts'. Ellis suggested making it a fourth volume, since the *Minstrelsy* was rapidly established as a 'library book' and 'in this bibliomaniac age, no one would think it perfect without the *preux chevalier*'.[4] But Scott had sold the copyright of the *Minstrelsy* to Longmans, and *Tristrem* continued to 'hang heavy on his hand'. In the end he hurried through the introduction and published an edition of a hundred and fifty copies at two guineas. Ellis and Robert Jamieson complained that the edition was small and the price high. But, like almost everything Scott did, it was an immediate success. It was regarded as equal in scholarship to Macpherson's edition of Wyntoun, and also likely to win more general readers by its lively introduction, its abstract of the story, and 'the variety of amusement comprehended in the notes'.[5] The *Annual Review* wrote, 'we have rarely or never seen a work so completely and admirably edited'. Frere thought it the most interesting early text so far published, and one that 'no one, *a priori*, could have supposed to exist'.[6] It is not surprising that the demand for the edition grew. In 1806, seven hundred and fifty copies were printed, and in 1811, a thousand. It was again printed in 1819. After 1833 it appeared in the *Collected Works*. In addition

[1] *Letters*, xii. 245.   [2] *Sir Tristrem*, p. lxv.   [3] *Letters*, xii. 217.
[4] Lockhart, ch. xi.   [5] *Letters*, xii. 251 n.   [6] *Letters*, xii. 271 n.

to the text, it contained a variety of illustrative material. The introduction gave an account of Thomas, a history of the various versions of the Tristram story, and an account of the Auchinleck text. Appendices contained the Welsh dialogue of Trystan and Gwalchmai, Ellis's translation of the *Lai de Chevrefeuil*, a full description of the contents of the Auchinleck manuscript, and Ellis's abstracts of Douce's manuscript. The notes are voluminous, and quote freely from other romances, with a wide range of information about the education and ideals of knights. The glossary was not a good one, depending as it did on Macpherson's glossary to Wyntoun and James Sibbald's to *Ane Satyre of the Thrie Estaits*. The problems of glossing were for Scott a game of ingenious guesswork, for which he felt his knowledge of the Scots dialect fitted him.[1] Leyden's transcript of the poem was not completely accurate; he omitted many final *e*'s, transcribed *u* as *v*, and made such errors of reading as 'merken' (for 'metten') and 'Y sain' (for 'Ysame'). The text was recollated for the later editions.[2]

One review, which should have disturbed Scott, was contributed by William Taylor of Norwich in *The Critical Review*. Taylor drew attention to Gottfried von Strassburg's translation about 1250 into German of a Norman-French *Tristan*. He argued that Thomas of Erceldoune was following a Norman and not a Celtic version, from his retention of French names exactly as found in the earlier French and German versions.[3] Scott did not respond to this until, in 1807, Gottfried's *Tristan and Isolt* was again brought to his attention, this time by Henry Weber. At once Scott realized that Gottfried's reference to 'Thomas' was 'a sort of knock-down blow' to his 'system about the Rhymer'.[4] To protect the system he was prepared to try to 'jostle Gottfried a little lower in chronology', and so, in the

[1] The many inaccuracies were pointed out by Francis Madden and Samuel Singer in *Gentleman's Magazine*, 103 (1833), 303–12, and New Series, 1 (1834), 167–70.

[2] In 1806 Scott added a postscript on the genealogy of Learmont, after Appendix IV.

[3] *Critical Review*, iii (1804), 45–52; Scott thought the review was by William Owen or Sharon Turner (*Letters*, xii. 264). See J. W. Robberd, *Memoirs of William Taylor* (1843), ii. 38.

[4] *Letters*, xii. 290–5. On Weber see Scott's account, printed in *Letters*, xii. 290 n. Gottfried's *Tristan* had been printed at Berlin in 1785.

third edition, he refers to him vaguely as 'a German minstrel of the thirteenth century' and uses him as further support for the claims of the Scots Thomas. In an additional appendix he printed Weber's *Account of German Romances on the Story of Sir Tristrem*. There was at least sufficient evidence here that the German poem derived from an Anglo-Norman romance by 'Thomas of Brittany'. Thomas of Erceldoune should therefore have been deprived of the 'early European celebrity' claimed for him by Scott. But by 1811 Scott's attention had moved far from the minutiae of the originator of *Sir Tristrem*. Richard Price with his usual acumen shed a great deal of light on the subject in a long note in his edition of Warton's *History* (1824).[1] Here the obvious conclusions that Scott had ignored were drawn, and the Rhymer left with only a possible claim to the Auchinleck *Tristrem*, and no share in the European dissemination of the Tristram legend. Scott's edition, however, even with its wild conjectures, still stands as the first great edition of a medieval romance. Diligence in collecting, taste in presentation, ingenuity in argument, and a wide scholarly understanding in ranging round his text for illustrative material, mark Scott as an editor of imagination. To transform the crabbed pages of the Auchinleck manuscript into the rich quarto was a feat that no mere antiquary could have performed. The edition pointed the way to the scholars who produced the Early English Text Society editions later in the century.

Though Scott 'put out his strength as an antiquary' in the edition of *Sir Tristrem*, his interest in other medieval romances is attested by the many references to them in the notes to the *Minstrelsy*, the *Lay of the Last Minstrel*, *Marmion*, and the novels. The correspondence with George Ellis shows him animated by the exchange of ideas and information about romances. He planned an edition of the sagas, 'selecting the most picturesque Incidents & translating the *Runic Rhymes*'.[2] When Thomas Johnes began a new translation of Froissart, Scott sent him information about the Battle of Otterburne. But when the edition appeared in 1804, Scott was disappointed with it. He

---

[1] Warton, *History* (1824), i. 181–98. Lockhart replied to this in the Advertisement to *Sir Tristrem* in Scott's *Poetical Works* (Edinburgh, 1833), v. pp. i–xiv.

[2] *Letters*, xii. 178.

would have preferred a reprint of Lord Berners' version.[1] In February 1809 he proposed to John Murray an edition of five hundred copies, with uniform spelling, notes, and corrections to the history. He had access to a French manuscript of Froissart in the possession of Lord Ancrum.[2] When this 'superb plan' came to nothing, he suggested Thomas Park or Sharon Turner as a suitable editor.[3] But in 1812 an edition by Utterson appeared. There were more schemes in Scott's mind than he could well accomplish. He proposed to fill in time whilst editing Swift by reprinting a collection of 'our English tales and Romances of wonder, with notes and critical prefaces' and a History of Romance.[4]

On the completion of his edition of Dryden, Scott assisted his young protegé, Henry Weber, in his plan for publishing an extensive edition of metrical romances.[5] The plan was one dear to Scott's heart, and in April 1808 he was hoping to persuade his friends in London to add notes and illustrations, and to subscribe five guineas for a set of three volumes.[6] In May he introduced Weber to Heber, and wrote, 'We [are] agitating despite of Ritson's failure a grand collection of Metrical Romances for which he is making researches in every direction'.[7] At the same time Weber was introduced to Douce. Douce delighted to talk with him about German romances, but he was deaf to Weber's hints about allowing his romances to be copied.[8] Six months later Scott declined to write a preface or to allow his name to appear on the title page,[9] and, according to Lockhart, both Scott and Ellis tried to convince Weber that Ellis's *Specimens* and Scott's *Tristrem* had not created an audience for a collection of texts.[10] Weber published his three volumes of *Metrical Romances* in Edinburgh in 1810, the second collection

---

[1] ibid., xii. 402 n., *Edinburgh Review*, v (1805), 361; vi (1805), 132.

[2] *Letters*, ii. 169. [3] ibid., xii. 402–3. [4] ibid., ii. 42–3.

[5] See Lockhart, ch. 17. For Scott's account of Weber, see *Letters*, xii. 290 n. and references in Lockhart.

[6] *Letters*, ii. 38 (to Surtees, 4 April 1808).

[7] ibid., xii. 301.

[8] ibid., 392 n. On 5 February 1810, Douce wrote to Ellis that Weber asked for too much information. See B.M. Add. ms 28099, f. 55^v–56, and f. 47^v (15 October 1808).

[9] ibid., ii. 93 (to Ellis, 8 October 1808).

[10] Lockhart, ch. 17.

of romances to be published, and, in the opinion of Scott, superior to Ritson's.[1]

In 1814, between finishing the first volume of *Waverley* and beginning the second, Scott wrote an *Essay on Chivalry* for Constable's supplement to the *Encyclopaedia Britannica*, and in 1823 he wrote an article on Romance for the same work.[2] By this time Scott's views were much more sober. He does not mention his earlier wild theories, but, as is suitable for an encyclopaedia, gives a correct account of the development of the word 'romance', the origin and history of the romances of chivalry in England and on the continent, with a brief note on the kinds of romance which superseded them.

In the eighteenth century Malory's *Morte Darthur* was valued simply as a compendious and reasonably accessible collection of Arthurian romantic material to be quoted when annotating Arthur's knights, ideals of chivalry or the education and discipline of knighthood. All the editions before 1634 were collector's pieces, since so few copies had survived, but the Stansby edition of 1634 was often a boy's book. Southey, for instance, possessed a battered copy when he was a boy,[3] and Scott made notes on Malory in a notebook he began in 1792, from a 1634 edition. This youthful acquaintance with Stansby's text endeared it to the early scholars, so that it was the first version to be reprinted in 1816. The two editions then printed themselves became rare, according to Thomas Wright. In these editions the generations between 1816 and 1868 made their first acquaintance with Malory, a fact which probably influenced Wright in again reprinting the 1634 edition in 1858 and 1866. Wright preferred this text to Caxton's as the latest of the old editions, and also because its orthography and phraseology 'with the sprinkling of obsolete words, not sufficiently numerous to be embarrassing, preserves a certain clothing of medieval character'.[4] Wright's reprint accurately follows a text which Sir Edward Strachey estimated had over

[1] Lockhart, ch. 68.
[2] Reprinted in *Miscellaneous Prose Works*, 3 vols. (1847). In the *Essay on Chivalry* are the germs of his last two novels, *Castle Dangerous* (in which *Thomas of Erceldoune* appears) and *Count Robert of Paris*.
[3] Southey's edition of *The Byrth, Lyf, and Actes of Kyng Arthur* (1817), i. p. xxviii.
[4] Thomas Wright, in Introduction to *Le Morte d'Arthure* (1858).

twenty thousand departures from Caxton's text. Stansby had remodelled the preface, divided the book into three parts, and modernized the spelling. The minor variants, Strachey suggested, probably arose 'from the printer reading a sentence and then printing it from recollection, without further reference to his "copy"', or from 'a desire to improve the original simplicity by what the editor calls "a more eloquent and ornate style".'[1]

It is well to remember that Caxton's Malory was available only in Southey's reprint in 1817, also a rare work until Strachey's edition in 1868. Until then, Stansby's version was the only one available to the ordinary reader, and indeed to many scholars. Rossetti, who described the Bible and the *Morte Darthur* as the 'two greatest books in the world', Edward Jones and William Morris, the Pre-Raphaelites whom Ruskin described as 'all gone crazy about the *Morte d'Arthur*', and Tennyson, probably all knew Malory in the 1816 and 1858 reprints of Stansby.[2]

The impetus to reprint the *Morte Darthur* came from Southey and Scott. The idea occurred to both simultaneously. On 11 October 1807 Scott wrote to the bookseller, Millar, that with the copy for Dryden he had handed to Ballantyne a copy of *Morte Darthur*. He hoped that his references to it in the notes to *Marmion* would help sell a small edition of five to seven hundred copies, and he asked Millar if he would like to publish the book and pay thirty guineas a volume to Scott in exchange for a preface and his name on the title-page.[3] If Millar was unwilling to publish, Scott urged him to keep the plan secret. On 18 November he described the project to Heber. Since no copy of Caxton's edition was then known to have survived, Scott planned not 'an antiquary's book' but a layman's, and if it succeeded, he intended to print many similar texts. But only two days earlier Southey had written to Heber and Williams Wynn about the edition he was preparing, which was to contain notes supplied by Sharon Turner, William Owen and

---

[1] Strachey in Introduction to *Morte Darthur* (1868), (ed. 1898, p. xxxii).

[2] Oswald Doughty, *A Victorian Romantic: Dante Gabriel Rossetti* (1949), pp. 207, 283.

[3] *Letters*, xii. 296.

Edward Williams.[1] Scott withdrew his suggestion and offered any help Southey might need. But in August 1809 Southey reported that Longman had again put off printing the text, and in October he resigned the edition to Scott.[2] In the meantime, a copy of Caxton's Malory had been discovered in the possession of Lady Jersey, and Scott decided to go ahead with a limited edition for antiquaries, 'with all the superstition and harlotrie which the castrator in the reign of Edward VI [i.e. Copland, 1557] chose to omit'.[3] Already he had decided that it should come out a year or two after Southey's popular edition, which Southey was, however, on the point of abandoning. In December 1810 Scott was planning to collate his Stansby with the Caxton, and in June 1812 he was interested in the de Worde Malory (1498) at the great Roxburgh sale. But after this Scott's edition is heard of no more.

The de Worde Malory was bought not by Scott but by Lord Spencer, who also bought the only other existing Caxton (for £325) at the sale of Mr Lloyd's books at Wygfair, near St Asaph, in January 1816. This copy wants eleven leaves. But during the twelve months after Lord Spencer's purchase of it, John Upcott supervised the printing of this text by Longman, supplying the missing leaves from Lord Spencer's copy of the de Worde Malory, which is the only known copy of this edition. Southey wrote an introduction and some notes, which, however, fall far short of his plan to indicate the source of every chapter.[4] This reprint of Caxton's Malory in two handsome volumes appeared in 1817.

In the previous year two separate reprints of Stansby's Malory were issued, one in three volumes duodecimo printed and published by R. Wilks, and one in two volumes, printed by J. Dove for a group of publishers that included Longman.

---

[1] Southey, *Life and Correspondence*, ed. C. C. Southey (1850), iii. 116, 125; Southey, *Letters*, ed. J. W. Warter (1856), ii. 27; Scott, *Letters*, i. 39c, 401; ii. 23.

[2] Southey, *Life and Correspondence* (1850), iii. 250–5.

[3] Scott to Southey, 10 September 1809 (*Letters*, ii. 236). Lady Jersey's copy is the only perfect one. It passed from the Harleian Library to Osborne, to Brian Fairfax, and then to Mr Child, Lady Jersey's grandfather. It is now in the Pierpont Morgan Library.

[4] On Southey's edition, see Sir Edward Strachey, *Morte Darthur* (ed. 1898). pp. xxxii f.

As Scott had intended, a popular reprint had preceded a scholar's edition. But Scott seems not to have been concerned in any of the reprints. Thus, after a lapse of nearly two centuries, Malory's work—or works, as the discovery of the Winchester manuscript has now made clear—were again in print. The appearance of two editions of Stansby's text in the same year is surprising, hardly less so than the long delay in reprinting. To the two unknown editors of these reprints readers were indebted for another forty years.

The task of reprinting our early poetry and romances, though well performed in its early stages by amateur scholars, was, with the rapidly developing interest of the nineteenth century, becoming too great for individuals. Scott thought it was 'worth the attention of the English Universitites', 'with their huge endowments and the number of learned men to whom they give competence and leisure'.[1] The universities should do for English literature what the French Benedictines had done for that of France. In this demand Scott was far ahead of his time. It is a clear indication of the seriousness with which he viewed the study of medieval literature. His interest was never lost. When he was at Naples in the last year of his life he copied an entire manuscript containing *Bevis* and *Libius*[2], in the Royal Library.

The inspiration which Scott derived from the romances is difficult to determine. Visual relics of the middle ages, its architecture, abbeys, castles, and its armour and weapons, have always been more potent than its literary products. But Scott had the power to translate what he read into vivid picture. The outcome in his poems and novels is not, however, the result of recreating the stories that the romances tell. It is rather the recreation of the audience for whom he imagined the stories were written. His imagination seized on the customs and manners the romances described, the dress, the modes of combat, the chivalrous attitudes, the social manners. Like Southey, he avoided retelling the tales the minstrels had already told. But he was himself regarded as the heir of the line of

[1] *Edinburgh Review*, vii (1806), 413; Scott, *Letters*, i. 259.
[2] Lockhart, *Life* (1836), vii. 351–2; *Letters*, xii. 46–7. The transcript is now at Abbotsford (see J. G. Cochrane's *Catalogue* (1838), p. 105).

Bards, Scalds and Minstrels whom Percy had brought into prominence.[1] From his critique of the medieval romance developed his theory of the modern 'romantic poem'. The medieval romance was 'the abstract and brief chronicle of the time'; its narrative generally rambling and desultory—'just a necklace of beads', so that the minstrel could abridge his recital at will. If its simple stanza and diction necessitated a loose and tedious style, and its incidents were sometimes improbable and awkwardly contrived, yet 'there is a sort of *keeping* in these ancient tales'. The 'gloom of superstition' added a wildness, occasionally mounting to the sublime, and, at their best, individual adventures were 'happily conceived and artfully executed'.[2]

For his *Lay of the Last Minstrel* Scott adopted 'the measured short line, which forms the structure of so much minstrel poetry, that it may be properly termed the Romantic stanza'.[3] In his Preface to the 1830 edition of the *Lay*, he also admitted that his choice of this form of the octosyllabic couplet had been influenced by hearing Coleridge's *Christabel* recited. When Coleridge published his poem in 1816, he noted that the measure had been used by Scott and Byron, but claimed it as his own invention. The new principle, he said, lay in 'counting in each line the accents, not the syllables'. Coleridge had used the metre for a narrative with a medieval setting. But, as Theodore Watts pointed out, it had been used by Chatterton for his 'Unknown Knight'.[4] It had the advantage of sounding like the metre in which a medieval poet would, and sometimes did, write.

When Scott wrote his *Lay* it was at once recognized by Jeffrey, reviewing it in the *Edinburgh Review*, as 'such a romance as we may suppose would have been written in modern times, if that style of composition had continued to be cultivated, and partakes consequently of the improvements which every branch of literature has received since the time of its desertion'.

[1] For example, by Ellis (Scott, *Letters*, xii. 199 n.).
[2] *Edinburgh Review*, vii (1806), 411–12 (reviewing Ellis's *Specimens*).
[3] Introduction to the *Lay* (1830).
[4] T. M. Ward (ed.), *The English Poets* (1880), iii. 401. See also E. L. Griggs's note in Coleridge, *Collected Letters* (Oxford, 1959), iii. 355–61.

Scott was able to indulge himself in the conduct of his poem, 'beginning and ending as he may judge best', and to excuse himself on the grounds that the original minstrel's poem had also been 'just a necklace of beads'. The medieval romance provided a primitive form of long narrative poem free from any restricting observation of critical 'rules'. Percy, analysing *Libius*, had concluded that the medieval poet had instinctively observed the 'rules' of strict narrative structure. Scott used the romances as an excuse to escape from any such narrow observation. He was eager to use new subject-matter for poetry, and to present it in a way which was not only in keeping with his own desire to be free from restraint, but which was also, he felt, the way a medieval poet would have chosen. Thereby he would fit the style and the shape of his poem to his matter. Accordingly he developed a definition of what the Romantic Poem should be:

a fictitious narrative, framed and combined at the pleasure of the writer; beginning and ending as he may judge best; which neither exacts nor refuses the use of supernatural machinery; which is free from the technical rules of *Epée*; and is subject only to those which good sense, good taste, and good morals, apply to every species of poetry without exception. The date may be in a remote age, or in the present; the story may detail the adventures of a prince or peasant. In a word, the author is absolute master of his country and its inhabitants, and everything is permitted to him, excepting to be heavy or prosaic, for which, free and unembarrassed as he is, he has no manner of apology.[1]

The medieval romance liberated the long narrative poem in the hands of Scott, and 'breathed a youthful spirit into English poetry'.[2]

[1] Preface to *The Bridal of Triermain* (1813).
[2] Obituary of George Ellis, *Gentleman's Magazine*, lxxxv (1815), 372.

CHAPTER VIII

WHAT THEN WAS ROMANTIC?

> We talk of schools . . . unscholarly; if schools
> Part the romantic from the classical.
>
> Landor, 'Epistle to the Author of *Festus*'

To conclude this survey of romance scholars with Scott is arbitrary but necessary. The medieval scholarship of the nineteenth century is too voluminous to be surveyed in any brief account, nor would it be easy to extract merely the work on the romances. Romance scholarship in the nineteenth century does not have the significance that it has in the eighteenth. The age of the amateur scholar was by no means ended with Scott, yet the study of medieval literature had reached a point at which, as Scott saw, it was desirable that the universities should take a hand. It was, in fact, a long time before they did. But various societies were founded in order to print medieval documents and literature, amongst them the Bannatyne Club, and the Percy, Camden, Chaucer, Shakespeare and Early English Text Societies. These societies performed a service on which modern scholars still rely. The nineteenth-century literary scholars considered the most valuable works of literary scholarship which they inherited from their immediate predecessors to be the great editions of Shakespeare and Warton's *History of English Poetry*. Indeed, for most of the following century, the latter provided, in the forms revised by Price (1824), Taylor (1840) and Hazlitt (1871), the only account of the history of poetry before Spenser. In scholarship, the nineteenth century built on the foundations laid, to a large extent, in the last forty years of the eighteenth.

Instead, however, of looking forward, it may be more useful to look back over the century and a half before Scott, and survey some of the contexts in which the word 'romantic' was used.[1] For in this period the word was first invented, as an

[1] For previous discussions of the word, see the list of works in the Bibliography, p. 243 below.

adjective to describe the qualities of the romances—medieval, Peninsular and modern. By the 1820s it was occasionally used in England to describe contemporary literature.[1] In 1829, for example, Kenelm Henry Digby castigated those students of literature who 'are only careful to determine between the classical and romantic schools'.[2] This, to him, was a way of talking about literature invented by those who were impervious to the inspiring quality of what they read. Sir Egerton Brydges in 1824 regarded Gray and Collins as belonging to the romantic school of poetry, because Collins 'loved fairies, genii, giants, and monsters', and because Gray had translated from Old Norse and Welsh.[3] Another author, anticipating Pater, remarked that it was possible to describe Homer as romantic, 'if by the word romantic be meant wild, abrupt, and grotesque sublimity, in opposition to beauty, elegance and pacific symmetry'.[4] This indeed was often what 'romantic' did mean, when applied to poetry. But in general Carlyle was right when, in 1831, he wrote that in England 'we are troubled with no controversies on Romanticism and Classicism—the Bowles controversy on Pope having long since evaporated'.[5] The poets we think of now as 'romantic' were in their own day divided into 'Lake schools, and Border-Thief Schools and Cockney and Satanic Schools'.[6]

To end with Scott is to draw back at the point where the medieval revival of the previous forty years begins to bear fruit. The probable nature of that fruit horrified at least one old-fashioned critic, Jeffrey. Reviewing *Marmion* in the *Edinburgh Review*, he warned the public against the establishment of 'an indiscriminate taste for chivalrous legends, and romances in irregular rhyme'. He feared that Scott would have 'as many

---

[1] The opposition between 'classical' and 'romantic' originated in Germany and developed later in France and Italy. See A. O. Lovejoy, 'The Meaning of "Romantic" in Early German Romanticism', and 'Schiller and the Genesis of German Romanticism', in *Essays in the History of Ideas* (Baltimore, 1948).

[2] *Godefridus* (1829), p. 31.

[3] Brydges, ed. Phillips, *Theatrum Poetarum* (1824), p. xxxv. See also *Cambrian Quarterly Magazine*, ii (1830), 2, 48–9.

[4] *Cambrian Quarterly*, iii (1831), 186. cf. Pater on 'Romanticism' in *Macmillan's Magazine*, xxxv.

[5] Carlyle on Schiller, in *Miscellaneous Essays* (1872), iii. 71.

[6] ibid., iv. 184.

copyists as Mrs Radcliffe or Schiller', and lamented the day 'when a gentleman of such endowments was corrupted by the wicked tales of knight-errantry and enchantment'. 'Romantic' poetry was Scott's poetry, poetry deliberately based on chivalrous story and told in the 'romantic stanza'.

If we look back from Scott instead of forward, we find in Hurd's criticism (itself an elaboration of Addison on 'the fairy way of writing') the first distinction between 'classical' and 'romantic', with a bias in favour of the 'romantic'. Even then Hurd generally used the term 'Gothic' rather than 'romantic'. 'Gothic' had historical associations—marking the period after the fall of Rome—and was opposed to 'classical' in architectural discussions. The Gothic was the modern, the post-classical, in historical, architectural and literary contexts. 'Romantic' for Hurd, was a narrower word, meaning 'such as is found in the romances', and in a literary context implied 'unnatural'. Only by showing 'Gothic' manners, the manners of people who lived in the later middle ages, to be natural, could he argue that 'romantic manners are to be accounted *natural*'.[1] What is romantic, that is, what is found in the romances, could then be discussed on the same grounds as what is classical, and be regarded as superior for the purposes of the poet. Tasso, Spenser and Milton could be seen as faced with a choice of models, the ancient and the modern, 'the fables of Greece' and 'the legends of Chivalry'.

Romance was regarded as the characteristic mode of modern literature by Hurd and Addison, and by all the critics who discussed epic and romance. Those who theorized about the origin of romance were looking for the starting point of 'modern' literature. And it was not to Greece and Rome that the more rigorous theorists looked. Thomas Warton excluded classical 'poetical novels' from his definition of romantic fictions.[2] Huet found no link between classical fiction and modern. Though all men are inclined to fabling, the particular quality of imaginative extravagance that characterized modern romance was not of European origin. This was the accepted

[1] Hurd, *Letters on Chivalry* (1762), Letter xi, *ad fin.*
[2] Warton, *History* (1774), i. sig. a1. What he admired in Dante did not derive from Greece and Rome, it 'must be traced to a different stock' (ibid., iii. 255).

view to the time of Warton. The collapse of Rome had left southern Europe open to the influence of an imagination wilder than any it could have produced for itself. Everything distinguishing European literature written after the fall of the Roman Empire, from that produced in 'classical' times, was regarded by many writers as deriving from the Arabs—where, of course, it was not simply the product of barbarism, ignorance and superstition. Scholars and critics recognized also the influence of that other eastern people, the Hebrews, whose imagination was tinged with the same extravagance. The Old Testament, as well as the superstitions of early Christians, had helped to encourage the romantic quality of 'modern' literature. The somewhat perfunctory borrowings from Eastern romance to be found in Greek and Latin literature—according to theorists like Huet—are as nothing compared with the flood of Oriental borrowings of the middle ages. An anonymous author, writing in 1695, summarized the then accepted view of the origin and development of romantic fiction:

The Arabians excelled the Hebrews in Metaphors, Similitudes, and Fictions, of which their Alcoran is a proof, as well as their troops of Poets, which afterwards infected Spain and Provence, with Rhodomontade and Knight-Errantry, Giants, Dragons, Enchanted Castles, and Such-like acts of Chivalry.

From these fountains the Christian Monks drunk in the Art of Lying, and composing of Legends; but they did not tell their Tales so finely as the Greeks and the Orientals.[1]

The original 'romantic' poetry was written by Arabs, who are described by Rymer:

Fancy with them is predominant, is wild, vast, and unbridled, o're which their *judgment* has little command or authority: hence their conceptions are monstrous, and have nothing of exactness, nothing of resemblance or proportion.[2]

The terms are those used to distinguish Gothic or Romantic poetry from ancient or classical.

[1] L.P., *Two Essays* (1695), p. 31. The preponderance of Eastern tales by Hawksworth in the periodical *The Adventurer* occasioned the description of it as 'the romantic *Adventurer* fresh from Eastern ground' in *The Miniature*, No. 1, 23 April 1804.

[2] Spingarn, *Critical Essays of the Seventeenth Century* (Oxford, 1908), ii. 165. cf. quotation from Riou, p. 14 above.

The indebtedness of post-classical Europe to the Arabs for the philosophy and science of the Greeks, gave added weight to the argument that modern Europe owed much to the East. To anyone who might ask why the Arabs did not also transmit a correct taste in literature by passing on the poetry of the Greeks, Thomas Warton replied that the Arabs ignored it, partly 'because it inculcated polytheism and idolatry, which were inconsistent with their religion', and partly because 'it was too cold and too correct for their extravagant and romantic conceptions'.[1] 'Metaphors, Similitudes, Fictions', and allegory, rhyme, and the pointed arch, were all traced to the East. 'Hyperbolical descriptions', and 'an infinity of marvellous tales', together with the 'superstitions of dragons, dwarfs, fairies, giants and enchanters'[2], combined to produce 'that extraordinary species of composition which has been called ROMANCE'.[3]

2

For the late seventeenth-century writer it was axiomatic that romantic fabling was the product of an extravagant imagination. The extravagance manifested itself in improbable and impossible fictions, in the creation of worlds outside Nature. But it was equally seen in an excessive fondness for hyperbole, metaphor and allegory. Extravagance of imagination uncontrolled by judgement produced, it was said, the style of Shakespeare, 'pestered' with figurative expressions, just as much as it produced the witches in *Macbeth*. 'Figuris liberis et audacibus utuntur', wrote Georg Neuman when defining romances.[4]

Addison found 'the fairy way of writing' not only in medieval and Elizabethan literature, but also in Ovid. That is, if we equate 'the fairy way of writing' with the 'romantic' in

[1] Warton, *History* (1774), i. Dissertation II, sig. b3ᵛ.

[2] ibid., i. 110.

[3] ibid.

[4] J. Georg Neuman, *Primitiae Dissertationum Academicarum* (Wittenberg, 1716), p. 441 (Dissertation X, *De Parabola*, dated 1690). Voltaire found the style of the English dramatists of the seventeenth century 'too closely copied from the Hebrew writers', i.e. too figurative after the manner of Eastern writings (*Letters concerning the English Nation* (1733), p. 177).

literature, it was seen as a quality which, while predominant in 'modern' European literature, was not confined to it, just as 'classical' qualities were not confined to 'ancient' literature. The ballad of *Chevy Chase* was for Addison 'classical', in the sense of being an accurate delineation of human manners, in the same way as Chaucer was for Dryden more of a 'classical' poet in this sense than was Ovid. The writer whose imagination was attracted by improbable fictions was also likely to be unable to exercise his judgement in the choice of appropriate figures of speech or thought. Novelty of subject-matter for its own sake was likely to be accompanied by novelty of figures, the whole being consonant with human experience neither in the events described nor in the language used. 'Epigrammatical turns and points of wit', whether in Cowley or Martial, are for Addison, 'the Gothic manner of writing'.[1] Here 'Gothic', though it derives its pejorative sense from its historical connotations, implies all 'wrong artificial taste' in contrast to the normal taste of 'the most unprejudiced, or the most refined' for simple and majestic 'copyings after nature'. This unnatural style which Addison calls 'Gothic', and which Johnson later discussed as 'metaphysical', is an extreme form of a style of writing usually associated with writers of romances. A great writer, like Shakespeare, when creating a 'romantic' world, one outside Nature, would have the judgement to create also a language natural to that imagined world. A lesser writer, like Collins, would be as unnatural in his style as in his subject-matter.

The romance-writer's 'unnatural' style was not usually one of epigram and wit. That it was easily recognizable as one associated with a subject-matter entirely imagined may be seen in *The Great Assize* (1645) where the journal called the *Post* is accused of presenting its invented 'news' in a style stolen from *Euphues* and the *Arcadia*.

> Such was his style, such tales he did endite,
> That he no newes, but *Romaunts* seem'd to write.[2]

[1] *Spectator*, Nos. 70 and 74; cf. no. 409, where Addison avers that the 'general taste in England is for epigram, turns of wit, and forced conceits', and calls it 'this gothic taste'.

[2] *The Great Assize* (1645), Luttrell Reprint, No. 6 (Oxford, 1948), p. 24.

James Arderne warned the sermon writer not to suffer his fancy 'to be tempted towards following of Poetick or Romantick writings'.[1] It was 'a mixt language between Poetry and Prose'.[2] We meet it again at the end of the century in the Gothic novels, where the peculiar style of such works is attributed to an imitation of that of the romances of chivalry. A reviewer in the *Monthly* for April 1773, for example, objected to *The Test of Friendship* as 'a tale truly romantic, and narrated in the unnatural, bombast style of the old chivalry books'.[3] To another writer, in 1804, the descriptions in the Gothic novels are 'somewhat delirious'. He goes on,

Horror must be heaped on horror, and darkness thicken upon darkness, amidst cold clammy carcases, accumulated skeletons, blood-stained daggers, &c. Our prose must now *run quite mad*; mobs of metaphors, unlike similes, and ill-paired figures jostling and supplanting each other, must add *new terrors to the terrific* description. Nor must our brains cease to be racked for fine words, far fetched expressions, half concluded periods, and sentences breaking off in the middle.[4]

Such was the style associated in the eighteenth century with 'romance'.

3

The unreal quality of the romances, the remoteness of their characters and action from real life, are reflected in the use of the term 'romantic love'. To be called 'romantic', love had to have the characteristics with which it is associated in seventeenth-century French romances, not those which are found in the Peninsular or medieval romances. To Vanessa, in Swift's poem, the behaviour of Cadenus is the distant, idealized adoration of the lover in romance. His discourse is couched in

---

[1] James Arderne, *Directions concerning the Matter and Style of Sermons* (1671), pp. 73–4.

[2] *Power and Harmony of Prosaic Numbers* (1749), p. 45. Clara Reeve, writing in 1785 of the French romances of the seventeenth century, notes that 'these books produced a particular kind of affectation in speaking and writing, which is still called the Romantic'. (*Progress of Romance* (Colchester, 1785), i. 66.)

[3] Quoted in J. M. S. Tompkins, *The Popular Novel in England*, 1770–1800 (1962), p. 207 n. See also p. 229.

[4] *The Miniature*, No. 2, 30 April 1804.

'exalted strains', with 'sublime conceits', 'raptures, flights and fancies'. Such love Vanessa regarded as Platonic, no more than 'devotion, duty and respect'; it was to her 'a high romantic strain', tormenting to one who desired her lover 'to act with less seraphic ends'. Romantic love was Platonic love,

> a pretty name
> For that romantic fire,
> When souls confess a mutual flame
> Devoid of loose desire.[1]

It was the unreal love of the characters of romance,

> In mad sublime did each fond lover woo,
> And in heroics ran each *billet-doux*:
> High deeds of chivalry their sole delight,
> Each fair a maid distrest, each swain a knight.[2]

Had the term 'romantic love' been in use in the sixteenth century, however, it would have signified the 'bold bawdry' which contemporary moralists found so shocking in *Morte Darthur* and *Amadis*. The ideal chastity to which it did refer was that assumed by the heroines of modern romances. The love which provided the chief motive to action in the seventeenth-century romances and in the heroic plays, though it had derived from the medieval and Peninsular romances, was a purer, a more 'unreal' thing. Richardson's Mr B., in *Pamela*, regarded Pamela's fantastic concern for her 'Honour' as romantic.[3]

4

It was the unrealistic quality of romances which impressed critics of the seventeenth and eighteenth centuries, and determined the usages of the epithet 'romantic'. We do not find

[1] 'Platonic Love', in *Scots Magazine*, October, 1741, p. 455.

[2] George Colman, Prologue to *Polly Honeycombe* (1760). Andrew Marvell, in *The Rehearsal Transprosed* (1672), ed. Grosart, iii. 49, refers to a 'Platonic knight-errant'.

[3] On romantic love as ideal chastity, see Ian Watt, *The Rise of the Novel* (1957), pp. 159–60, 165. Mr B. uses such terms as 'a very pretty romantick Turn for Virtue, and all that', and 'Romantick Idiot' when speaking of Pamela. Cf. 'the delicate adoration, the platonic purity, which marks the love of the Hero, and suits the sensibility of his Mistress' (*The Microcosm*, no. 26, 14 May 1787) and Hurd's account of the idealization of chastity by Germanic peoples and in the romances (Letter III).

allegory referred to specifically as romantic, for instance, though critics counted a love of metaphor and allegory with a love of fabling as qualities of the Eastern peoples from whom Europe derived romance. Addison discussing 'the fairy way of writing' includes not only giants and enchanters, but also allegorical figures, like Milton's Sin and Death.[1] These also are 'persons who are not to be found in being', creations of the poet's imagination which makes 'new worlds of its own'. Allegory is but an extension of metaphor, a 'continuous Metaphor' as Daniel Waterland calls it,[2] and both are characteristic products of the unbridled imagination of the East and of 'romantic' writers. Thus when, in 1650, we first meet the word 'Romantick' on the title page of Thomas Bayly's allegorical romance *Herba Parietis, or The Wall-Flower. As it grew out of the Stone-Chamber Belonging to the Metropolitan Prison of London, called Newgate. Being a History Which is Partly Romantick, Morally Devine whereby a Marriage Betweene Reallity & fancie is Solemnied by Devinity*,[3] it is not accidental that the aspect of the work that is called 'romantic' is allegorical. It was in the allegorical figures that Bayly's imagination was free to create a world outside Nature. The parts of his romance that were 'romantic' were not 'true', not records of events which had actually happened. They were imagined or invented, as were romances, the product of the 'fancie'. 'That imagination which is most free', wrote Henry More in 1659, is 'such as we use in Romantick Inventions'.[4]

Bayly's use of 'romantic' is simply descriptive, and means 'freely invented', not as an imitation of real events, but newly created by the imagination. In his work he was using the mode

---

[1] *Spectator*, 419. In no. 357 he explains why allegorical figures are not suitable for epic poetry, 'which ought to appear credible in all its principal parts'.

[2] D. Waterland, *A General Preface to Scripture Vindicated* (1732), p. vi.

[3] During the seventeenth century, when the reading of the voluminous French romances, and their English translations and imitations, was at its height, the need for an adjective that would mean 'like the romances', led to the development of many forms—romanza (1640); romance (as adj.) (1653); romancial (1653); romancist (1653); romancer (1654); romancy (1654); romancicall (1656); romanical (1665); romantically (1668); romanticly (1681); romancing (1695)—in addition to 'romantic'. 'Romantics' as a noun, meaning 'features suggestive of romance', is used of the *Arcadia* in 1628. See OED. s.v. Romantic.

[4] Henry More, *The Immortality of the Soule* (1659), ii. p. ix.

of romance for spiritual ends. In Bunyan's *Pilgrim's Progress* (1670) we have another example of the completely spiritual romance. Much of Bunyan's scenery—the Enchanted Ground, the Castle of Despair, the Valley of the Shadow, with their hobgoblins, satyrs, invisible foes and unseen dangers—and such a character as Mr Greatheart, protector of damsels in distress and conqueror of giants, derives from the romances.[1] Yet to the Puritan the use of the romantic mode for conveying spiritual truths was abhorrent. 'But it is feigned', Bunyan imagines him objecting because St Paul had warned against fiction and old wives' tales.[2] The objection extended even to the use of metaphor as single figures, or in expanded form as allegory— 'They drown the weak; metaphors make us blind'.[3] This distrust of fiction, metaphor and allegory, the products of the imagination, was not confined to the Puritan. In an age distrustful of the 'Imaginative Powers' as 'breathing a gross dew upon the pure Glass of our Understandings', it was natural that the term 'romantic' should be launched on its career as 'an exploding word'. Romance was the child of the unbridled imagination. Obadiah Walker, a Roman Catholic, makes clear the link between 'romance' as the literature produced by the imagination at its most free, and 'romance' as indicating the ascendancy of Imagination over Judgement in the ordinary exercise of human thought; 'romances in thought' is his term for the 'false notions of things . . . wandering and insignificant fancies *in the brain*' which were the product of the imaginative faculty, stifling clear thought.[4]

'Every ass that's romantick', writes Robert Wolseley in 1685, that is, that gives free rein to his imagination, 'believes he's inspired'.[5] The 'fantastics' the 'enthusiasts', victims of their imaginations, were 'romantic'. Shaftesbury's Philocles, in *The*

[1] On Bunyan's debt to the romances, see H. Golder, 'Bunyan's Valley of the Shadow', *JEGP*, xxx (1931), 55–72.

[2] In I *Timothy*, 1:4; 4:7; II *Timothy*, 4:1–4.

[3] *Pilgrim's Progress*, 'The Author's Apology for his Book'.

[4] See p. 39 above. William Gunn, in 1819, writes: 'the *anticipations* of *tomorrow*, are little more than *romances of the mind*, which, in a greater or less degree, subject the understanding to the imagination'. (W. Gunn, ed. The '*Historia Brittonum*' *commonly attributed to Nennius* (1819), p. xxviii.)

[5] Preface to *Valentinian* in Spingarn, *Critical Essays of the Seventeenth Century* (Oxford, 1908), iii. 12.

Moralists: A Philosophical Rhapsody (1709) listens to an enthusiastic prose-poem (i.e. in a 'romantic' style) in praise of 'Glorious Nature'. He is persuaded to admire 'romantic' scenery—'rude *Rocks*, the mossy *Caverns*, the irregular unwrought *Grotto's*, and broken *Falls* of Waters, with all the horrid Graces of the *Wilderness* itself'—but he is uneasy to think that those who are 'deep in this *romantick* way' are looked on 'as a People either plainly out of their wits, or overrun with *Melancholy* and Enthusiasm'.[1] To be romantic was to be mad, or melancholy, or 'enthusiastic'.

One form of the melancholy, if we may judge from the words of Thomson and Gray, was a gentle sweet sadness, a 'fine romantic kind of melancholy, on the fading of the year', says Thomson;[2] a mixed feeling of sadness and joy, such as Gray felt on reading a description of Mount Lebanon (not unlike the scenery admired by Philocles), 'The country about is peculiarly romantick, an uncommon Mixture of Woods, Waters, Grotto's, Rocks, Ruins, and the Sea'.[3]

5

When the epithet 'romantic' was introduced, romances were not simply associated with stories of knights and chivalry. Such stories, versions of the medieval and Peninsular romances, were normally called 'Histories', and were not the principal romances with which those who coined the epithet were acquainted.[4] Scenery, for example, was 'romantic' if it was like the scenery described in, for example, Sidney's *Arcadia*, or Spenser's *Faerie Queene*, or French romances such as *Clelia* and *Astrea*—a pastoral scenery with 'flocks of sheep and nut-brown shepherdesses'.[5] Romance-writers idealized such scenes, which were not often to be met with in real nature. Thomas Sprat accused Sorbière of writing

---

[1] Shaftesbury, *Works* (1727), ii. 393–4.
[2] Letter to William Cranstoun, September 1725, quoted in A. D. McKillop, *Background to Thomson's 'Seasons'* (1942), p. 3.
[3] Notebook, 1744, quoted in W. P. Jones, *Thomas Gray, Scholar* (Cambridge, Mass., 1937), p. 75.
[4] See below, Appendix 3.
[5] J. Britton, *Memoirs of John Aubrey* (1845), pp. 32–3.

so Romantically of the *Vallies*, the *Hills*, and the *hedges* of *Kent*, that the *Authors* of *Clelia*, or *Astrea*, scarce ever venture to say so much on the like occasion.[1]

Evelyn described Guy of Warwick's grotto as

A squalid den made in the rock, croun'd yet with venerable Oakes, & respecting a goodly streame, so as, were it improv'd as it might be, 'twere capable of being render'd one of the most romantique & pleasant places imaginable.[2]

It required the imagination of a poet to create out of nature's raw material a scene which could be called 'romantic'. The idealized scenery beloved of the romance writers of the seventeenth century included not only pastoral landscapes, but also woods, rugged hills and castles, deserts, streams, caves, precipices, cataracts, hermitages, and scenes of wild and irregular beauty. 'Romantic' was a simple descriptive term indicating such scenes 'as a writer of romance might have delighted to feign',[3] or 'qui rapellent les descriptions des poèmes et des romans'.[4] It was not, therefore, an 'exploding word', but one which, when not simply descriptive, expressed approval.

Other things apart from scenery were 'romantic'. In the translator's preface to Charles Sorel's *The Extravagant Shepherd. The Anti-Romance* (1653) J. Davies uses 'romantic' more than once—'*Lysis*'s contempt of good Books, shews he esteems all pedantry that is not Romantick', 'As for *Lysis*'s carrying away of his Mistress, 'tis an ordinary Romantick humour', 'your *Romantick Shepherds* being all Beggars'.[5] Sir William Lower,

[1] *Observations on Sorbière's Relation d'un Voyage en Angleterre* (1665), p. 43.

[2] *Diary*, 3 August 1654, ed. E. S. de Beer (Oxford, 1956), iii. 121. See also entries under 22 July 1654, 27 June 1654, 23 June 1679, and Evelyn's letter to Sir Thomas Browne, 28 January 1660, in *Works of Browne*, ed. G. Keynes (1928–31), vi. 305. Romantic scenery was first discussed by L. P. Smith, *Four Words, Romantic, Originality, Creative, Genius*, S.P.E. Tract, No. 17. 1924.

[3] Johnson, *Journey to the Western Isles* (1775), ed. R. W. Chapman (Oxford, 1924), pp. 35, 69, 141. cf. *Adventurer*, 108, 17 November 1753. See also *Spectator*, 74; Thomson, *Spring*, ll. 941–2, *Summer*, l. 381, *Autumn*, ll. 894 f., and Preface to *Winter*; Sterne, *Tristram Shandy*, Book vii, ch. 29, Book viii, ch. 1; Uvedale Price, *Essays on the Picturesque* (1810), i. 88, 248–9, ii. 361 n. For Gilpin's distinction between 'romantic' and 'picturesque' see W. P. Ker, *Art of Poetry* (Oxford, 1923), pp. 73–4. For descriptions of romantic scenery, see A. O. Lovejoy, 'The Chinese Origin of a Romanticism', *Essays in History of Ideas* (Baltimore, 1948), pp. 130–1.

[4] J. Garner, *Le Nouveau Dictionnaire universel* (Rouen, 1802), s.v. romantique.

[5] *The Extravagant Shepherd* (1653), sig. a3ᵛ, d1, d1ᵛ.

translating R. de Cerizier's *The Triumphant Lady: or The Crowned Innocence* in 1656, refers to the heroine as 'a Romantick Lady'.[1] Francis Kirkman, considering the improbabilities of romances, writes in 1661, 'I am sure in most Romantic Plays there hath been more probability, than in our true (though sad) Stories'.[2]

6

Romances were regarded as the product of the unbridled imagination, 'the great general distinction of these works has been the ascendancy of imagination over judgment' wrote Foster.[3] They were written by men who were capable of the wildest excess without being conscious of any excess at all. 'They did not perceive any want of consistency and probability in descriptions of objects, and narrations of actions, which a sound judgment would have convicted of monstrous absurdity.'[4] Since the ascendancy of imagination over judgement is the great distinction of romances, it must also be the foundation of whatever is called 'romantic' in human character. To be 'romantic' a person must be possessed of a weak judgement and a strong imagination. Such a person does not 'exercise' his imagination but indulges it

till it usurp an entire ascendancy over the mind, and then every subject presented to that mind will excite imagination, instead of understanding, to work; imagination will throw its colours where the intellectual faculty ought to draw its lines; imagination will accumulate metaphors where reason ought to deduce arguments; images will take the place of thoughts, and scenes of disquisitions.[5]

When the imagination was given free rein in the invention of a fable, its product was 'romantic'; the resulting work was made up of impossibilities, whether in the form of 'impenetrable

---

[1] *The Triumphant Lady* (1656), sig. A3.

[2] Preface to Webster and Rowley's *Thracian Wonder* (1661), quoted in H. E. Rollins, 'The English Commonwealth Drama', *Studies in Philology*, xviii (1921), 289 n.

[3] John Foster, 'On the Application of the Epithet Romantic', in *Essays in a Series of Letters to a Friend* (1806), i. 243 (subsequently referred to as Foster). cf. Sir Richard Blackmore, quoted on p. 8 above.

[4] ibid., p. 245.   [5] ibid., p. 248.

armour, Inchanted Castles, invulnerable bodies, Iron Men, Flying horses',[1] or of platonic lovers, and idealized or imaginary scenery. But not all that was 'romantic', as we have seen in the case of scenery, was despised. Addison, for example, praises Milton's account of Thammuz as 'finely romantic',[2] when listing particular beauties in *Paradise Lost*. There is a wild improbability about the story of 'Thammuz yearly wounded', while the river Adonis runs 'purple to the sea' and the Syrian damsels lament. Shakespeare's most 'romantic' play naturally called forth the praise of Joseph Warton. Writing of *The Tempest* he comments,

He has there given the reins to his boundless imagination and has carried the romantic, the wonderful and the wild, to the most pleasing extravagance. The scene is a desolate island; and the characters the most new and singular that can be well conceived: a prince who practises magic, an attendant spirit, a monster, the son of a witch, and a young lady who had been brought to this solitude in her infancy, and had never beheld a man except her father.[3]

To be 'romantic', a work had to contain the elements typical of a romance; there was nothing vague in the use of the term. Spenser was 'a romantic poet' ,wrote Thomas Warton, because he undertook 'a recital of chivalrous atchievements'.[4]

7

The remoteness of the world of the romance writer was at once the source of critical objection to the romances, and the reason for regarding them as morally harmless, since 'the reader was in very little danger of making any applications to himself'.[5] But where a person did indulge in behaviour or hopes which could be related to the actions and ideals of characters in romance, then the epithet 'romantic' was applied. Thus, according to John Foster, who in 1805 summarized the usages of the term, whatever seemed singular, impracticable, or foolishly adventurous, was stigmatized as 'romantic'. Perhaps, Foster asks those who use the term,

[1] Hobbes, in Spingarn, *Critical Essays of the Seventeenth Century* (Oxford, 1908), ii. 61.
[2] *Spectator*, 303.   [3] *Adventurer*, 93, 25 September 1753.
[4] *Observations on the Faerie Queene* (1762), ii. 88.
[5] *Rambler*, 4.

you mean that the ideas . . . associate in your mind with the fantastic images of romance, and that you cannot help thinking of enchanted castles, encounters with giants, solemn exorcisms, fortunate surprises, knights and wizards, dragons and griffins. You cannot distinguish what the absurdity in any notion *is*, but you fancy what it is *like*. You therefore condemn it, not by giving a definition, but by applying an epithet which assigns it to a class of things already condemned.[1]

Ruskin, nearly half a century later, pleaded for the abandonment of 'romancing' as a synonym for 'lying', and of 'romantic' as the equivalent of 'weak, foolish, speculative, unpractical, unprincipled'.[2]

Foster explains the usages of 'romantic', by distinguishing between various modes of uncontrolled imagination, each one of which he dubs 'romantic' from the presence of the same mode in romances.[3] First, since romances 'display a destiny and a course of life totally unlike the common condition of mankind', those are *romantic* who believe that they are 'born to some peculiar and extraordinary destiny, while there are no extraordinary indications in the person or his circumstances'. Or, connected with this, a romantic person expects a 'life of singular felicity', in spite of the evidence around him of the evils which harass others. Such a person 'takes no deliberate account of what is inevitable in the lot of humanity, of the sober probabilities of his own situation, or of those principles in the constitution of his mind which are perhaps unfavourable to happiness'. Secondly there is the sentimentally romantic person, who believes 'that his peculiar lot is to realise all the wonders of generous, virtuous, noble, unalienable friendship, and of enraptured, uninterrupted, and unextinguishable love, that fiction ever talked of in her dreams'. The third type of romantic person is the man in whom extravagant imagination is linked with a passion for variety and novelty. He will refuse to consider a life of 'confined regularity, and common plodding occupations', and will believe that he 'was born for an

---

[1] Foster, pp. 242–3.

[2] Ruskin, *Lectures on Architecture and Painting* (1853), opening of Lecture II.

[3] Foster, pp. 255 f. What follows in the text is a synopsis of Foster's explanation of the meanings of 'romantic', not my own.

adventurer, whose story will one day amaze the world'. Persons of these three types, who regard themselves as exceptions to the usual lot of humanity, are notable for their affectation of manners—disdaining 'regular hours, usual dresses and common forms of transacting business'. The ideals they entertain are not uncongenial with the human mind, but are absurd when held by adults who neglect the factors which show that the ideals cannot be realized.

This also is the folly of a fourth type of romantic, who forms schemes or indulges expectations 'essentially incongruous with the nature of man'—schemes for retiring from society, and for promoting wisdom and nobility by new systems of education. Equally romantic, because they are unadapted to human nature, are the speculations of philosophers and philanthropists who believe in systems based on 'equality of property and modes of life throughout society'. Until men have been stripped of their ambition, craft, avarice, stupidity, indolence and selfishness, 'these beautiful theories' will be read as 'romances'. The age of chivalry itself shows, in many of its practices, especially those relating to love, the same incongruity with the simplest principles of human nature. To the modern *romantic* the attractiveness of ideal schemes may be occasioned, or at least augmented, by 'an exclusive taste for what is grand'.[1] 'They cut out the grand objects, to dispose them into a world of their own. All the images in their intellectual scene must be colossal and mountainous.' Such a taste will lead a man to thoughts of revolution in the state in order to achieve his grandiose schemes

The man will wish to summon the world to throw aside its tame accustomed pursuits, and adopt at once more magnificent views and objects, and will be indignant at mankind that they cannot or will not be sublime. Impatient of little means and slow processes, he will wish for violent transitions and entirely new institutions. He will perhaps determine to set men the example of performing something great, in some ill-judged sanguine project that will fail . . .

The utopian philosopher and the idealist-revolutionary are both 'romantic'.

[1] cf. Coleridge, quoted above, p. 37.

The sixth application of the epithet 'romantic' may be explained in terms of one of the qualities of works of romance—'the utter violation of all the relations between ends and means'. Sometimes the ends proposed seem impossible, sometimes the means used for achieving probable ends are fantastic and improbable. When this absurdity prevails 'in the calculations of real life, you may justly apply the epithet, romantic'. This tendency is encouraged by novels, which, 'though more like real life than the romances which preceded them (and which are now, with some alterations, partly come into vogue again)' are still full of lucky incidents and adventures. They encourage readers to entertain hopes which cannot be fulfilled. In real life romantic schemes for civilizing barbarous nations without the intervention of conquest are indulged in by animated young philanthropists. Similarly men overvalue teaching and instruction as a means in forming the character of youth, without realizing that 'external circumstances' (environment) are the main formative influence. It is *romantic* to expect that inadequate means can produce a desired effect.

Foster also gives examples of applications of the epithet which he considers to be improper. A man who 'contemplates with emotion' and proposes to himself, in all humility, to imitate, 'the class of men who have been illustrious for their excellence and their wisdom'[1] is not properly *romantic*. Nor is the man who, at the dictate of reason and conscience, attempts to do good and to follow a virtuous discipline, against the normal conduct of his class in society.

The irreligious will apply this epithet to the determination to make, and the zeal to inculcate, great exertions and sacrifices for a purely moral ideal reward . . . The epithet will often be applied to a man who feels it an imperious duty to realize, as far as possible, and as soon as possible, everything which in theory he approves and applauds.

Lastly,

it may be very romantic for a man to promise himself to effect such designs upon others as it may be very reasonable to meditate for

[1] Foster, p. 335.

himself... But the schemes of eminent personal attainments... are romantic only when there is some fatal intellectual or moral defect in the mind itself which has adopted them.

Foster's treatment of 'romantic', as an 'exploding word, of more special deriding significance than the other words of its order, such as wild, extravagant, visionary, ... a standard expression of contemptuous dispatch',[1] covers most of the uses of the word as applied to behaviour, and shows how the usages grew out of long-standing attitudes towards the romances. It systematizes the various types of behaviour that eighteenth-century writers usually saw as the outcome of a person's attempting to imitate in real life the attitudes of heroes or heroines of romance.[2]

8

'Romantic' was 'so variously and disapprovingly applied'[3] and had gathered to itself such an aura of disapproval that its use as a term to describe contemporary literature was only possible in the vocabulary of a hostile critic. Of contemporary criticisms of the novel of the last thirty years of the century, Miss Tompkins comments,

'Romantic', in its general sense of extravagant, was applied to scenes in books where probability has been sacrificed to produce some thrilling effect or satisfactory conclusion. Thus, all sorts of recognitions, escapes, providential reunions and resuscitations of the dead count as romantic, however baldly presented; and the word was transferred to such incidents of real life as lie outside reasonable expectation. It is this sense of extravagance, for which they perceive no adequate motive and no adequate compensation, that accounts for its tart flavour on the tongue of many a critic. They flung it as a rebuke to bring to heel a writer who forsook 'nature'...[4]

---

[1] ibid., i. 240.

[2] Attacks on romances and novels are common in the periodical essays, sometimes taking the form of anecdotes illustrating 'romantic' behaviour and its unhappy consequences. See the accounts of the 'romantic' husband and wife in *The Lounger*, Nos. 74, 92, and George Colman the Elder, *Polly Honeycombe, A Dramatic Novel in One Act* (1760).

[3] *The Popular Novel*, p. 212.　　　　[4] ibid.

But in spite of the critics, the romantic came in with a rush in the novel. However much Richardson was thought of by some as an author who borrowed none of his 'Excellencies from the romantick Flights of unnatural Fancy',[1] many writers in the second half of the century saw his works as encouraging romantic notions in the heads of readers. In addition, the spate of Gothic romances after Walpole's *Castle of Otranto* (1765) brought before an avid reading public the marvellous, the terrible and the superstitious, 'fictions of the most wild and horrible grandeur', whose appeal was heightened by their being set in medieval and renaissance scenes unhampered by the restraint of authenticity.

'Romantic' was applied to works as diverse as *Pamela* and *The Castle of Otranto*, *Clelia*, *The Faerie Queene*, and *Guy of Warwick*, which have in common only their tenuous connection with the real world. Literature of this type appealed to the untrained reader; the chapbook romances to children and the least literate in the community; Richardson and the Gothic novel to the growing reading public of the lower middle classes. We can apply to the late eighteenth century Bagehot's description of the middle of the nineteenth, as a realm of the half-educated, lacking a literary aristocracy to guide its taste amongst a mass of books. And left to itself it chose a 'showy' art, a '*glaring* art which catches and arrests the eye for a moment', but which cannot hold the attention for long. The hasty reader 'passed on to some new excitement, which in its turn stimulates for an instant, and then is passed by for ever'. The growing importance of women readers was also noted by Bagehot as influencing the growth of an art of 'delicate unreality'.[2] Reading for such classes was not a strenuous exercise but a transient source of unthinking pleasure, a pursuit of the author 'with much hurry and impatience to his last page'.[3]

The romances of whatever age were ideally suited for this

---

[1] *Pamela* (1740). The first Recommendatory Letter.

[2] Walter Bagehot, *Wordsworth, Tennyson and Browning* (1864) in *English Critical Essays (Nineteenth Century)*, ed. E. D. Jones (1924), p. 490; cf. Ian Watt, *The Rise of the Novel* (1957), pp. 43–5.

[3] Steele, *The Guardian*, No. 60.

type of reader, for they 'are to be comprehended without any great labour of the mind, or the exercise of our rational faculty, and where a strong fancy will serve the turn, with little or no burden to the memory'.[1] At different periods, Steele, Carlyle and Bagehot all wrote against such an unguided taste for mere excitement from print. During the last quarter of the eighteenth century, when the novelists supplied the works demanded by this taste, the aristocracy of letters was engaged in advocating for poetry a return to the fables of the middle ages. Whatever guidance in taste, therefore, the lower classes of readers had merely conformed to their own predilection for the excitement of the strange.

Joseph Warton, for instance, encouraged the view of poetry as divided into two schools, the 'lovers and imitators of Spenser and Milton', and 'those of Dryden, Boileau, and Pope'.[2] The deepest reverence was reserved for the former; 'no man of a true poetical spirit, *is master of himself while he reads* them',[3] whereas Pope, 'whatever poetical enthusiasm he actually possessed, he withheld and stifled', 'imagination was not his predominant talent, because he indulged it not', '*good sense* and *judgment* were his characteristical excellences'. The value, to a reader, of not being master of himself as he reads, is not defined. But by implication the 'more genuine flights of poetry' are appreciable only by men of 'true poetical spirit', a narrower audience than Pope is thought to have attained. His poems are 'fit for universal perusal', 'adapted to all ages and stations; for the old and the young, the man of business and the scholar'.[4] The encouragement of the indulgence of the imagination in poetry, of invention, new manners and images, in place of morality and comment on contemporary events, people, follies and evils, could not but provide the sensational novelists with an impetus to turn the novel in the same direction. The

[1] Huet, *Of the Origin of Romances*, in Croxall, *Select Collection of Novels* (1720), i. xlv.

[2] V. Knox, *Essays, Moral and Literary* (1782), ed. 1823, iii, 51. 'On the prevailing Taste in Poetry'. Knox writes of the two schools, the 'English Antique' and 'the school of Pope'.

[3] J. Warton, *Essay on the Genius and Writings of Pope* (ed. 1806), ii. 403.

[4] This is how Addison had described 'genuine' poetry when discussing *Chevy Chase*.

effect, both in poetry and the novel, was not to narrow the audience to those of 'true poetical spirit'—though doubtless many of the multitude of readers congratulated themselves on their superior sensibility—but to widen it. The aristocracy of letters turned attention to the past, as the source from which materials and inspiration were to be drawn for a more imaginative and inventive poetry. The scholars laboriously cast light on the manners and customs of that past. And those who reaped the harvest of popularity took the encouragement and the materials and produced on the pattern of Horace Walpole. The new 'fairy way of writing', like the old, turned its back on the present, on adherence to the observed experiences of men, and indulged imagination to produce new worlds outside nature, which appealed widely—as all romances always have— to readers who have not been arduously trained to derive their pleasure from the 'reflection and remembrance of what one has read'. Their enjoyment came from the 'transient satisfaction of what one does'.[1]

Wordsworth renounced the old 'Romantic tale by Milton left unsung', 'dire enchantments', chivalry and the migration of Odin,

> The moving accident is not my trade;
> To freeze the blood I have no ready arts.[2]

But Southey, Scott, Byron, Moore and Campbell, to name only the most successful of the new writers, turned to the distant in time or place for their narratives, and pleased their many readers, if less violently than Walpole, Mrs Radcliffe or 'Monk' Lewis had done, yet equally by appealing to the fascination of whatever was remote from contemporary experience.

The medieval romances themselves were a very small part of the stream which fed the new taste. The world of romance that the scholars investigated was, until the publication of George Ellis's prose versions, not accessible to those without

---

[1] Steele, *Guardian*, No. 60.
[2] 'Hart-Leap Well' (1800), Part II, ll. 1–2. cf. 'Peter Bell', Prologue, ll. 136–7.

> The dragon's wing, the magic ring,
> I shall not covet for my dower.

cf. his comments on *Marmion*, quoted in Lockhart, *Life of Scott*, ch. xvi.

the inclination to master Middle English. The pseudo-Spenserian language used by Chatterton in the Rowley poems was more easily intelligible than the language of *King Horn*, while the rhythmical prose of Macpherson's Ossian poems ensured a wide audience among those with a taste for the out-pourings of a 'primitive' bard who would never have troubled themselves with 'a phraseology so obsolete as that of Lydgate'.[1] The 'scholars of taste and genius' encouraged the use of 'antiquarian lore' in poetry and in the Gothic novel so success-fully that Malone, writing to Percy in 1809, could observe, 'the whole world is to be "bespread with the dust of antiquity" and what was formerly thought a good subject of ridicule, is now quite the fashion'.[2] Scott's poems, for instance, 'brought chivalry again into temporary favour'.[3] But time has shown that Carlyle and Bagehot were right in their attack on 'the doctrine that poetry is a light amusement for idle hours, a metrical species of sensational novel'.[4] In their attempt to revivify poetry, Percy and the Wartons directed attention to what Carlyle called 'external circumstances', to the customs and manners of the middle ages, to stories of chivalry and enchantment, to the excitement of a past age which was idealized in their minds. Looking back on what had been the outcome of this enthusiasm, Carlyle characterized the wrongness of this seeking for new subject-matter for poetry.

The ordinary poet, like the ordinary man, is forever seeking in external circumstances the help which can be found only in him-self. In what is familiar and near at hand, he discerns no form or comeliness: home is not poetical but prosaic; it is in some past, distant, conventional heroic world, that poetry resides; were he there and not here, were he thus and not so, it would be well with him. Hence our innumerable host of rose-coloured Novels and iron-mailed Epics, with their locality not on the Earth, but somewhere nearer to the Moon. Hence our Virgins of the Sun, and our Knights of the Cross, malicious Saracens in turbans, and copper-coloured Chiefs in wampum, and so many other truculent figures from the heroic

[1] George Ellis, in G. L. Way, *Fabliaux or Tales* (1800), ii. 297.
[2] *Percy–Malone Correspondence*, p. 260.
[3] Jeffrey's phrase, in his critique of *Marmion* in *Edinburgh Review*, April 1808, quoted by Lockhart, *Life of Scott*, ch. xvi.
[4] W. Bagehot, p. 433.

times or the heroic climates, who on all hands swarm in our poetry. Peace be with them! But yet, as a great moralist proposed preaching to the men of this century, so would we fain preach to the poets, 'a sermon on the duty of staying at home'. Let them be sure that heroic ages and heroic climates can do little for them. That form of life has attraction for us, less because it is better or nobler than our own, than simply because it is different; and even this attraction must be of the most transient sort. For will not our own age, one day, be an ancient one, and have as quaint a costume as the rest; not contrasted with the rest, therefore, but ranked along with them, in respect of quaintness? Does Homer interest us now, because he wrote of what passed beyond his native Greece, and two centuries before he was born; or because he wrote what passed in God's world, and in the heart of man, which is the same after thirty centuries? Let our poets look to this: is their feeling really finer, truer, and their vision deeper than that of other men,—they have nothing to fear, even from the humblest subject; is it not so,—they have nothing to hope, but an ephemeral favour, even from the highest.[1]

9

'No age', wrote Carlyle, 'ever seemed the Age of Romance to *itself*',[2] yet all ages are Ages of Romance. To be romantic is to feel the 'otherness' of the past. The scholars I have studied felt this intensely. Their work is not only the prologue to the growth of modern literary scholarship; it is the basis of the revival of interest in medieval literature and society which looms so large in the following century. Wherever we turn we stumble on their influence and their successors—hosts of scholars editing medieval texts, and later on of undergraduates studying their editions; political thought pervaded by ideas caught from a study of feudalism, in Carlyle's *Past and Present*, in Francis Palgrave's *The Merchant and the Friar* (1837), in the New England Movement; novelists like Peacock in *Crotchet Castle* (1831), mocking at the taste for medievalism, or using a romance as a mirror-image of a modern tale, as Mrs Gaskell does in *Sylvia's Lovers* (1863); poets whether they be Tennyson or the vicar of Morwenstow, Lytton or Swinburne, choosing

[1] Carlyle, reviewing Lockhart's *Life of Burns*, in *Edinburgh Review* (1828), reprinted in *Miscellaneous Essays* (1872), ii. 12–13.
[2] *The Diamond Necklace* (1837), ch. 1.

Arthur as their theme; others, like Morris, retelling Nordic legends, or, like Rossetti, translating Dante and his contemporaries; the Pre-Raphaelite Brotherhood; art critics of the school of Ruskin. The romance scholars from Percy to Scott left as their legacy the realization that the middle ages originated or perfected 'nearly all the inventions and social institutions, whereby we yet live as civilized men'.[1]

[1] Carlyle, reviewing William Taylor's *Historic Survey of German Poetry* (1830), *Miscellaneous Essays* (1872), iii. 240.

1

English Medieval Scholarship before Percy

The 'fonder, more earnest looking back into the Past' which Carlyle saw as beginning about the middle of the eighteenth century in Germany, France and England, had its roots in the accumulated work of the antiquaries, scholars and collectors of the previous two centuries. The foundations were laid by those scholars who rescued from destruction the manuscripts cast out of the monasteries and cathedral libraries throughout France, Germany and England in the sixteenth century, as a result of the Huguenot Wars in France, the Peasants' War in Germany, and the Dissolution of the Monasteries in England.

In France such scholars as Pierre Pithou (1539–96) and André Duchesne (1584–1640) collected manuscripts illustrating medieval history. In England, the collectors were Archbishop Parker, Camden, Selden, Spelman, Sir Robert Cotton, Sir Kenelm Digby, Bishop Moore, and later on Robert and Edward Harley. The material assembled by Leland in the sixteenth century, some of which was used by Bale for his bibliographical account of English writers,[1] was to prove invaluable to later scholars when it was finally published in the eighteenth century.[2] Anglo-Saxon studies began in the middle of the sixteenth century, among a group of scholars surrounding Archbishop Parker. In the following century they were pursued in Cambridge, under Abraham Wheloc, and later at Oxford under Edward Thwaites.

Even though the middle ages were regarded from the early sixteenth century as ignorant, barbarous and superstitious, yet, according to Leland, even before 1540 'the antiquities of the Saxon Church were being studied as a source of reformation propaganda'.[3] Many antiquaries of Elizabeth's reign were interested

[1] John Bale, *Scriptorum Illustrium Majoris Britanniae Catalogus* (Basle, 1559).
[2] John Leland, *Commentarius de Scriptoribus Britannicis* (Oxford, 1709); *De Rebus Britannicis Collectanea* (1770); *Itinerary* (1744–5).
[3] T. D. Kendrick, *British Antiquity* (1950), p. 115.

in topics that took them to medieval documents[1]—the history and antiquity of laws, institutions, titles, customs, privileges and land-tenure, local and ecclesiastical history, from Roman Britain to their own day. Bacon noted that Martin Luther had been 'enforced to awaken all antiquity and to call former times to his succours . . . so that the ancient authors, both in divinity and humanity, which had a long time slept in libraries, began generally to be read and re-solved'.[2] An antiquarian bias was characteristic of the English Reformation,[3] and much of the research into medieval history in the sixteenth and seventeenth centuries was motivated by a desire to 'establish the antiquity of the thought and customs of the Reformed Church'. Pre-Conquest England was not simply interesting in itself, but a source of valuable ammunition for contemporary controversy. 'By the ancient Saxon Monuments', wrote John Fortescue-Aland in 1714, 'we are able to demonstrate that the Faith, Worship and Discipline of our Holy Church is in great measure the same with that of the primitive Saxons.'[4] The contemporary urgency to establish a sense of continuity in ecclesiastical and constitutional affairs produced a steady stream of publications of medieval documents. Collections were made of monastic annals and charters, chronicles, registers, muniments, genealogies, monumental inscriptions, heraldic achieve-ments. Some of this material issued in county histories, like Sir William Dugdale's *Antiquities of Warwickshire illustrated from Records, Leiger-Books, Manuscripts, Charters, Evidences, Tombes and Armes* (1656).[5] Some issued as collections of documents, giving an account of English Monastic life, like Dugdale's *Monasticum Anglicanum* (1655-73).

The immense erudition, enthusiasm and labour of so many antiquaries engaged on research into medieval documents hardly allows us to regard the scholars of the later eighteenth century as the discoverers of the middle ages. They were interested in an aspect of the middle ages that the previous workers in the field had ignored. They were loud in their praises of such works as the *Linguarum Veterum Septentrionalum Thesaurus* of George Hickes, that had begun

---

[1] See the essays collected by Hearne in *A Collection of Curious Discourses* (Oxford, 1720), papers read to a Society of Antiquaries that flourished from 1590 on.

[2] Bacon, *Advancement of Learning* (1605), I, iv, 2.

[3] See Douglas, p. 19; Kendrick, p. 115.

[4] J. Fortescue-Aland, *The Difference between an Absolute and Limited Monarchy* (1714), p. lxviii.

[5] Similar work was done by Anthony Wood on the University and City of Oxford, by John Aubrey on Surrey, William Burton on Leicestershire, Robert Plot on Oxfordshire and Staffordshire, Elias Ashmole on Berkshire, Robert Thorston on Nottinghamshire, Peter le Neve on Norfolk, Ralph Thoresby on Leeds, Francis Drake on York, and so on.

in 1703. It 'never had nor will have its equal' wrote Ritson.[1]
Later scholars used the information in it, about Anglo-Saxon and
Norse literature, its Anglo-Saxon grammar, and Wanley's list of
Anglo-Saxon manuscripts. But, apart from Edward Lye, whom
Percy called 'the first in the world for northern literature', they were
not engaged on research in the fields of Old English and Old Norse.
Instead they raided the earlier scholars for specific pieces of infor-
mation, as Percy did when compiling an account of English mins-
trels, in which he quotes from Leland, Bale, Camden, Junius, Wood,
Dugdale, Plot, Smith's edition of Bede, Gibson's edition of the
Saxon Chronicle, Wharton's *Anglia Sacra*, Rymer's *Foedera*, Du
Cange, Hearne, and many others. They considered the long line of
chronicles so carefully edited by Hearne to be, at best, the result of
misplaced energy. Thomas Warton condemned the 'antiquaries of
former times' for employing 'their industry in reviving obscure
fragments of uninstructive morality or uninteresting history'.[2]
Warton went on to explain that 'in the present age we are beginning
to make ample amends: in which the curiosity of the antiquarian is
connected with taste and genius, and his researches tend to display
the progress of human manners, and to illustrate the history of
society'.

The scholar and antiquary was now more likely to turn his
attention to the plays of Shakespeare, and as the century progressed,
editions steadily accumulated the information gleaned by many
different scholars. The plays started many lines of historical investigation—the history of the stage, the development of the drama
before Shakespeare, the beliefs and customs of the Elizabethans,
the sources of Shakespeare's plots—which were regarded as suitable
topics for a man of taste to pursue because they served to illuminate
the genius of Shakespeare. The poems of Spenser and Milton were
regarded in the same way, and lovingly annotated and edited.
The scholars of 'taste and genius' took for their 'documents'
not monastic annals and charters, or bare chronicles, but works of
great creative literary genius. In medieval literature the works of
Chaucer and the romances formed the centre of interest. The texts
that had been 'overlooked or rejected' by earlier antiquaries, and
'despised as false or frivolous' became intensely interesting. It was
partly because the earlier scholars had so thoroughly worked over
the sources of medieval ecclesiastical history, and edited so many of

[1] Ritson, *Observations* (1782), p. 48. On Hickes, see Douglas, ch. iv; J. A. W.
Bennett, 'Hickes's "Thesaurus": a study in Oxford Book Production'. *English
Studies* (1948), pp. 28–45.
[2] *History* (1774), i. 209; cf. *Reliques* (1765), iii. p. ix.

the chronicles, that the later generation found it necessary to turn to other texts.

Throughout the eighteenth century there was a growing public for antiquarian literature, provided that it was presented in a humane manner. Such readers were more inclined to read Maurice Shelton's English translation (1735 and 1737) of Wotton's epitome of Hickes's *Thesaurus* than the great work itself. Month by month they were offered, in the *Gentleman's Magazine*, articles on archaeological remains, architecture, coins, monuments, epitaphs and sculpture. Most of the remains discussed are 'medieval'. Interest in Roman antiquities was, in comparison, small; so small that in 1722 William Stukeley formed a short-lived Society of Roman Knights for the study of Roman Britain. Stukeley and Alexander Gordon seem to have found the Society of Antiquaries, founded in 1718, too little interested in Roman Britain, and its members 'busying themselves to restore their Gothic Remnants'.[1] One at least of the results of the investigation of medieval works as a part of the political and religious controversies of the sixteenth and seventeenth centuries had been to direct attention to the real origins of English life. The regret, expressed so often, for the Gothic barbarism that had swept Roman life aside, and the ardent resolve to mould modern civilization and art in the pattern of the classical world, had in two centuries produced 'a great deal of good sense'. But natural curiosity about the 'Millennium of Darkness' had never been stifled. The antiquary-historian found many attractions in the middle ages. First, the genealogy of princes, and the social, commercial and governmental structure of modern nations had their foundations here, and not in classical antiquity. Secondly, there was ample opportunity for the discovery of documents historical and literary. Thirdly, it was a period which confirmed in the historian a sense of superiority instead of inferiority, to the past. Compared with the Rome of Augustus, modern man might appear puny and barbarous; compared with any moment of the Dark Ages, modern man exhibited all the signs of a steady progress towards civility.

[1] S. Piggot, *William Stukeley* (Oxford, 1950), pp. 15, 55.

2

Manuscripts of English Metrical Romances known to the Early Scholars

The romances are listed here in the order in which they are given in the *Cambridge Bibliography of English Literature*, i. 130–60. Under each romance I have given only those manuscripts or printed texts which were known to Percy, Warton, Ritson, Ellis, Scott and a few other scholars before 1810. The absence of a romance or a manuscript from this list means that, as far as I am aware, it was not used by any of these scholars. References are to Percy's list in volume three of the *Reliques* (numbered according to the 1794 list), to Warton's *History* in the 1824 edition, to Ritson's manuscript *Catalogue of Romances* (B.M. Add. MS 10, 285) and his *Metrical Romanceës* (1802), and to Ellis's *Specimens of Romances* (ed. 1811).

	Percy	Warton	Ritson	Others
RTHOUR				
Ɔ MERLIN				
Auchinleck MS	No. 13 (1767)		f. 311	
Lincoln's Inn Library, MS 150			f. 311	Ellis abstract, i. 203–323
Percy Folio MS	No. 13 (1765)			
Douce MS 236				Once owned by Edward Lhwyd
IR TRISTREM				
Auchinleck MS	Blair sent details of the MS for *Reliques* (1767) but missed this romance	At iii. 126n. presumed existence of a Tristrem romance from de Brunne's reference	f. 311^v, and quoted in glossary to *Ancient Songs* (1792)	Ellis (*Specimens of Early Poets* (1801), iii. 409) says Ritson discovered this romance Edited by Scott (1804)

	Percy	Warton	Ritson	Others
3 YWAIN AND GAWAIN				
(a) MS Cotton, Galba E IX		iii. 394–418	f. 311 i. 1–169	The MS was transcribed by J. W. Reed in 1777, the transcript being now Dou MS 65
4 LIBEAUS DESCONUS				
(a) Caligula A II	No. 7 (1765)	ii. 31, 40	f. 312, ii. 1–90	
(b) Lincoln's Inn Library, MS 150			f. 312	
(c) Royal Library, Naples, XIII B 29				Scott, *Letters*, xii. 47; Lockhart, vii. 351–2; *Abbotsford Library Catalogue* (1838), p. 105
(d) Percy Folio MS	No. 7 (1765)			
(e) Lambeth MS 306				H. J. Todd, *Illustrations of Chaucer and Gower* (1810), p. 167
5 JOSEPH OF ARIMATHIE				
(a) Vernon MS (Bodleian 3938)				Percy knew of the text of *The King of Tars* in this M but does not mention *Jose*
6 SIR GAWAYNE AND THE GRENE KNIGHT				
(a) Cotton, Nero A X 4				Price, in Warton (1824), i. (17) n., 187–8
7 AWNTYRS OFF ARTHURE				
(a) Douce MS 324	No. 39 (1794)		ff. 132ᵛ, 311	Printed in Pinkerton, *Scottish Poems* (1792) from transcript (now Douce MS 309) of this MS which was then owned by Ritson. Earlier in collections of Jo Baynes and Joseph Ames
(b) Thornton MS (Lincoln Cathedral Library, A, 5, 2)			ff. 132ᵛ, 311	Ritson knew the MS and presumably its contents
8 MORTE ARTHURE (Alliterative)				
(a) Thornton MS			f. 132ᵛ	Ritson knew the MS and presumably its contents

	Percy	Warton	Ritson	Others
R PERCYVELLE F GALLES Thornton MS			iii. 245	Ellis (i. 204) unable to obtain a transcript
LE MORTE ARTHUR (Stanzaic) Harley MS 2252	No. 8 (1765)	ii. 38–40	f. 311; i. p. cv	Ellis abstract, i. 324–408
HENRY LOVELICH'S HISTORY OF THE HOLY GRAIL MS Corpus Christi College, Cambridge, 80		i. 153 (from Emendations and Additions)	f. 311	Warton used lines transcribed by Nasmith
GOLAGRUS AND GAWAIN Edition pr. Edinburgh, 1508	No. 38 (1794)		f. 316	
JEASTE OF SYR GAWAYNE Douce MS 261				In Douce's possession but not known to other scholars until 1839
OTUEL Auchinleck MS	No. 33 (1767)	i. 92 n.		Ellis abstract, ii. 324–55. Douce MS 367 is Leyden's transcript of the Auchinleck text of this
Fillingham MS (B.M. Add. MS 37492)				Ellis abstract, ii. 355–68. This MS also contains *Sir Ferumbras*
ROLAND AND VERNAGU Auchinleck MS	No. 32 (1767) '*Rouland Louth*; quere'			Ellis abstract, ii. 302–23 as *Roland and Ferragus*

	Percy	Warton	Ritson	Others
16 SOWDONE OF BABYLONE (a) Fenwick MS			f. 311ᵛ	Ellis abstract, ii. 369–419 as *Sir Ferumbras*. He used transcript made by Georg Steevens when the MS was owned by Richard Farme This transcript is now Douce MS 175
17 TAILL OF RAUF COILZEAR (a) Robert Lekprevik's edition, 1572			ff. 316ʳ·ᵛ *Letters* (1830), ii. 94	
18 KYNG ALISAUNDER (a) Laud MS Misc. 622 (b) Lincoln's Inn Library MS 150 (c) Auchinleck MS		ii. 53 f. iii. 140	f. 313ᵛ	Printed in Weber, from Park's transcript
19 ALLITERATIVE ALEXANDER FRAGMENTS (a) Bodley MS 264 (b) Ashmole MS 44 (c) Trinity College, Dublin, MS D. 4, 12		ii. 145 f. ii. 145 n.	f. 313ᵛ	
20 SCOTTISH ALEXANDER BUIK (a) Unique printed copy, 1580				Examined by Scott in 18c (*Letters*, i. 252–3) and analysed by him in Webe *Metrical Romances* (1810), i. pp. lxxii f.
21 SEEGE OF TROY (a) Harley MS 525 (b) Lincoln's Inn Library MS 150			f. 313ᵛ f. 313ᵛ	

	Percy	Warton	Ritson	Others
Egerton MS 2862				The MS was owned by Farmer, later by Munro, later by General John Leveson Gower, who gave it to the Marquis of Stafford. It was examined by Captain Lord Mark Robert Kerr between 1805 and 1810. See Weber, ii. 73; H. J. Todd, *Illustrations of Chaucer and Gower* (1810), pp. 162–8
LAUD TROY BOOK Laud MS 595		ii. 406		Warton also used Lydgate's *Troy-Book* and the prose *Recuyell*
CHEVALERE ASSIGNE Caligula A II	No. 16 (1765)	ii. 149	f. 313	
ed. pr. Copland and de Worde	}No. 16 }(1765)			
KING HORN Camb. U.L. MS Gg. IV. 27.2 MS Laud Misc. 108				Discovered by J. M. Kemble (Warton, ed. 1840, i. 41 n.) Discovered by Sir Frederic Madden (Warton, ed. 1840, i. 41 n.)
Harley MS 2253	No. 1 (1765)	i. 40–6	f. 313; ii. 91–155	
HORN CHILDE AND MAIDEN RIMNILD Auchinleck MS	No. 1 (1767)	i. 45 n.	f. 313; iii. 282–320	
KING PONTUS AND THE FAIR SIDONE Ed. de Worde 1511		iii. 60	iii. 277	Recognized as version of Horn story by Price in Warton, *History* (1824), i. 46. Douce MS 384 is a fragment of *Ponthus of Galyce*

	Percy	Warton	Ritson	Others
25 HAVELOK				
(a) MS Laud Misc. 108			i. p. lxxxviii (Gaimar's version)	The Laud MS discovered Madden
26 GUY OF WARWICK				
(a) Auchinleck MS (two versions and *Reinbrun*)	No. 4,5 (1767)		f. 312	Ellis abstract, ii. 3–94
(b) Caius College, Camb., MS 107	No. 3 (1765)		f. 312; i. p. xciii	
(c) Cambridge U.L. MS Ff. II. 38	No. 3 (1765)			
(d) Copland's edition	Introd. to 'The Legend of Sir Guy' in vol. iii	ii. 1 f.	f. 51; i. p. xciii	
(e) Lydgate's *Guy* in MS Laud D. 31		i. 91 n.		
27 BEUES OF HAMTOUN				
(a) Auchinleck MS	No. 6 (1767)		f. 312; i. p. xciv	
(b) Caius College, Camb., MS 175	No. 6 (1765)	ii. 40	f. 312; i. p. xciv	Ellis abstract, ii. 95–174
(c) Cambridge U.L. Ff. II. 38	No. 6 (1765)		f. 312; i. p. xciv	
(d) Egerton MS 2862				Ellis, ii. 96. This belonge to Richard Farmer. See Todd, *Illustrations of Chau and Gower* (1810), pp. 16:
(e) Royal Library, Naples, XIII B 29				Scott, *Letters*, xii. 47; Lockhart, vii. 351–2; *Abbotsford Library Catalog* (1838), p. 105
(f) Copland editions Pynson edition	*Percy–Warton Corresp.* p. xxiii	*Observations,* ii. 40, *History,* iii. 426	f. 52; i. p. xciv	
28 RICHARD COER DE LYON				
(a) Auchinleck MS	No. 25 (1767)		i. p. lxxxvi	
(b) Egerton MS 2862				Todd, pp. 162–8
(c) Harley MS 4690			f. 53; i. p. lxxxvi	
(d) Caius College, Camb., MS 175		i. 122 n.	f. 53; i. p. lxxxvi	Ellis abstract, ii. 177–29 (using also Douce MS an de Worde)

	Percy	Warton	Ritson	Others
Douce MS 228				Imperfect, olim Richard Farmer
de Worde ed. 1528	No. 25 (1765)	i. 162 f.	i. p. lxxxvi	
LAI LE FREINE Auchinleck MS			iii. 333	Ellis abstract, iii. 291–307
SIR ORFEO Auchinleck MS Harley MS 3810			{f. 313^v; {ii. 248–69	
EMARE MS Cotton, Caligula A II	No. 15 (1765)	iii. 418	f. 313; ii. 204–47	
SIR LAUNFAL MS Cotton, Caligula A II	No. 12 (1765)	i. p. ccxxvi; ii. 409 (transcript from Percy)	f. 312; i. 170–215	Printed by Ellis in G. L. Way, *Fabliaux or Tales* (1796, 1800), ii. 298–340
SIR DEGARE Auchinleck MS			f. 312	
Cambridge U.L. Ff. II 38	No. 22 (1765)	ii. 13 n.	f. 312	
Percy Folio MS	No. 22 (1765)			
Egerton MS 2862				Todd, pp. 162–8
Douce MS 261				Imperfect
Printed edition, John King, 1560	No. 22 (1765)	ii. 13–17	f. 49	
Copland edition	No. 22 (1765)	ii. 13 n.	f. 49	Ellis abstract, iii. 358–81
SIR GOWTHER Nat. Lib. Scotland, MS 19.3.1				MS discovered by Southey, see Scott, *Letters*, i. 262–3, xii. 278; Southey, *Letters*, ed. Warter (1856), i. 340–3
MS Royal 17. B. 43		ii. 430–1	f. 315	
de Worde ed. of *Robert the Devil*			f. 158	A MS copy with coloured miniatures (temp. Eliz. I) owned by Thomas Allen, sold to J. Herbert in 1795. Edition of 50 copies, August 1797 (dated 1798). See Douce's MS note in his copy of Warton's *History* (1778), ii, Emendation to i. 190

	Percy	Warton	Ritson	Others
35 EARL OF TOULOUS				
(a) Cambridge U.L. MS Ff. II 38	No. 27 (1765)	ii. 410–12	f. 313; iii. 93–144	
(b) Ashmole MS 45	No. 27 (1775)	ii. 410–12; iii. 407	f. 313;	
(c) Thornton MS			iii. 342	
36 FLORIS AND BLAUNCHEFLUR				
(a) Auchinleck MS			f. 313	Ellis abstract, iii. 105–47
(b) Cotton MS., Vitellius D. III			f. 313	
(c) Egerton MS 2862				Todd, pp. 162–8
37 AMIS AND AMILOUN				
(a) Auchinleck MS	No. 37 (1767) Identified by S. Pegge, v. Note T in 1794 ed. to 'Essay on Minstrels'		f. 313	
(b) Douce MS 326				Olim S. Pegge. Used for Ellis abstract, iii. 396–432
(c) Harley MS 2386	No. 31 (1765)	i. 92	f. 313	
(d) Egerton MS 2862				Todd, pp. 162–8
38 KING OF TARS				
(a) Auchinleck MS	No. 34 (1767)		f. 313	
(b) Vernon MS	No. 34 (1775)	ii. 23 f.	f. 313; ii. 156–203	
39 THE SEVEN SAGES OF ROME				
(a) Auchinleck MS				Ellis abstract, iii. 3–101 (end from Galba E IX)
(b) Galba E IX		ii. 298 n.		
40 IPOMYDON				
(a) Harley MS 2252	No. 23 (1765)	ii. 31 f.	f. 312^v	Ellis abstract, iii. 215–65
(b) Printed copy in Lincoln Cathedral Library	No. 23 (1765)	ii. 31 f.	f. 49	
41 OCTAVIAN				
(a) Caligula A II	No. 19 (1765)	ii. 40 n.	f. 313	

	Percy	Warton	Ritson	Others
Cambridge U.L. MS Ff. II. 38	No. 19 (1765)	ii. 40 n.	f. 313	
WILLIAM OF PALERNE MS King's College, Camb. 13				J. Bryant, *Observations on the Poems of Thomas Rowley* (1781), pp. 14–22, 73. George Steevens was refused permission to see the MS. C. H. Hartshorne printed 560 ll. in *Ancient Metrical Tales* (1829). Douce and Ritson owned the French text in the edition printed by Nicolas Boufous (n.d.)
SIR ISUMBRAS Caius College, Camb, MS 175	No. 14 (1765)	iii. 9	f. 48	Ellis abstract, iii. 158–81
Caligula A II	No. 14 (1765)	iii. 9	f. 48	
Copland edition	No. 14 (1765)	iii. 9	f. 48	
Nat. Lib. Scotland, MS 19. 3, 1				Discovered by Southey in 1805, see Scott, *Letters*, i. 262–3; xii. 278; Southey, *Letters*, ed. Warter (1856), i. 340–3 Douce MS 261 (imperfect) contains this romance. The MS is dated 1564
ROBERT OF CISYLE Vernon MS		ii. 17	f. 315	
Cambridge U.L. MS Ff. II 38	No. 28 (1765)	ii. 17	f. 315	
Caius Coll. Cam. MS 174		ii. 17	f. 315	
Harley MS 525		ii. 17		
Harley MS 1701 (3)	No. 28 (1765) as '1703 (3)'		f. 315	
SIR EGLAMOUR OF ARTOIS Cotton, Caligula A II			f. 48	
Cambridge U.L. MS Ff. II 38	No. 20 (1765)		f. 48	
Printed editions		i. 149	f. 48	Ellis abstract, iii. 266–90
Percy Folio MS				

	Percy	Warton	Ritson	Others
(e) Egerton MS 2862				Todd, pp. 162–8 Douce MS 261 (imperf.) contains this romance.
46 TITUS AND VESPASIAN				
(a) Cotton, Caligula A II	No. 17 (1765)		f. 315	
(b) Laud MS 622		ii. 50		
(c) Douce MS 78				
(d) Douce MS 126				
47 SIR DEGREVANT				
(a) Cambridge U.L. MS Ff. I. 6			f. 312	
48 LEBONE FLORENCE DE ROME				
(a) Cambridge U.L. MS Ff. II 38	No. 29 (1765)		f. 313; iii. 1–92	
49 SIR CLEGES				
(a) Nat. Lib. Scotland, MS 19.3.1				See entry for item 43 (d)
50 SIR TRIAMOUR				
(a) Cambridge U.L. MS Ff. II 38	⎱ No. 21 ⎰ (1765)			
(b) Percy Folio MS				
(c) Copland ed.		i. 149	f. 48	Ellis abstract, iii. 182–214
51 SIR TORRENT OF PORTYNGALE			f. 50 lists four leaves in Cambridge U.L. and printed fragments owned by Farmer, later Douce	
52 SQYR OF LOWE DEGRE				
(a) Percy Folio MS	⎱ No. 24 ⎰ (1765)			
(b) Copland ed. 1555–60		ii. 7 f.	f. 49; iii. 145–92	

	Percy	Warton	Ritson	Others
NIGHT OF OURTESY				
Copland ed. 1568	No. 26 (1765)	ii. 45	iii. 193–218	
ELUSINE				
is Royal 18 B II			f. 313ᵛ	
IR EGER, SIR RIME, AND SIR RAYSTEELE				
Percy Folio MS	No. 12 (1794)			
ed. Aberdeen, 711			f. 317	Ellis abstract, iii. 308–57 from Douce's copy
OSWALL AND ILLIAN				
Printed Edinburgh, 1775			f. 317	Ellis abstract, iii. 382–95 from Douce's copy

APPENDIX

3

'History', 'Romance' and 'Novel'

In the eighteenth century the term 'romance' refers to the medieval, Peninsular and modern narratives built out of detached and independent adventures. It is distinguished from epic not so much by its subject-matter as by its structure—or lack of it. Until the end of the century a 'novel' was 'a kind of abbreviation of a romance'. According to George Colman, the novel was the 'younger sister of romance', 'Less solemn in her air, her drift the same', two neat pocket-volumes instead of a folio,

> Plot and elopement, passion, rape and rapture,
> The total sum of every dear, dear chapter.[1]

Congreve, in the Preface to *Incognita: A Novel* (1692), describes Romances as 'composed of the Constant Loves and invincible Courages of Hero's, Heroins . . . where lofty Language, miraculous Contingencies and impossible Performances, elevate and surprize the Reader into a giddy Delight'. But Novels 'are of a more familiar Nature; come near us, and represent to us Intrigues in practice . . . but not such as are wholly unusual or unpresidented'. By 1780 Thomas Holcroft, in the preface to *Alwyn*, distinguishes between romance and novel on formal grounds, demanding of the novel unity of design, which necessitates the exclusion of all incidents which do not further the story. Both Clara Reeve and Scott differentiate romance from the novel on the grounds of subject-matter, the novel being 'a picture of real life and manners, and of the times in which it is written', a romance describing in lofty and elevated language what never happened nor was likely to happen. The definition of the novel—if it can be called a definition—is gradually extended by demanding of it the structural qualities either of the epic or the drama, and by distinguishing its subject-matter as the natural events of contemporary society. The distinction between novel and romance

---

[1] Colman, Prologue to *Polly Honeycombe* (1760); Chesterfield, *Letters* (ed. 1792), i. 185; Tompkins, *Popular Novel*, p. 212 n.

was firmly established when the *Critical Review* began, in 1794, to index them separately. At the end of the seventeenth century, prose fictions were entered in the *Term Catalogues* under *History*, together with chronicles, biographies, antiquarian collections, and accounts of contemporary political events.

When Scott wrote his first prose fiction, he was exercised by the problem of how to describe it clearly. He solved it neatly, with the title *Waverley, or, 'Tis Sixty Years Since*. His first chapter indicates how he had to avoid the sub-title 'A Tale of other Days' and other forms involving 'Tale' or 'Romance'. The use to which they had already been put was likely to excite expectations in the reader which his work would not satisfy. Its setting in the past precluded the use of the term 'novel'.

Sixty years earlier the problem had been equally acute. Fielding had difficulty in assigning *Joseph Andrews* to a category. He did not want it to be associated with works like *Clelia* 'commonly called Romances'. He was prepared to link it with such works as Fénelon's *Télémaque*, which he considered to be a type of epic poem in prose, presumably on the grounds of structure and of its serious combination of entertainment with instruction. 'Comic romance' and 'comic epic poem in prose' were for him synonymous. On his title page he called it *The History of the Adventures of Joseph Andrews*, and in his first chapter ironically connects it with such fictitious biographies as *Jack the Giant-Killer*, *Guy of Warwick* and *The Seven Champions*. These, he sarcastically declares, offer delight mixed with instruction. A glance at the prefaces to the editions of these works shows that this is what they invariably offer.

There is, I suggest, more to Fielding's choice of the term 'History' than at first appears. It means, of course, simply 'narrative', whether true or false. But when Fielding was writing it had collected particular associations from its use on the title page of fictitious narratives. During the sixteenth century, medieval romances such as *Guy of Warwick* were referred to by Tyndale for example as 'histories', and by Puttenham as 'old Romances or historicall rimes'. In the seventeenth century 'History' is commonly used for fictitious biographies, the commonest forms of which were the medieval and Peninsular romances—*Guy, Bevis, Valentine and Orson, Don Bellianis* and so on. The title pages of these always read 'The Most Famous History', or a variant of this. Francis Kirkman, in his preface to *Don Bellianis* (1671), distinguishes between 'histories', which he lists as *The Destruction of Troy, The Seven Champions of Christendom, Arthur of Little Britain*, and 'another sort of Historyes, which are called Romances', these being such works as *Arcadia* and the French romances of the seventeenth century, which are always described as 'A Romance' on their title-pages. Richard Baxter in 1660 and 1673 writes of the medieval romances as 'old feigned stories' and 'History-Fables', and of the modern as 'Romances'.[1] In the book-trade 'Histories' became a technical term to describe the abbreviated medieval romances which were so frequently reprinted.[2]

'History' on the title-page of a fictitious work implied a feigned biography, and Fielding in his first chapter exploited this. Later, in the opening chapter of Book III, he again plays with the term, *this* time in its sense of 'true narrative of political events'. He finds such 'histories' less 'true' than either the feigned biographies of Marivaux or romances such as *Don Quixote*. And the latter he also finds superior, in truthfulness to human experience, to modern romances—the voluminous examples of the seventeenth century—or 'the modern novel', that is the abbreviated form of these romances. When Fielding was writing, the abbreviated forms of the medieval romances were called 'Histories', the short forms of the modern romances were called 'novels'. In writing *Joseph Andrews* and *Tom Jones* Fielding kept to the 'historical arrangement', that is, as a fictitious biographer he followed the plan not of the epic, beginning *in medias res*, but of the 'histories' and of Marivaux, giving a continued narrative of the life of his hero from his birth to his establishment in the world.[3]

The epic has somehow disappeared from view. (Epic structure is that used in *Amelia*, which in its first four books follows the *Aeneid* closely.) Perhaps one should have been warned when, in the Preface to *Joseph Andrews*, Fielding omitted to mention in his references to the epic the two most important aspects of that form for the critics, its structure and its machinery. His title-page drew attention to the romantic aspect of Parson Adams, the quixotic knight-errant sallying out against contemporary evils in society. But it also pointed through the term 'History' to the other knight, Joseph, who is conducting his lady safely to her home, like Spenser's Red Cross Knight or Richard Johnson's St George and the Fair Sabra. The romantic material is translated into comic terms—the forests of

---

[1] Baxter, *Treatise of Self-Denyall* (1660), p. 126; *Christian Directory* (1673), p. 61. 'Historical Novel' is common on title pages, to describe brief imaginative accounts of actual historical persons, e.g. *Tudor, Prince of Wales. An Historical Novel* (1678), on the love of Owen Tudor and Henry V's widow. All that I have seen are translated from the French where the term is 'Nouvelle Historique'.

[2] C. Stowey, *The Printer's Grammar* (1808), p. 481.

[3] James Beattie, *Dissertations Moral and Critical* (1783), p. 309.

romance become the road to the West Country, the castles become inns, the armed combats become bouts of fisticuffs, the temptations of the knight to be unfaithful to his lady are translated into the episodes of Lady Booby and Betty. The 'open manslaughtre and bold bawdry' of romance—and of such romantic epics as the *Odyssey*—are transformed. The result is a 'comic romance'. Perhaps a 'comic history' would be a more accurate title than 'a comic epic in prose'. It is a more successful venture than Smollett's more blatant attempt to translate knight-errantry into modern terms in *Sir Lancelot Greaves.*[1]

[1] On the elements of romance in *Tom Jones*, see E. M. W. Tillyard, *The Epic Strain in the English Novel* (1958), pp. 52-4.

BIBLIOGRAPHY

In addition to the sources from which I quote, for which references are given in the footnotes, there are many useful studies which are more generally related to my topic. Some of these are listed below under the bibliography for Chapter I. The titles of others, together with titles of books and articles about the scholars and scholarship of the period, are accessible in the Sections headed 'Medieval Influences' and 'Literary Historians and Antiquaries' in the *Cambridge Bibliography of English Literature* (vol. ii, supplemented in vol. v). Valuable bibliographies are also found in Brinkley, Dunlop and Wellek, cited below.

CHAPTER I.   INTRODUCTION

BEER, E. S. de, 'Gothic: Origin and diffusion of the Term; The Idea of Style in Architecture', *Journal of the Warburg and Courtauld Institutes*, xi (1948), 143–62.

BEERS, H. A., *A History of Romanticism in the Eighteenth Century* (1898, rev. 1910).

BRINKLEY, R. F., *The Arthurian Legend in the Seventeenth Century* (Baltimore, 1932).

BRUCE, J. D., *The Evolution of Arthurian Romance* (Göttingen, 1928).

CHAMBERS, E. K., *Arthur of Britain* (1927).

CLARK, KENNETH, *The Gothic Revival. An Essay in the History of Taste* (1928).

CRANE, R. S., 'The Vogue of "Guy of Warwick" from the close of the Middle Ages to the Romantic Revival', *PMLA*, xxx (1915).

—, *The Vogue of Medieval Chivalrous Romance during the English Renaissance* (Menasha, Wisconsin, 1919).

DICKSON, A., *Valentine and Orson. A study in Late Medieval Romance* (New York, 1929).

DOUGLAS, D., *English Scholars, 1660–1730*. Second edition (1951).

DUNLOP, J. C., *The History of Fiction* (1814), rev. H. Wilson (1846).

EASTLAKE, C. L., *History of the Gothic Revival* (1872).

ESDAILE, A., *A List of English Tales and Prose Romances printed before 1740* (1912).

FARLEY, F. E., *Scandinavian Influences on the English Romantic Movement* (Boston, 1903).

FRIEDMAN, A. B., *The Ballad Revival* (Chicago, 1961).

JONES, ERNEST, *Geoffrey of Monmouth, 1640–1800* (Berkeley, 1944).

KENDRICK, T. D., *British Antiquity* (1950).

KER, W. P., 'The Literary Influence of the Middle Ages', *Cambridge History of English Literature*, x (1913), 217–41.

MACCALLUM, M. W., *Tennyson's Idylls of the King and Arthurian Story from the Sixteenth Century* (Glasgow, 1894).

MCKILLOP, A. D., 'A Critic of 1741 on Early Poetry', *SP*, xxx (1933).

PHELPS, W. L., *The Beginnings of the English Romantic Movement* (Boston, 1893).

RENWICK, W. L. and ORTON, H., *The Beginnings of English Literature to Skelton, 1509* (1939, rev. 1952).

SCHWERING, J., 'Amadis und Faustbuch in den Hexenprozessen', *Zeitschrift für Deutsche Philologie*, li (1926).

SNYDER, E. D., *The Celtic Revival in English Literature, 1760–1800* (Cambridge, Mass., 1923).

THOMAS, H., *Spanish and Portuguese Romances of Chivalry* (Cambridge, 1920).

THOMPSON, J. W., *History of Historical Writing* (New York, 1942).

WARD, H. L. D., *Catalogue of Romances in the Department of Manuscripts in the British Museum* (1883–93).

WASSERMAN, E. R., *Elizabethan Poetry in the Eighteenth Century* (Urbana, 1947).

WATKINS, W. B. C., *Johnson and English Poetry before 1660* (Princeton, 1936).

WEISINGER, H., 'The Middle Ages and the late Eighteenth-Century Historians', *PQ*, xxvii (1948).

WELLEK, R., *The Rise of English Literary History* (Chapel Hill, 1941).

WILLARD, R., 'Layamon in the Seventeenth and Eighteenth Centuries', *Studies in English* (Texas), xxvii (1948).

WURTSBAUGH, J., *Two Centuries of Spenserian Scholarship, 1609–1805* (Baltimore, 1936).

CHAPTER II.   EPIC AND ROMANCE: RICHARD HURD

See *CBEL*, ii. 852–3 and E. J. Morley's edition of *Letters on Chivalry and Romance* (1911).

EVANS, A. W., *Warburton and the Warburtonians* (Oxford, 1932).

HAMM, V. M., 'A Seventeenth-Century French Source for Hurd's *Letters on Chivalry and Romance*', *PMLA*, lii (1937).

KILVERT, F., *Memoirs of the Life and Writings of Bishop Hurd* (1860).

SMITH, A. L., 'Richard Hurd's *Letters on Chivalry and Romance*', *ELH*, vi (1939).

TROWBRIDGE, H., 'Bishop Hurd: a Reinterpretation', *PMLA*, lviii (1943).

CHAPTER III.   THOMAS PERCY

See *CBEL*, ii. 74, 78–9; v. 381–2.

The Percy Letters, ed. D. Nichol Smith and Cleanth Brooks (Baton Rouge, 1944–57).

Percy–Malone, ed. A. Tillotson, 1944.

Percy–Farmer, ed. C. Brooks, 1946.

Percy–Warton, ed. M. G. Robinson and L. Dennis, 1951.

Percy–Hailes, ed. A. F. Falconer, 1954.

Percy–Evans, ed. A. Lewis, 1957.

Percy–Paton, ed. A. F. Falconer (New Haven, 1961).

Other letters in J. Nichols, *Illustrations of the Literary History of the Eighteenth Century*, vi (1817), vii (1848), viii (1858). The more directly relevant modern studies are:

BATE, W. J., 'Percy's Use of his Folio-Manuscript', *JEGP*, xliii (1944).

BRONSON, B. H., 'A Sense of the Past', *Sewanee Review*, 67 (Winter, 1959), 145–55.

BROOKS, C., 'The Country Parson as Research Scholar: Thomas Percy, 1760–1770', *Papers of the Bibliographical Society of America*, liii (1959).

DENNIS, L., '"Blandamour" in the Percy–Ritson controversy', *MP*, xxix (1931).

—, 'Percy's Essay "On the Ancient Metrical Romances"', *PMLA*, xlix (1934).

—, 'Percy: Antiquarian versus Man of Taste', *PMLA*, lvii (1942).

GAUSSEN, A. C. C., *Percy, Prelate and Poet* (1908).

MARWELL, H., *Thomas Percy: Studien zur Entstehungsgeschichte Seiner Werke* (Göttingen, 1934).

OGBURN, V. H., 'Thomas Percy's Unfinished Collection, "Ancient English and Scottish Poems"', *ELH*, iii (1936).

CHAPTER IV. THOMAS WARTON

See *CBEL*, ii. 384–5; v. 431–2.

HAVENS, R. D., 'Thomas Warton and the Eighteenth-Century Dilemma', *SP*, xxv (1928).

KER, W. P., 'Thomas Warton' in *Collected Essays*, i (1925).

MANT, R., 'Memoirs of the Life and Writings of Thomas Warton', in *Poetical Works of Thomas Warton* (Oxford, 1802).

MILLER, F. S., 'The Historic Sense of Warton', *ELH*, v (1938).

SMITH, D. NICHOL, *Warton's History of English Poetry*, British Academy Lecture, 1929.

—, 'Warton's Miscellany: The Union', *RES*, xix (1943).

RINAKER, C., *Thomas Warton* (Urbana, 1916).

WELLEK, R., *Rise of English Literary History* (Chapel Hill, 1941), ch. 6.

CHAPTER V. JOSEPH RITSON

There are two full-length studies of Ritson, by Burd and Bronson; both give bibliographies of Ritson's works. See *CBEL*, ii. 905–7.

BURD, H. A., *Joseph Ritson, a Critical Biography* (Urbana, 1916).

BRONSON, B. H., *Joseph Ritson, Scholar at Arms*, 2 vols. (Berkeley, 1938).

—, 'The Caledonian Muse', *PMLA*, xlvi (1931).

—, 'Ritson's "Bibliographia Scotica"', *PMLA*, lii (1937).

[FRANK, J.], *Letters of Joseph Ritson* (with a Memoir by Sir Harris Nicholas), 2 vols. (1833).

HASLEWOOD, J., *Some Account of Joseph Ritson* (1824) (the B.M. copy contains much MS material, press mark G. 13123).

HOPKINS, A. B., 'Ritson's "Life of King Arthur"', *PMLA*, xliii (1928).

CHAPTER VI. GEORGE ELLIS

Since there is no full study of Ellis, I shall give a fuller list of his works and sources of information about him.

WORKS:

Bath; Its Beauties and Amusements (1777).

Poetical Tales of Sir Gregory Gander (1778).

Criticisms on the Rolliad, Papers 1, 2; *Probationary Odes* (1785) (Contributions by Ellis).

Memoir of a Map of the Countries comprehended between the Black Sea and the Caspian (1788).

History of the Late Revolution in the Dutch Republic (1789) (transl. into French by 'Monsieur', afterwards Louis XVIII). Contributions to *The Anti-Jacobin, or Weekly Examiner* (20 November 1797 to 9 July 1798).

Fabliaux or Tales . . . Selected and translated in English Verse [by G. L. Way]. Ellis provided introduction and notes and edited the second volume after Way's death. Vol. i, 1796; reissued 1800; vol. ii, 1800; repr. 3 vols. 1815. Reviewed in *Critical Review*, xxx (1800), 413–17; *Monthly Magazine*, x (1801), 609; *Monthly Review*, xxiii (1797), 174–6 (by W. Taylor) and xxxvi (1801), 276–8 (by Charles Burney).

Specimens of the Early English Poets (1790).

Specimens of the Early English Poets, to which is prefixed An Historical Sketch of the Rise and Progress of the English Poetry and Language. 3 vols. 1801; reprinted in 1803, 1811, 1845, 1851. Rev. by Southey in *Annual Rev.*, ii (1804), 548; *Monthly Rev.*, xlii (1803), 154–7 (by Ferriar); *Critical Rev.*, iii (1804), 51.

Specimens of Early English Metrical Romances. 3 vols. 1805, repr. Edinburgh, 1811; revised J. O. Halliwell, 1847. Reviews in *Monthly Rev.*, v (1806), 281–7 (by Muirhead); *Edinburgh Rev.*, vii (1806), 387–413 (by Scott); *Annual Rev.*, iv (1805), 536–44 (by Southey).

Ellis's reviews include the *Edinburgh Review* (1804) of Scott's *Sir Tristrem*, and twenty-eight articles for the *Quarterly* before 1815, including *Lady of the Lake* (1811), *Childe Harold* (1812), *Bride of Abydos, Corsair, Lara* (1814).

Diary of William Windham, 1784–1810, ed. Mrs H. Baring (1866), contains Preface by Ellis (pp. xv–xl).

BIOGRAPHY

See the articles in *D.N.B.*, *Encyclopaedia Britannica*, Gorton's *Biographical Dictionary* (1830), i. 699. Obituary in *Gentleman's Magazine*, lxxxv (1815), 371–2; R. A. Austen-Leigh, *Eton College Register, 1753–1790* (Eton, 1921), p. 179; G. Festing, *J. H. Frere and his Friends* (1899); F. MacCunn, *Sir Walter Scott's Friends* (1909), pp. 241 ff.; J. Bagot, *Canning and his Friends* (1909); W. Partington, *Sir Walter's Post-Bag* (1932); *Life and Letters of Sir Gilbert Elliot*, i. 189–190, 388–402; *Diaries and Correspondence of the First Earl of Malmesbury*, iii. 429 ff.; *Percy-Malone Correspondence*, p. 91.

Letters from Ellis to William Owen-Pughe are in National Library of Wales MS 13221, f. 163; MS 13222, f. 105; MS 13223, ff. 227, 231, 315, 883, 895, 909. Letters from Ellis to Douce are in Bodley MS Douce d 34 (Douce's replies in B.M. Addit. MS 28099). Letters to W. Rose are in B.M. Addit. MS 31022. The correspondence with Scott (extracts from which are printed in footnotes to Scott's *Letters*) are in National Library of Scotland MS 865, ff. 48–58; MS 870, f. 16; MS 873; MS 3875, f. 170; MS 3876, f. 209; MS 3877, ff. 43, 134, 168, 211–14, 223; MS 3878, ff. 164, 232; MS 3879, ff. 29, 137, 222; MS 3880, ff. 1, 209; MS 3884, f. 47; MS 962, f. 72. Ellis's letters to John Sneyd were at one time in the possession of the Bagot family at Keele Hall.

STUDIES

HOLLOWAY, O. E., 'George Ellis, *The Anti-Jacobin* and the *Quarterly Review*.' *RES*, x (1934), 55–66.

KITCHEN, G., *Survey of Burlesque and Parody in English* (Edinburgh, 1931).

RICE OXLEY, L., *The Poetry of the Anti-Jacobin* (Oxford, 1924).

CHAPTER VII. WALTER SCOTT

BALL, M., *Sir Walter Scott as a Critic of Literature* (New York, 1907), pp. 32–45.

COCHRANE, J. G., *Abbotsford Library Catalogue* (Edinburgh, 1838).

CORSON, J. C., *A Bibliography of Sir Walter Scott. A Classified and Annotated List of Books and Articles relating to his Life and Works*, 1797–1940 (Edinburgh, 1943).

GRIERSON, H. J. C., *Letters of Sir Walter Scott*. 12 vols. (1932–7).

PARTINGTON, W., *Sir Walter's Post-Bag* (1932).

SCOTT, W., *Miscellaneous Prose Works*. 3 vols. (1847) for the Essays on Chivalry and on Romance. *Minstrelsy of the Scottish Border* (Edinburgh, 1801–3). See the 1830 edition for 'Introductory Remarks on Popular Poetry' and 'Essay on the Imitations of the Ancient Ballad'.

Sir Tristrem

Scott's edition (Edinburgh, 1804) was reprinted in 1806, 1811, 1819 and in the *Poetical Works* (1833, 1848). Additional material is in the second and third edition. For Price on Scott's theories see Warton, *History* (1824), i. 181–98. Lockhart's reply is in Scott's *Poetical Works* (1833), v. Garnett's reply to Lockhart is in Warton, *History* (1840), 109–12. For inaccuracies in Scott's Glossary see *Gentleman's Magazine*, October 1833, pp. 303–12 and February 1834, pp. 167–70. Modern editions of the Auchinleck *Tristrem* by E. Kölbing (Heilbronn, 1882) and G. P. McNeill (Scottish Text Society, 1886). For the French texts see J. Bédier, *Le Roman de Tristan* (Paris, 1902–5), Bédier, *La Folie Tristan* (Paris, 1907), F. Michel, *Poetical Romances of Tristan* (1835).

BIBLIOGRAPHY

The Auchinleck Manuscript

For description of the MS and identification of the number of scribes engaged on it, see E. Kölbing, 'Vier Romanz Handschriften', *Englische Studien*, vii (1884), 177–201, and A. J. Bliss, 'Notes on the Auchinleck MS', *Speculum*, xxvi (1951), 652 f. On the date of the MS see *Speculum Gy de Warewyke*, ed. G. L. Morrill (*E.E.T.S.* E.S. 75, 1898), p. clxxxix; J. M. Booker, *A Middle English Bibliography* (Heidelberg, 1912), pp. 54–5; C. R. Borland, *Catalogue of the Medieval MSS in the Library of the Faculty of Advocates*, iii. 601 f. On the dialect of *Sir Tristrem* see Warton, *History* (1840), i. 110; F. Madden in *Gentleman's Magazine*, 103 (1833), p. 308; B. Vogel, 'The Dialect of Sir Tristrem', *JEGP*, xl (1941), 538 f.; xli (1942).

For discoveries of leaves which once formed part of the MS see [David Laing], *A Penni-Worth of Witte* (1857), Preface, and G. V. Smithers, 'Two newly-discovered fragments from the Auchinleck MS', *Medium Aevum*, xviii (1949), 1–11. For general discussion of the compilation and sources used, see L. H. Loomis, 'Chaucer and the Auchinleck MS', in *Essays in Honor of Carleton Brown* (New York, 1940), pp. 111–28, and *SP* (1941); 'The Auchinleck MS and a possible London Bookshop of 1330–1340', *PMLA*, lvii (1942), 595 f., and 'The Auchinleck *Roland and Vernagu* and the *Short Chronicle*', *MLN*, lx (1945), 94 f.; R. N. Walpole, 'The source MS of *Charlemagne and Roland* and the Auchinleck Bookshop', *MLN*, lx (1945), 22 f.; H. M. Smyser, '*Charlemagne and Roland* and the Auchinleck MS', *Speculum*, xxi (1946), 275 f. For Ritson's description of the MS see H. M. Smyser, 'The List of Norman Names in the Auchinleck MS', in *Medieval Studies in Honor of J. D. M. Ford* (Cambridge, Mass., 1948), p. 261.

Malory's Morte Darthur

For Southey's interest see his *Correspondence* (ed. C. C. Southey, 5 vols., 1850, and ed. J. W. Warter, 1856), and his edition of *The Byrth, Lyf and Actes of Kyng Arthur*, 2 vols. 1817. See the introductions to the editions of Malory by Thomas Wright (1858), Edward Strachey (1868), Oskar Sommer (1890) and E. Vinaver (1947). For the interest of Warton, Johnson, etc. see Mary Lascelles, 'Sir Dagonet in Arthur's Show', *Shakespeare Jahrbuch*, 96 (1960), 145–54.

CHAPTER VIII. WHAT THEN WAS ROMANTIC?

On the early development of the word 'romance' see J. D. Bruce, *Evolution of Arthurian Romance*, 2 vols. Göttingen, 1928, i. 67 n. 63; Voelker, P., 'Die Bedeutungsentwickelung des Wortes Roman', *Zeitschrift für romanische Philologie*, x (1887), 485 f. Two eighteenth-century discussions which I have not mentioned elsewhere are W. Drake, 'On the Origin of the word "Romance"', *Archaeologia*, iv (1786), 142–8, and J. Bowle, 'Remarks on the word "Romance"', *Archaeologia*, v. 267. J. Foster discusses the application of the epithet 'romantic' in *Essays in a Series of Letters to a Friend*, 2 vols. 1805.

243

BIBLIOGRAPHY

On the word 'romantic' the standard works are:

BALDENSPERGER, F., '"Romantique", ses Analogues et ses Equivalents: Tableau Synoptique de 1650 à 1810', *Harvard Studies and Notes in Philology and Literature*, xix (1937), 13–105.

BRIDGES, ROBERT, *Pictorial, Picturesque, &c.* S. P. E. Tract No. 15, 1923, pp. 15 f.

HOOPS, R., 'Der Begriff "Romance" in der mittel-englischen und früh-neuenglischen Literatur', *Anglistische Forschungen*, vol. 68, Heidelberg, 1929.

SMITH, L. P., *Four Words, Romantic, Originality, Creative, Genius.* S. P. E. Tract No. 17, 1924.

These may be supplemented by the following: T. L. Ustick in *Times Literary Supplement*, 21 December 1933; W. P. Ker, 'Romantic Fallacies' in *Art of Poetry* (Oxford, 1923); Mario Praz, *The Romantic Agony* (1933), pp. 17–21; A. Warren and R. Wellek, *Theory of Literature* (1949), pp. 345, 381; A. O. Lovejoy, *Essays in the History of Ideas* (Baltimore, 1948); F. L. Lucas, *The Decline and Fall of the Romantic Ideal* (Cambridge, 1936); J. M. S. Tompkins, *The Popular Novel in England*, 1770–1800 (1932; re-issued 1962), ch. 6; F. W. Bateson, *English Poetry* (1950), p. 95.

INDEX

Title references to the romances are followed by the numbers (bracketed) under which they are listed in Appendix 2.

Seege of Troye (21), 97n, 226
Seven Champions of Christendom, vii, 28, 30, 37, 87, 90, 103, 104, 122, 235
Seven Sages of Rome (39), *see Seven Wise Masters*
Seven Wise Masters, 29, 32, 161, 169, 173, 230
Shakespeare, William, 3, 7, 12n, 28, 33, 42–6, 47, 61, 73, 81, 92, 108n, 115, 200, 208, 221
Shelley, Percy Bysshe, 50
Shenstone, William, 62, 76, 78–80, 82, 86, 146
Shurley, John, 29, 30, 31
Smith, Edmund (Neale), 28
Smith, John, 39
Smithson, Samuel, 30
Smollett, Tobias, 72, 237
Southey, Robert, 2, 29, 37n, 49, 50, 64, 124, 127, 138, 146–7, 149, 151, 156–8, 171, 174, 177, 189f, 192, 215
Sowdone of Babylone (16), 170–1, 226
Spenser, Edmund, 3, 5, 6, 7, 8, 28, 33, 40, 42–6, 89, 92, 115, 118, 132, 152, 197, 221, 236; Hurd on, 61f; Warton on, 90, 100f
Sqyr of Lowe Degre (52), 13, 45, 90, 91, 93, 97, 106, 112, 141, 151, 232
Steele, Richard, vii, 7, 30–1, 214
Steevens, George, 132
Sterling, Joseph, 24
Strutt, Joseph, 26, 181
Stuart, Gilbert, 56
Stukeley, William, 14, 222

Tars, King of (38), 93n, 112, 113, 140, 141, 230
Tasso, 5, 7n, 66, 70, 73, 87, 197
Taylor, William, 49, 175–6, 186
Temple, William, 18
Thomson, James, 8, 49, 62, 205, 206n
Titus and Vespasian (46), 91, 232
Tom a Lincoln, 30
Torrent of Portyngale, Sir (51), 232
Triamore, Sir (50), 76, 91, 159–60, 169, 232

Tristrem, Sir (2), 40, 41, 49, 59, 97n, 115, 132–3, 158, 161, 162, 168, 169, 175, 178f, 223, 242
Troy Book, Laud (22), 227
Turner, Sharon, 58n, 129, 156, 157, 158, 188, 190
Two Children in the Wood, 3
Tyrwhitt, Thomas, 19, 58, 88, 113–14, 126, 131, 137, 142, 151

Valentine and Orson, 3, 5, 28, 29, 31, 76, 87, 88, 122, 235
Vernon MS, 93, 115, 117n, 133
Virgil, 10, 48, 51, 63, 70, 71

Walker, Joseph, 123–5, 126, 127
Walker, Obadiah, 39, 204
Wanley, Humphrey, 19, 41, 111, 130, 221
Warburton, William, 14, 18–19, 26n, 44, 45, 53, 60, 107, 130
Warton, Joseph, 23, 26, 49, 64, 67, 208, 214
Warton, Thomas, 4, 23, 24, 25, 26, 27, 32, 40, 41, 42, 43, 44, 45, 49, 68, 76, 82, 85, 88, 100–19, 137, 142, 169, 199, 208, 240 *and see* App. 2; on origin of romances, 14, 17–19, 52f, 64, 197–8; on romances, 103f, 110f; ideal of scholarship, 108–9, 117–18, 221; correspondence with Percy, 45–6, 53–5, 80, 89–90, 91n, 106, 107, 109, 118; *Observations on the Faerie Queene*, vii, 44, 53, 60, 62, 83, 90, 100f, 108–10, 118; *History of English Poetry*, 19, 38n, 107f, 121, 128–30, 150, 151, 165, 178, 187, 195
Watson, William, 29
Way, Gregory Lewis, 26n, 135, 152–5
Weber, Henry, 94, 135, 174, 186–7, 188–9
Wilkie, John, 61
William of Palerne (42), 231
Wordsworth, William, 1, 2, 37f, 49, 80, 150, 176n, 177, 215
Wren, Christopher, 14

Ywain and Gawain (3), 113, 114, 130, 141, 174, 224